FAULTLINES

Debating the Issues in American Politics

Fourth Edition

A brief edition of *The Enduring Debate*, Seventh Edition

David T. Canon
University of Wisconsin–Madison

John J. Coleman
University of Wisconsin–Madison

Kenneth R. Mayer
University of Wisconsin–Madison

W. W. Norton & Company
New York London

W. W. Norton & Company has been independent since its founding in 1923, when William Warder Norton and Mary D. Herter Norton first published lectures delivered at the People's Institute, the adult education division of New York City's Cooper Union. The Nortons soon expanded their program beyond the Institute, publishing books by celebrated academics from America and abroad. By mid-century, the two major pillars of Norton's publishing program—trade books and college texts—were firmly established. In the 1950s, the Norton family transferred control of the company to its employees, and today—with a staff of 400 and a comparable number of trade, college, and professional titles published each year—W. W. Norton & Company stands as the largest and oldest publishing house owned wholly by its employees.

Previous editions (1990–2002) published as Readings for AMERICAN GOVERNMENT

Composition: Westchester Book Composition
Production manager: Ashley Horna
Manufacturing by Sheridan Books

Library of Congress Cataloging-in-Publication Data
Canon, David T.
    Faultlines : debating the issues in American politics / [edited by] David T. Canon, University of Wisconsin, Madison, John J. Coleman, University of Wisconsin, Madison Kenneth R. Mayer, University of Wisconsin, Madison. — Fourth edition.
        pages cm
    Includes bibliographical references.
    ISBN 978-0-393-92159-5 (pbk.)
    1. United States—Politics and government.   I. Title.
    JK31.F37 2014
    320.973—dc23   2013018581

W. W. Norton & Company Inc., 500 Fifth Avenue, New York, N.Y. 10110
www.wwnorton.com
W. W. Norton & Company Ltd., Castle House, 75/76 Wells Street, London W1T 3QT

1 2 3 4 5 6 7 8 9 0

Contents

1

Political Culture: What Does It Mean to Be an American?

What does it mean to be an American? This deceptively simple question is challenging to answer. Because the United States encompasses a vast array of ethnicities, religions, and cultures, it can be difficult to define "American" by reference to those criteria. The country's geography differs dramatically from area to area, and the economic way of life accordingly differs greatly as well. In many ways, diverse groups of Americans have experienced American history differently, so a common historical identity is not obviously the answer either. One popular argument is that the United States is united by a set of political ideals. As far back as the early nineteenth century, scholars have tried to identify the nature of American political culture: Is it a commitment to individualism? A belief in equality? A shared set of values about the appropriate role of government? Openness?

Eric Liu wonders whether Americans have lost their way in having any shared identity. To Liu, "America is always in flux, but the flux today seems more disorienting than usual." He sees contemporary Americans as having a shared identity influenced heavily by the ideas and images presented by various media, oriented around commercial touchstones such as the Super Bowl, and ultimately not one of permanence. And although America has a strong story and history dating from the Declaration of Independence onward, Liu argues that its grip on the public is weak and that "these days, talk of citizenship is thin and tinny." Believing that a robust sense of nationhood and civic life is important for the future, Liu contends that a new Americanization campaign is necessary to breathe life back into the American creed. The effort must avoid the problems of past efforts at Americanization, particularly efforts to minimize differences and diversity in the quest for national unity. The modern effort to promote the American creed, character, and culture should, in Liu's view, be led by progressives, rather than being seen by progressives as a threat.

Steven Warshawsky argues that American identity centers around a commonly held set of ideas that can be considered the American way of life. This way of life includes beliefs in liberty, equality, property rights, religious freedom, limited government, and a common language for conducting political and economic affairs. Although America has always been a nation of immigrants, from the original European settlers to the mass immigration of the late nineteenth and early twentieth centuries, Warshawsky sees assimilation into American political culture as critical to American national identity. He also notes that America, including the scope and reach of government, has changed dramatically over time. Warshawsky asks whether these changes have also changed what it means to be an American. He argues this is a difficult question but concludes that straying too far from the principles of the Founders means "we will cease to be 'Americans' in any meaningful sense of the word."

Daniel Elazar provides a different way of approaching the question of what it means to be an American. He argues that political beliefs in the United States are distributed unevenly across the country. In large part, this has to do with migration patterns. Once certain ethnic groups and nationalities predominated in a particular area, the institutions they built and the practice of politics tended to become ingrained with their political and cultural beliefs. Elazar sees three types of value systems across the country: moralism, individualism, and traditionalism. Moralism is focused on the community and engaging in politics to do good. Individualism focuses on individual rights and tends to view governing as a set of transactions among various individuals and groups. Traditionalism attempts to use government to preserve existing social arrangements. These three approaches vary in their prevalence across the country, and even within states there may be variation as to which of the three predominates. Some areas have a mixture of two of these value systems, whereas other areas are more purely of one type.

Eric Liu

Sworn-Again Americans

Last December I went to Taiwan to visit my grandmother. Like the Republic of China itself, she had turned 100 earlier in the year. During the trip I spent a day at the National Palace Museum in Taipei. Set among lush, green, mist-draped mountains, the museum holds the world's most spectacular collection of Chinese artifacts—spirited away in wartime by the Nationalists who fled to Taiwan when Mao's Communists took over the mainland.

On display that morning was a centennial exhibit of 100 masterpieces from the museum's holdings: famous calligraphic scrolls, priceless porcelain vases, finely carved jadeite cabbages. Each exquisite object was surrounded by a welter of tourists, many from the mainland. Even more stirring than the exhibit was its ambition, the belief that something as vast as Chinese culture and tradition could be captured in a selection of iconic things. The objects, from across dynasties and millennia, *were* Chineseness; the exhibit, an act of re-Sinicization. It was heritage reinforcement for an audience presumed Chinese.

I wondered, on the long flight home, whether Americanness could be so captured and so reinforced. I don't doubt that the Smithsonian could create a comparable show with 100 special objects. What I doubt is whether we have today a strong enough sense of shared identity, of common cultural and civic roots, for such an exhibit to capture the country's imagination.

America is always in flux, but the flux today seems more disorienting than usual. As China emerges rapidly and confidently, as Americans begin to wonder aloud about relative decline, as the center of gravity in our electorate shifts away from white men, as globalization enables immigrants to stay more wedded than ever to their homelands and not their new land, as political paralysis calls into question the durability of our constitutional design—as all these trends converge, a question arises: What is the content of American identity?

Without bonds of blood or tribe or sect to pull its people together, America has always tended toward the centrifugal. We are held together by Black Friday and "I'm lovin' it," by bowl games and March Madness, by reality television and virtual water coolers. America's story of self today is not so much a story as a Twitter feed. Heavily mediated, mainly commercial, and shockingly perishable is the sense of the republic that our public has today.

Of course, from the Revolution onward, America has had available a real story and a great unifying force: the self-evident ideals enshrined in the Declaration of Independence, encoded, even if imperfectly, in the Constitution, and embodied in amendments that made citizenship of the United States something transcendent and vital. Because our country began as an idea, the status of the citizen here has always been more than simply ministerial. It is, at least in theory, a trust; half a social contract. Citizens are promised liberty, and we, in turn, promise to earn it—by sustaining it.

These days, however, talk of citizenship is thin and tinny. The word has a faintly old-fashioned feel to it when used in everyday conversation. When evoked in national politics, it's often accompanied by the shrill whine of a descending culture-war mortar. Hence the debates in recent years about birthright citizenship and whether such status ought to be denied to so-called "anchor babies," mostly of Mexican descent. Or, less seriously but no less menacingly, the efforts to push the President of the United States out of the boundaries of American citizenship with a fervently wished-for foreign birth certificate.

When citizenship is drained of content by a commoditizing market and polarized politics, America suffers. Our ability as a people to maintain the democracy we've inherited diminishes, as does our ability to adapt to new challenges. We have to revive a spirit of citizenship if we want to remain a people.

That is why it is time now for a movement to re-Americanize Americans. This means reanimating our creed, cultivating the character needed for civic life, and fostering a culture of strong citizenship. Each of these imperatives is subject to abuse and co-optation by those who take a narrow view of what this country is. Which is why I argue that a twenty-first-century Americanization movement must be catalyzed by progressives.

Americanization, Last Time

A hundred years ago, as the great wave of European immigration to the United States peaked, there was a push for Americanization that crossed sector and institution. In public schools, the curriculum was changed to emphasize more American history and to teach patriotic anthems and parables. In urban slums, settlement houses like Jane Addams's Hull House and hundreds like it taught immigrant adults how to speak English and to assimilate into the "melting pot" of the city. Historic preservation took on greater prominence. From the pulpit came more lessons about American providence. Genealogy became a phenomenon and "heritage" a cultural obsession.

Today, at the end of another great migration to the United States, the will to Americanize is much weaker. That is in part proper. The nineteenth-century Americanizers, in their frantic eagerness, were stifling even when they meant well. As the First World War approached, much of the earnest patriotism of the movement curdled into jingoism and nativism. Excluded altogether from the Americanizing embrace were most people of color, who, whether deemed black, brown, yellow, or red, were the anvil against which various European ethnicities were forged into dominant whiteness.

In ensuing generations, with the emergence of the civil rights movement and multiculturalism, the descendants of those new-century immigrants came to reject the melting-pot ideal and its obliteration of differences. They instead learned to embrace a cosmopolitan pluralism—an identity libertarianism—in which to be American is to be what you want. Out went assimilation, in came authenticity.

Much has been gained in this revolution. Identity libertarians have freed us all to express and create our true selves and enabled the marketplaces of ideas, style, cuisine, and commerce to benefit from real diversity. But what's been lost is the core of American citizenship. It's no exaggeration to say that America has never been more confused about what its own citizenship entails—and never more timid about imparting the values, knowledge, and skills needed to be a citizen in the broadest sense.

Citizenship in this nation is many things. It is a legal status conferred by the accident of birth or by the process of naturalization. It is a set of privileges and immunities. But it is also a cultural inheritance, an ethical standard, an implied set of responsibilities, a collective story and memory.

At its core, citizenship in America is an act of claiming. *What* is being claimed is a creed that emanates from the declaration and finds restatement in the Gettysburg Address and yet again in "I Have a Dream." *How* it is claimed is by a combination of collective belief and deeds.

To pour content again into the vessel of citizenship, we need to Americanize anew. To do that, we must reinvent the very notion of Americanization. What I write of is not a deracinating assimilation to a white man's way. It is not enforcement of partisan orthodoxy. It is taking profoundly seriously how we make an *unum* from the *pluribus*. It is about having confidence in what is exceptional about our experiment.

Americanization, This Time

The word "Americanization," like the word "exceptionalism," pushes the buttons of many people, especially on the left. To them, it can sound like a cover for white privilege and warmongering. It suggests arrogance and groupthink. In short, Americanization conjures up for some folks the worst of America.

But these connotations are not fixed. It is in our power to reshape them by recalling the best of America, including our capacity to face our history in full. Americanization should mean, "to keep trying to live up to our promise." Redeeming the idea of Americanization is the very kind of redemptive act that America stands for. Not "my country right or wrong," but, as the German immigrant and U. S. senator Carl Schurz said a century ago, "our country—when right to be kept right; when wrong to be put right."

This is true patriotism. To Americanize means to ask people to commit to a set of values. Rights come with responsibilities and opportunities with obligations. You have the right to burn the flag in America—but you should honor the fact that the flag symbolizes that right. You have to be willing to work hard and be enterprising—but if you are, you should be promised a fair chance at success. You are free to sustain the traditions of your ancestral lands—but you should contribute to the development of *this* land and its rituals.

A new Americanization movement will reinforce these principles. It will instill in young people a sense of why being here is special, even in a networked and transnationalizing age, and what they owe this country. It will sharpen for Americans of all ages a sense of appreciation and responsibility for the institutions of our democracy—and thus our ability to participate in those institutions. It will enable us to face an era of demographic transition with more unity of purpose. And it will prove to us and to the world that for all its profound and tragic flaws, the United States still has a confounding ability to convert its shortcomings into strengths and to remix itself.

This new Americanization program, importantly, is not just for immigrants. It is for everyone. It is for the longstanding citizens who have forgotten or never appreciated the full measure of their inheritance. It is for the chieftains of global companies who think their fates are no longer tied to the fate of this nation. It is for romantics of the far left and far right who think nations and states are obsolete until they need one—this one—to provide for their needs.

A new Americanization program must also be created by everyone. Government can be involved, but so must community foundations, schools, business leaders, union organizers, film and TV producers, social-media mavens. There should be a spirit of wiki to it all, of popular movement, with ideas emerging from the bottom up and not only from experts. Throughout, it should focus on three core elements of a civic religion: creed, character, and culture.

Creed

To be Americanized is first to be immersed in the tenets of our democratic faith, expressed in seminal texts, speeches, and stories, from Jefferson's time to our own.

> As the patriots of seventy-six did to the support of the Declaration of Independence, so to the support of the Constitution and Laws, let every American pledge his life, his liberty, and his sacred honor. . . . Let reverence for the laws . . . be preached from the pulpit, proclaimed in legislative halls, and enforced in the courts of justice. And, in short, let it become the political religion of the nation; and let the old and the young, the rich and the poor, the grave and the gay, of all sexes and tongues, and colors and conditions, sacrifice unceasingly upon its altars.

When a young Abraham Lincoln spoke these words at the Young Men's Lyceum in Springfield, he meant by "reverence for the laws" not mere obedience to authority. He meant reverence for democracy itself—and for the obligations that democratic freedom entails.

To Americanize is to be comfortable telling everyone that what separates this nation from others is that it has a *moral* identity. Others have history and tradition. We do too, but more than anything, our nation is dedicated to a proposition. That distinction cannot be emphasized enough. When Jefferson proclaimed the truth of human equality "self-evident," he was not recording a timeless fact; he was asserting one into being. His saying so, as he declared America, helped make it so.

It falls on us to keep it so. Only continuous renewal of a commitment to the creed keeps the creed alive. Naming it matters: rediscovering the words, saying them again, assaying their meaning. In classrooms, boardrooms, kitchens, and churches, in corner stores and today's settlement houses, on TV and on Twitter, it's time to shake off the sleep of cynicism and to awaken in earnest as Americans. It is time to appreciate the content of our creed as if we were all newcomers: with wonder and awe at the world-changingness of it all.

To reanimate the creed we need to focus in part on revitalizing civic education in our schools. The Campaign for the Civic Mission of Schools is one advocacy group working to do this. Even though public education in America is a matter largely left to the states, there can and should be a federal requirement that the basic texts and ideas of our nation's civic creed be taught, in an upward spiral of sophistication, every year from kindergarten to twelfth grade. After all, as Justice Sandra Day O'Connor notes, this was the very point of creating free and compulsory public education: to make citizens.

The responsibility belongs not only to schoolteachers or education policymakers. Leaders in every community should take it upon themselves to start contests and public conversations about the American creed: what's in it, what challenges it, how we honor it, how we have fallen short. The answers will be staggeringly varied—as they are on the DefineAmerican.com website started by the Pulitzer Prize-winning journalist (and undocumented immigrant) Jose Antonio Vargas—but they will have a unifying thread of *reckoning*.

Character

Our standard of citizenship in America is centered, constitutionally and rhetorically, on rights. But with rights come duties and with liberty, responsibility; else freedom decays into mere free-for-all. So a second dimension of a new Americanization is the cultivation of citizenship as a matter of character. This is citizenship in the sense of good or great citizenship: living in a pro-social way; showing up for one another; making an adaptive asset of our diversity. Civic character is therefore more than industry, perseverance, and other personal virtues. It is character in the collective: team-spiritedness, mutuality, reciprocity, responsibility, empathy, service, cooperation. It is acting as if you believed that society becomes how *you* behave—because it does. Character is the thread that ties creed and deed together. What acts instantiate our stated values? With what understanding of our system of self-government? Making what kind of contribution?

The cultivation of strong citizens does not happen automatically, any more than the cultivation of healthy plants does. Democracy is a garden in which the organisms are interdependent. Developing civic character is the work of gardening—of tending the plot. In a multiethnic market democracy like ours, we cannot rely on a myth of rugged individualism to hold us together. We have to seed and feed trust. We reap what we sow.

Educators need to teach not just civic facts and history but also the elements of civic character: what it means to be in union with others. That requires doing real things together and reflecting on the shared experience. In schools, it means more service learning that's tied to an understanding of American institutions. Take students to serve in a church food bank, for instance, but also discuss the civic role of faith-based groups. What can citizens make happen with and without government, with and without each other?

In government policy, cultivating civic character means adding more resources for AmeriCorps and other national service programs—but also grounding them more explicitly in elements of American citizenship. In parenting and child rearing, it means teaching and rewarding even the smallest acts of courtesy and cooperation because they compound. In philanthropy and community life, it means creating more opportunities for *adults* to learn how to do democracy.

During the Great Depression, grassroots citizenship schools like the Highlander Folk School in Appalachia emerged for just this purpose. Highlander is where Rosa Parks was trained to organize. It was where she learned that civic character is expressed in the choices we make. She was prepared by her teachers to make the right choice as a citizen when the time came. What institutions prepare us now?

Culture

As it happens, the Highlander School is also where an old black spiritual was adapted and then popularized into a movement anthem called "We Shall Overcome." American democracy makes us a promise that only we can keep. This faith requires a rich, suffusing culture of unity: anthems, rituals, colors, civic scripture set and reset in new creative contexts.

The third aspect of Americanization, then, is introducing Americans to the patterns of our civic culture—how we have governed ourselves, by law or custom, and lived in community over 200 years. One such pattern is promise, failure, and redemption. This is the foundational story of slavery and civil rights. Another is the generation of hybrid innovations from our miscegenated gene and meme pool. This is the story of American music, of Silicon Valley's ingenuity.

I believe the new Americanization agenda must reveal and express both these story patterns: the profound ways, past and present, that we have fallen short of our stated ideal; and our resilient, adaptive ability to take our failures as the stuff of new invention. Slavery's legacy is evident in de facto segregation and in the severe inequality of our schools. It is found too in the voice of every American, in the warp and woof of the American vernacular. *We Shall Overcome.*

To teach Americanness is to celebrate the ideal and the real as one, without irony or ambivalence. It is to use a shared language in public life—American English, with a democratic accent—so that we may transcend unshared private histories. It is to invoke a civic religion that infuses our many narratives with common purpose. In 1982, the liberal producer Norman Lear created a pageant for ABC called "I Love Liberty" that grabbed hold of both the cultural patterns I described above. With the Muppets and multicultural celebrities, with earnestness and absurdity, it depicted the turmoil and contradiction of our founding—and the insistent promise of our future.

We need to have the self-assurance to create new pageants, to invoke and remix the rituals and symbols our own way: the flag, the hymns, the oaths. We can't fear causing offense. A people scared to say the Pledge of Allegiance is nearly as unhealthy as one scared not to. What we must remember is that we get to continually reinvent and rewrite that pledge, this *culture*.

That's why recently I helped launch a civic-artistic project called Sworn-Again American. It mashes up aspects of a naturalization ceremony, a multicultural festival, and a revival tent to make a playful public experience in which Americans recommit to the content of their citizenship. What we should celebrate more than diversity is what we *do* with it. How do we bring everyone in the tent and create something together? In a twenty-first century way that activates our true potential, we all need to become sworn-again.

The Role of Progressives

What I've called for here may cause many progressives heartburn. I admit that this new Americanization agenda sounds like—indeed, is—something conservatives promote. But I disagree that it should be something *only* conservatives promote. Progressives should be front and center.

Why? The promise of American life is a promise of justice, requiring action not passivity, challenge not complacency; and is therefore progressive. The effort to nudge the country toward alignment with its stated ideals is asymptotic: We can keep halving the distance to perfection, but it remains infinitely out of reach. With the goal never fully attainable, the pursuit becomes then an act of faith, and therefore *progressive*. Progressivism is nothing if not the belief that something "more perfect" is worth striving for.

Some progressives contest the very idea of citizenship and dispute the need even for nation-states. They are too Utopian. Other progressives hold the

American nation-state in low regard because of a track record of racism and war and empire. They are too cynical. They do not see that inherent in the hypocrisy of so many American acts—in fact, what makes hypocrisy hypocrisy and not mere iniquity—is the existence of a higher professed standard.

We are called still, all of us, to live up to that standard. The best tradition of the American left is a tradition of love for America: insistent, impatient, often disappointed, but unrelenting. And the best hope for America tomorrow is that across lines of left and right we find ways to articulate common purpose—not by glossing over hypocrisies but by unpacking them; by treating them as the beginning of a chapter rather than the end of the story.

It's time for a civic synthesis that speaks to the tension between a Western WASP inheritance and a diverse multicultural present; between words in marble and a more sordid reality; between liberty and equality; freedom from and freedom to—because that tension is what is American. In every setting we can, progressives and conservatives must teach to the tension *together*. And progressives should initiate the dialectic—because in America we always have.

There are some progressives who say that conservatives, consumed with culture war, are incapable of teaching to the tension. Maybe. But they should take a look at *What So Proudly We Hail*, a recent anthology of American stories and songs whose editors include Leon Kass, the conservative scholar and former adviser to President George W. Bush. Every prefatory note in that collection speaks to the tension and complexity of American identity. Not a note incites culture war.

There are some conservatives who would double over laughing at the notion of progressives leading the charge to reanimate a love of American citizenship. But I would refer them to *A Patriot's Handbook*, a similar and similarly powerful anthology of civic religious texts assembled by Caroline Kennedy.

Together, these collections remind us that the most useful way to be progressive is to conserve: to honor and maintain the deeply revolutionary, once-in-a-world tradition of our creed and culture. And the most useful way to be conservative is to progress: to enable the American idea to adapt to changing times so that the idea itself may endure forever and ever.

Lines of Descent and Ascent

At the National Palace Museum, beholding those objects made epochs ago—ten or 12 Americas ago—I marveled at the continuity of the line. But that line of

Chineseness, a shared sensibility expressed in brushstrokes and carvings and in ratios of form to space, is in the end rooted in the soil and heart of China.

A European, an African, or a black or white American can appreciate those lines. They cannot claim them. When an American of Chinese descent like me can, it only sharpens the realization that of the two identities I might claim, only one is by design universal. Only one is an open operating system inviting people from anywhere to rewrite the code. Only one asks humans to be better.

American exceptionalism in this age of great tectonic shifts does not depend on our forever having the largest economy or the mightiest military. It does depend on our having the planet's most adaptive and resilient concept of citizenship, one that rises above land and blood, that commits us to a national lifetime of striving, failing, renewing, striving again to dedicate ourselves to our proposition.

We live in a great country. It's time again to get religion about it.

Steven M. Warshawsky

What Does It Mean to Be an American?

"Undocumented Americans." This is how Senate Majority Leader Harry Reid recently described the estimated 12–20 million illegal aliens living in America. What was once a Mark Steyn joke has now become the ideological orthodoxy of the Democratic Party.

Reid's comment triggered an avalanche of outrage among commentators, bloggers, and the general public. Why? Because it strikes at the heart of the American people's understanding of themselves as a nation and a civilization. Indeed, opposition to the ongoing push for "comprehensive immigration reform"—i.e., amnesty and a guest worker program—is being driven by a growing concern among millions of Americans that massive waves of legal and illegal immigration— mainly from Mexico, Latin America, and Asia—coupled with the unwillingness of our political and economic elites to mold these newcomers into red-white-and-blue Americans, is threatening to change the very character of our country. For the worse.

I share this concern. I agree with the political, economic, and cultural arguments in favor of sharply curtailing immigration into the United States, as well as refocusing our immigration efforts on admitting those foreigners who bring the greatest value to—and are most easily assimilated into—American society. * * * But this essay is not intended to rehash these arguments. Rather, I wish to explore the question that underlies this entire debate: What does it mean to be an American? This may seem like an easy question to answer, but it's not. The harder one thinks about this question, the more complex it becomes.

Clearly, Harry Reid has not given this question much thought. His implicit definition of "an American" is simply: Anyone living within the geopolitical boundaries of the United States. In other words, mere physical location on Earth determines whether or not someone is "an American." Presumably, Reid's definition is not intended to apply to tourists and other temporary visitors. Some degree of permanency—what the law in other contexts calls "residency," i.e., a subjective intention to establish one's home or domicile—is required. In Reid's view, therefore, a Mexican from Guadalajara, a Chinese from Shanghei [sic], an Indian from Delhi, or a [fill in the blank] become "Americans" as soon as they cross into U.S. territory and decide to live here permanently, legally or not. Nothing more is needed.

This is poppycock, of course. A Mexican or a Chinese or an Indian, for example, cannot transform themselves into Americans simply by moving to this country, any more than I can become a Mexican, a Chinese, or an Indian simply by moving to their countries. Yet contemporary liberals have a vested interest in believing that they can. This is not just a function of immigrant politics, which strongly favors the Democratic Party (hence the Democrats' growing support for voting rights for non-citizens). It also reflects the liberals' (and some libertarians') multicultural faith, which insists that it is morally wrong to make distinctions among different groups of people, let alone to impose a particular way of life—what heretofore has been known as the American way of life—on those who believe, speak, and act differently. Even in our own country.

In short, diversity, not Americanism, is the multicultural touchstone.

What's more, the principle of diversity, taken to its logical extreme, inevitably leads to a *rejection* of Americanism. Indeed, the ideology of multiculturalism has its roots in the radical—and anti-American—New Left and Black Power movements of the 1960s and 1970s. Thus the sorry state of U.S. history and civics education in today's schools and universities, which are dominated by adherents of this intellectual poison. Moreover, when it comes to immigration, multiculturalists actually *prefer* those immigrants who are as unlike ordinary Americans as possible. This stems from their deep-rooted opposition to traditional American society, which they hope to undermine through an influx of non-western peoples and cultures.

This, in fact, describes present U.S. immigration policy, which largely is a product of the 1965 Immigration Act (perhaps Ted Kennedy's most notorious legislative achievement). The 1965 Immigration Act eliminated the legal preferences traditionally given to European immigrants, and opened the floodgates to immigration from less-developed and non-western countries. For example, in 2006 more immigrants came to the United States from Columbia, Peru, Vietnam, and Haiti (not to mention Mexico, China, and India), than from the United Kingdom, Germany, Italy, and Greece. And once these immigrants arrive here, multiculturalists believe we should accommodate *our* society to the needs and desires of the newcomers, not the other way around. Thus, our government prints election ballots, school books, and welfare applications in foreign languages, while corporate America asks customers to "press one for English."

Patriotic Americans—those who love our country for its people, its history, its culture, and its ideals—reject the multiculturalists' denuded, and ultimately subversive, vision of what it means to be "an American." While the American identity is arguably the most "universal" of all major nationalities—as evidenced by the millions of immigrants the world over who have successfully assimilated into our country over the years—it is not an empty, meaningless concept. It has substance. Being "an American" is *not* the same thing as simply living in the United States. Nor, I would add, is it the same thing as holding U.S. citizenship. After all, a baby born on U.S. soil to an illegal alien is a citizen. This hardly guarantees that this baby will grow up to be *an American*.

So what, then, does it mean to be an American? I suspect that most of us believe, like Supreme Court Justice Potter Stewart in describing pornography, that we "know it when we see it." For example, John Wayne, Amelia Earhart, and Bill Cosby definitely are Americans. The day laborers standing on the street corner probably are not. But how do we put this inner understanding into words? It's not easy. Unlike most other nations on Earth, the American nation is not strictly defined in terms of race or ethnicity or ancestry or religion. George Washington may be the Father of Our Country (in my opinion, the greatest American who ever lived), but there have been in the past, and are today, many millions of patriotic, hardworking, upstanding Americans who are not Caucasian, or Christian, or of Western European ancestry. Yet they are undeniably as American as you or I (by the way, I am Jewish of predominantly Eastern

European ancestry). Any definition of "American" that excludes such folks—
let alone one that excludes me!—cannot be right.

Consequently, it is just not good enough to say, as some immigration restrictionists do, that this is a "white-majority, Western country." Yes, it is. But so are,
for example, Ireland and Sweden and Portugal. Clearly, this level of abstraction
does not take us very far towards understanding what it means to be "an American." Nor is it all that helpful to say that this is an English-speaking, predomi-
nately Christian country. While I think these features get us closer to the answer,
there are millions of English-speaking (and non-English-speaking) Christians in
the world who are not Americans, and millions of non-Christians who are. Certainly, these fundamental historical characteristics are important elements in
determining who we are as a nation. Like other restrictionists, I am opposed to
public policies that seek, by design or by default, to significantly alter the nation's
"demographic profile." Still, it must be recognized that demography alone does
not, and cannot, explain what it means to be an American.

So where does that leave us? I think the answer to our question, ultimately,
must be found in the realms of ideology and culture. What distinguishes the
United States from other nations, and what unites the disparate peoples who
make up our country, are our unique political, economic, and social values,
beliefs, and institutions. Not race, or religion, or ancestry.

Whether described as a "proposition nation" or a "creedal nation" or simply
just "an idea," the United States of America is defined by *our way of life*. This
way of life is rooted in the ideals proclaimed in the Declaration of Independence; in the system of personal liberty and limited government established by
the Constitution; in our traditions of self-reliance, personal responsibility, and
entrepreneurism; in our emphasis on private property, freedom of contract, and
merit-based achievement; in our respect for the rule of law; and in our commitment to affording equal justice to all. Perhaps above all, it is marked by our
abiding belief that, as Americans, we have been called to a higher duty in human
history. We are the "city upon a hill." We are "the last, best hope of earth."

Many immigration restrictionists and so-called traditionalists chafe at the
notion that the American people are not defined by "blood and soil." Yet the
truth of the matter is, we aren't. One of the greatest patriots who ever graced this
nation's history, Teddy Roosevelt, said it best: "Americanism is a matter of the
spirit and of the soul." Roosevelt deplored what he called "hyphenated Americanism," which refers to citizens whose primary loyalties lie with their particular

ethnic groups or ancestral lands. Such a man, Roosevelt counseled, is to be "unsparingly condemn[ed]."

But Roosevelt also recognized that "if he is heartily and singly loyal to this Republic, then no matter where he was born, he is just as good an American as anyone else." Roosevelt's words are not offered here to suggest that all foreigners are equally capable of assimilating into our country. Clearly, they aren't. Nevertheless, the appellation "American" is open to anyone who adopts our way of life and loves this country above all others.

Which brings me to the final, and most difficult, aspect of this question: How do we define the "American way of life"? This is the issue over which our nation's "culture wars" are being fought. Today the country is divided between those who maintain their allegiance to certain historically American values, beliefs, and institutions (but not all—see racial segregation), and those who want to replace them with a very different set of ideas about the role of government, the nature of political and economic liberty, and the meaning of right and wrong. Are both sides in this struggle equally "American"?

Moreover, the "American way of life" has changed over time. We no longer have the Republic that existed in TR's days. The New Deal and Great Society revolutions—enthusiastically supported, I note, by millions of white, Christian, English-speaking citizens—significantly altered the political, economic, and social foundations of this country. Did they also change what it means to be "an American"? Is being an American equally compatible, for example, with support for big government versus small government? The welfare state versus rugged individualism? Socialism versus capitalism? And so on. Plainly, this is a much harder historical and intellectual problem than at first meets the eye.

Personally, I do not think the meaning of America is nearly so malleable as today's multiculturalists assume. But neither is it quite as narrow as many restrictionists contend. Nevertheless, I am convinced that being *an American* requires something more than merely living in this country, speaking English, obeying the law, and holding a job (although this would be a very good start!). What this "something more" is, however, is not self-evident, and, indeed, is the subject of increasingly bitter debate in this country.

Yet one thing is certain: If we stray too far from the lines laid down by the Founding Fathers and the generations of great American men and women who built on their legacy, we will cease to be "Americans" in any meaningful sense of the word. As Abraham Lincoln warned during the secession era, "America will never be destroyed from the outside. If we falter and lose our freedoms, it will be because we destroyed ourselves." Today the danger is not armed rebellion, but the slow erasing of the American national character through a process of political and cultural redefinition. If this ever happens, it will be a terrible day for this country, and for the world.

Daniel J. Elazar
The Three Political Cultures

The United States is a single land of great diversity inhabited by what is now a single people of great diversity. The singleness of the country as a whole is expressed through political, cultural, and geographic unity. Conversely, the country's diversity is expressed through its states, subcultures, and sections. In this section, we will focus on the political dimensions of that diversity-in-unity—on the country's overall political culture and its subculture.

Political culture is the summation of persistent patterns of underlying political attitudes and characteristic responses to political concerns that is manifest in a particular political order. Its existence is generally unperceived by those who are part of that order, and its origins date back to the very beginnings of the particular people who share it. Political culture is an intrinsically political phenomenon. As such, it makes its own demands on the political system. For example, the definition of what is "fair" in the political arena—a direct manifestation of political culture—is likely to be different from the definition of what is fair in family or business relationships. Moreover, different political cultures will define fairness in politics differently. Political culture also affects all other questions confronting the political system. For example, many factors go into shaping public expectations regarding government services, and political culture will be significant among them. Political systems, in turn, are in some measure the products of the political cultures they serve and must remain in harmony with their political cultures if they are to maintain themselves.

* * *

Political-culture factors stand out as particularly influential in shaping the operations of the national, state, and local political systems in three ways: (1) by molding the perceptions of the political community (the citizens, the politicians, and the public officials) as to the nature and purposes of politics and its expectations of government and the political process; (2) by influencing the recruitment of specific kinds of people to become active in government and politics—as holders of elective offices, members of the bureaucracy, and active political workers; and (3) by subtly directing the actual way in which the art of government is practiced by citizens, politicians, and public officials in the light of their perceptions. In turn, the cultural components of individual and group behavior are manifested in civic behavior as dictated by conscience and internalized ethical standards, in the forms of law-abidingness (or laxity in such matters) adhered to by citizens and officials, and in the character of the positive actions of government.

* * *

The national political culture of the United States is itself a synthesis of three major political subcultures. These subcultures jointly inhabit the country, existing side by side or sometimes overlapping one another. All three are of nationwide proportions, having spread, in the course of time, from coast to coast. Yet each subculture is strongly tied to specific sections of the country, reflecting the streams and currents of migration that have carried people of different origins and backgrounds across the continent in more or less orderly patterns.

Given the central characteristics that define each of the subcultures and their centers of emphasis, the three political subcultures may be called individualistic, moralistic, and traditionalistic. Each reflects its own particular synthesis of the marketplace and the commonwealth.

It is important, however, not only to examine this description and the following ones very carefully but also to abandon the preconceptions associated with such idea-words as individualistic, moralistic, marketplace, and so on. Thus, for example, nineteenth-century individualistic conceptions of minimum intervention were oriented toward *laissez-faire*, with the role of government conceived to be that of a policeman with powers to act in certain limited fields. And in the twentieth century, the notion of what constitutes minimum intervention has been drastically expanded to include such things as government regulation of utilities, unemployment compensation, and massive subventions to maintain a stable and growing economy—all within the framework of the same political culture. The demands of manufacturers for high tariffs in 1865 and the demands of labor unions for worker's compensation in 1965 may well be based on the same theoretical justification that they are aids to the maintenance of a working marketplace. Culture is not static. It must be viewed dynamically and defined so as to include cultural change in its very nature.

The Individualistic Political Culture

The *individualistic political culture* emphasizes the conception of the democratic order as a marketplace. It is rooted in the view that government is instituted for strictly utilitarian reasons, to handle those functions demanded by the people it serves. According to this view, government need not have any direct concern with questions of the "good society" (except insofar as the government may be used to advance some common conception of the good society formulated outside the political arena, just as it serves other functions). Emphasizing the centrality of private concerns, the individualistic political culture places a premium on limiting community intervention—whether governmental or nongovernmental—into private activities, to the minimum degree necessary to keep the marketplace in proper working order. In general, government action is to be restricted to those areas, primarily in the economic realm, that encourage private initiative and widespread access to the marketplace.

The character of political participation in systems dominated by the individualistic political culture reflects the view that politics is just another means by which individuals may improve themselves socially and economically. In this sense politics is a "business," like any other that competes for talent and offers rewards to those who take it up as a career. Those individuals who choose political careers may rise by providing the governmental services demanded of them and, in return, may expect to be adequately compensated for their efforts.

Interpretation of officeholders' obligations under the individualistic political culture vary among political systems and even among individuals within a single political system. Where the standards are high, such people are expected to provide high-quality government services for the general public in the best possible manner in return for the status and economic rewards considered their due. Some who choose political careers clearly commit themselves to such norms; others believe that an office-holder's primary responsibility is to serve him- or herself and those who have supported him or her directly, favoring them at the expense of others. In some political systems, this view is accepted by the public as well as by politicians.

Political life within an individualistic political culture is based on a system of mutual obligations rooted in personal relationships. Whereas in a simple civil society those relationships can be direct ones, those with individualistic political cultures in the United States are usually too complex to maintain face-to-face ties. So the system of mutual obligation is harnessed through political parties, which serve as "business corporations" dedicated to providing the organization necessary to maintain that system. Party regularity is indispensable in the individualistic political culture because it is the means for coordinating individual enterprise in the political arena; it is also the one way of preventing individualism in politics from running wild.

In such a system, an individual can succeed politically, not by dealing with issues in some exceptional way or by accepting some concept of good government and then by striving to implement it, but by maintaining his or her place in the system of mutual obligations. A person can do this by operating according to the norms of his or her particular party, to the exclusion of other political considerations. Such a political culture encourages the maintenance of a party system that is competitive, but not overtly so, in the pursuit of office. Its politicians are interested in office as a means of controlling the distribution of the favors or rewards of government rather than as a means of exercising governmental power for programmatic ends; hence competition may prove less rewarding than accommodation in certain situations.

Since the individualistic political culture eschews ideological concerns in its "business-like" conception of politics, both politicians and citizens tend to look upon political activity as a specialized one—as essentially the province of professionals, of minimum and passing concern to laypersons, and with no place for amateurs to play an active role. Furthermore, there is a strong tendency among the public to believe that politics is a dirty—albeit necessary—business, better left to those who are willing to soil themselves by engaging in it. In practice, then, where the individualistic political culture is dominant, there is likely to be an easy attitude toward the limits of the professional's perquisites. Since a fair amount of corruption is expected in the normal course of things, there is relatively little popular excitement when any is found, unless it is of an extraordinary character. It is as if the public were willing to pay a surcharge for services rendered, rebelling only when the surcharge becomes too heavy. Of course, the judgments as to what is "normal" and what is "extraordinary" are themselves subjective and culturally conditioned.

Public officials, committed to "giving the public what it wants," are normally not willing to initiate new programs or open up new areas of government activity on their own initiative. They will do so when they perceive an overwhelming public demand for them to act, but only then. In a sense, their willingness to expand the functions of government is based on an extension of the *quid pro quo* "favors" system, which serves as the central core of their political relationships. New and better services are the reward they give the public for placing them in office. The value mix and legitimacy of change in the individualistic political culture are directly related to commercial concerns.

The individualistic political culture is ambivalent about the place of bureaucracy in the political order. In one sense, the bureaucratic method of operation flies in the face of the favor system that is central to the individualistic political process. At the same time, the virtues of organizational efficiency appear substantial to those seeking to master the market. In the end, bureaucratic organization is introduced within the framework of the favor system; large segments of the bureaucracy may be insulated from it through the merit system, but the entire organization is pulled into the political environment at crucial points through political appointment at the upper echelons and, very frequently, also through the bending of the merit system to meet political demands.

* * *

The Moralistic Political Culture

To the extent that American society is built on the principles of "commerce" (in the broadest sense) and that the marketplace provides the model for public relationships, all Americans share some of the attitudes that are of great importance in the individualistic political culture. At the same time, substantial segments of the American people operate politically within the framework of two political cultures—the moralistic and traditionalistic political cultures—whose theoretical structures and operational consequences depart significantly from the individualistic pattern at crucial points.

The *moralistic political culture* emphasizes the commonwealth conception as the basis for democratic government. Politics, to this political culture, is considered one of the great human activities: the search for the good society. True, it is a struggle for power, but it is also an effort to exercise power for the betterment of the commonwealth. Accordingly, in the moralistic political culture, both the general public and the politicians conceive of politics as a public activity centered on some notion of the public good and properly devoted to the advancement of the public interest. Good government, then, is measured by the degree to which it promotes the public good and in terms of the honesty, selflessness, and commitment to the public welfare of those who govern.

In the moralistic political culture, individualism is tempered by a general commitment to utilizing communal (preferably nongovernmental, but governmental if necessary) power to intervene in the sphere of "private" activities when it is considered necessary to do so for the public good or the well-being of the community. Accordingly, issues have an important place in the moralistic style of politics, functioning to set the tone for political concern. Government is considered a positive instrument with a responsibility to promote the general welfare, although definitions of what its positive role should be may vary considerably from era to era.

As in the case of the individualistic political culture, the change from nineteenth- to twentieth-century conceptions of what government's positive role should be has been great; for example, support for Prohibition has given way to support for wage and hour regulation. At the same time, care must be taken to distinguish between a predisposition toward communal activism and a desire for federal government activity. For example, many representatives of the moralistic political culture oppose federal aid for urban renewal without in any way opposing community responsibility for urban development. The distinction they make (implicitly, at least) is between what they consider legitimate community responsibility and what they believe to be central government encroachment; or between communitarianism, which they value, and "collectivism," which they abhor. Thus, on some public issues we find certain such representatives taking highly conservative positions despite their positive attitudes toward public activity generally. Such representatives may also prefer government intervention in the social realm—that is, censorship or screening of books and movies—over government intervention in the economy, holding that the former is necessary for the public good and the latter, harmful.

Since the moralistic political culture rests on the fundamental conception that politics exists primarily as a means for coming to grips with the issues and public concerns of civil society, it embraces the notion that politics is ideally a matter of concern for all citizens, not just those who are professionally committed to political careers. Indeed, this political culture considers it the duty of every citizen to participate in the political affairs of his or her commonwealth.

Accordingly, there is a general insistence within this political culture that government service is public service, which places moral obligations upon those who participate in government that are more demanding than the moral obligations of the marketplace. There is an equally general rejection of the notion that the field of politics is a legitimate realm for private economic enrichment. Of course, politicians may benefit economically because of their political careers, but they are not expected to *profit* from political activity; indeed, they are held suspect if they do.

Since the concept of serving the community is the core of the political relationship, politicians are expected to adhere to it even at the expense of individual loyalties and political friendships. Consequently, party regularity is not of prime importance. The political party is considered a useful political device, but it is not valued for its own sake. Regular party ties can be abandoned with relative impunity for third parties, special local parties, or nonpartisan systems if such changes are believed to be helpful in gaining larger political goals. People can even shift from party to party without sanctions if such change is justified by political belief.

In the moralistic political culture, rejection of firm party ties is not to be viewed as a rejection of politics as such. On the contrary, because politics is considered potentially good and healthy within the context of that culture, it is possible to have highly political nonpartisan systems. Certainly nonpartisanship is instituted not to eliminate politics but to improve it, by widening access to public office for those unwilling or unable to gain office through the regular party structure.

In practice, where the moralistic political culture is dominant today, there is considerably more amateur participation in politics. There is also much less of what Americans consider to be corruption in government and less tolerance of those actions considered to be corrupt. Hence politics does not have the taint it so often bears in the individualistic environment.

By virtue of its fundamental outlook, the moralistic political culture creates a greater commitment to active government intervention in the economic and social life of the community. At the same time, the strong commitment to *communitarianism* characteristic of that political culture tends to channel the interest in government intervention into highly localistic paths, such that a willingness to encourage local government intervention to set public standards does not necessarily reflect a concomitant willingness to allow outside governments equal opportunity to intervene. Not infrequently, public officials themselves will seek to initiate new government activities in an effort to come to grips with problems as yet unperceived by a majority of the citizenry. The moralistic political culture is not committed to either change or the status quo *per se* but, rather, will accept either depending upon the morally defined ends to be gained.

The major difficulty of this political culture in adjusting bureaucracy to the political order is tied to the potential conflict between communitarian principles and the necessity for large-scale organization to increase bureaucratic efficiency, a problem that could affect the attitudes of moralistic culture states toward federal activity of certain kinds. Otherwise, the notion of a politically neutral administrative system creates no problem within the moralistic value system and even offers many advantages. Where merit systems are instituted, they are rigidly maintained.

* * *

The Traditionalistic Political Culture

The *traditionalistic political culture* is rooted in an ambivalent attitude toward the marketplace coupled with a paternalistic and elitist conception of the commonwealth. It reflects an older, precommercial attitude that accepts a substantially hierarchical society as part of the ordered nature of things, authorizing and expecting those at the top of the social structure to take a special and dominant role in government. Like its moralistic counterpart, the traditionalistic political culture accepts government as an actor with a positive role in the community, but in a very limited sphere—mainly that of securing the continued maintenance of the existing social order. To do so, it functions to confine real political power to a relatively small and self-perpetuating group drawn from an established elite who often inherit their "right" to govern through family ties or social position. Accordingly, social and family ties are paramount in a traditionalistic political culture; in fact, their importance is greater than that of personal ties in the individualistic political culture, where, after all is said and done, a person's first responsibility is to him- or herself. At the same time, those who do not have a definite role to play in politics are not expected to be even minimally active as citizens. In many cases, they are not even expected to vote. In return, they are guaranteed that, outside of the limited sphere of politics, family rights (usually labeled "individual rights") are paramount, not to be taken lightly or ignored. As in the individualistic political culture, those active in politics are expected to benefit personally from their activity, though not necessarily through direct pecuniary gain.

Political parties are of minimal importance in a traditionalistic political culture, inasmuch as they encourage a degree of openness and competition that goes against the fundamental grain of an elite-oriented political order. Their major utility is to recruit people to fill the formal offices of government not desired by the established power-holders. Political competition in a traditionalistic political culture is usually conducted through factional alignments, as an extension of the personalistic politics that is characteristic of the system; hence political systems within the culture tend to have a loose one-party orientation if they have political parties at all.

Practically speaking, a traditionalistic political culture is found only in a society that retains some of the organic characteristics of the pre-industrial social order. "Good government" in the political culture involves the maintenance and encouragement of traditional patterns and, if necessary, their adjustment to changing conditions with the least possible upset. Where the traditionalistic political culture is dominant in the United States today, political leaders play conservative and custodial rather than initiatory roles unless pressed strongly from the outside.

Whereas the individualistic and moralistic political cultures may encourage the development of bureaucratic systems of organization on the grounds of "rationality" and "efficiency" in government (depending on their particular situations), traditionalistic political cultures tend to be instinctively anti-bureaucratic. The reason is that bureaucracy by its very nature interferes with the fine web of informal interpersonal relation-ships that lie at the root of the political system and have been developed by following traditional patterns over the years. Where bureaucracy is introduced, it is generally confined to ministerial functions under the aegis of the established power-holders.

* * *

The Distribution and Impact of Political Subcultures

Map 1 on pages 26–27 shows how migrational patterns have led to the concentration of specific political subcultures in particular states and localities. The basic patterns of political culture were set during the period of the rural-land frontier by three great streams of American migration that began on the East Coast and moved westward after the colonial period. Each stream moved from east to west along more or less fixed paths, following lines of least

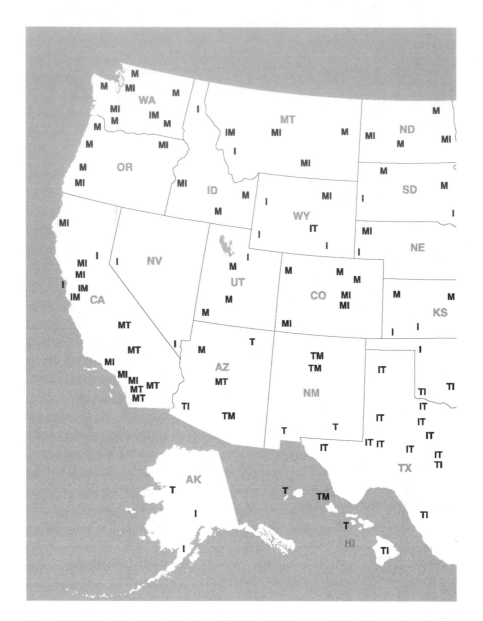

Map 1 The Regional Distribution of Political Cultures Within the States. *Source:* Daniel J. Elazar, *American Federalism: A View from the States*, 3d ed. (New York: Harper and Row Publishers, 1984), pp. 124–25. Reprinted by permission of HarperCollins Publishers.

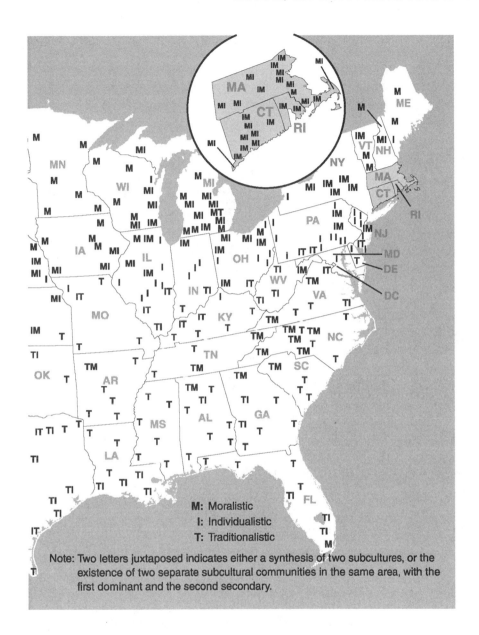

M: Moralistic
I: Individualistic
T: Traditionalistic

Note: Two letters juxtaposed indicates either a synthesis of two subcultures, or the existence of two separate subcultural communities in the same area, with the first dominant and the second secondary.

resistance that generally led them due west from the immediately previous area of settlement.

* * *

Political Culture: Some Caveats

By now the reader has no doubt formed his or her own value judgments as to the relative worth of the three political subcultures. For this reason a particular warning against *hasty* judgments must be added here. Each of the three political subcultures contributes something important to the configuration of the American political system, and each possesses certain characteristics that are inherently dangerous to the survival of that system.

The moralistic political culture, for example, is the primary source of the continuing American quest for the good society, yet there is a noticeable tendency toward inflexibility and narrow-mindedness among some of its representatives. The individualistic political culture is the most tolerant of out-and-out political corruption, yet it has also provided the framework for the integration of diverse groups into the mainstream of American life. When representatives of the moralistic political culture, in their striving for a better social order, try to limit individual freedom, they usually come up against representatives of the individualistic political culture, to whom individual freedom is the cornerstone of their pluralistic order, though not for any noble reasons. Conversely, of course, the moralistic political culture acts as a restraint against the tendencies of the individualistic political culture to tolerate anything as long as it is in the marketplace.

The traditionalistic political culture contributes to the search for continuity in a society whose major characteristic is change; yet in the name of continuity, its representatives have denied African Americans (as well as Native Americans and Latinos) their civil rights. When it is in proper working order, the traditionalistic culture has produced a unique group of first-rate national leaders from among its elites; but without a first-rate elite to draw upon, traditionalistic political-culture systems degenerate into oligarchies of the lowest level. Comparisons like these should induce caution in any evaluation of a subject that, by its very nature, evokes value judgments.

It is equally important to use caution in identifying individuals and groups as belonging to one cultural type or another on the basis of their public political behavior at a given moment in time. Immediate political responses to the issues of the day may reveal the political culture of the respondents, but not necessarily. Often, in fact, people will make what appear to be the same choices for different reasons—especially in public affairs, where the choices available at any given time are usually quite limited. Deeper analysis of what is behind those responses is usually needed. In other words, the names of the political cultures are not substitutes for the terms *conservative* and *liberal*, and should not be taken as such.

* * *

DISCUSSION QUESTIONS

1. Should the United States, as Liu argues, engage in a new Americanization process? If so, how? What are the potential benefits and potential problems with such a process? Is it important for the country to have a sense of "shared values" or not?

2. Political scientists and historians often refer to "American exceptionalism," or the idea that the United States is unique. For example, compared to other democratic countries, Americans place more emphasis on individual rights, and the United States features much greater decentralization of political power across the branches and levels of government. Do these outcomes *require* the kind of shared beliefs discussed by Warshawsky?

3. Consider the definitions Elazar presents in his analysis. What would you say are the fundamental differences and similarities among the three approaches?

4. A visitor from another country asks you, "What does it mean to be an American?" What do you say?

2

The Founding and the Constitution: How Democratic Is the Constitution?

Veneration for the Constitution is a classic American value; indeed, it is often said that the essence of being an American is a set of shared values and commitments expressed within the four corners of that document, most notably equality and liberty. The Constitution is the embodiment of those values, celebrated as the first, and most enduring, written constitution in human history. We celebrate the first words of the preamble, "We the people," salute the framers as men of historic wisdom and judgment, and honor the structures and processes of government.

We also note the practical wisdom of the framers, in their ability to reconcile competing tensions in creating a government powerful enough to function, but not at the risk of giving majorities the right to trample minority rights. Political theory at the time held that efforts to create democracies inevitably devolved into one of two end results: either mob rule, as majorities took control and used their power to oppress political minorities; or autocracy, as elites assumed control and did not give it up. The many carefully considered elements of constitutional structure—bicameralism, the balance between federal and state power, the equilibrium of checks and balances—have lasted for more than two centuries. And apart from one exceptional period of civil war, the structures have channeled political conflict peacefully.

Is that veneration truly warranted? Sanford Levinson, a professor at the University of Texas Law School, thinks not. He considers the Constitution to be a seriously flawed document in need of fundamental change. As originally written, the Constitution came nowhere near the aspirations of the Preamble, explicitly allowing slavery, and even after amendments retains several antidemocratic elements, including the electoral college; the vastly unequal representation in the Senate, in which Wyoming (population 576,000) has the same voting power as California (population 38 million, over sixty-five times as large); and lifetime tenure for judges. These features fail to live up to the Preamble, which Levinson considers to be the foundation of the rest of the Constitution—the whole point of the constitutional enterprise. Levinson points out that several key figures of the American founding—Thomas Jefferson especially—believed that the Constitution would require frequent updating. This was the purpose of Article V, which sets out the process for amending the document. And, Levinson notes, many of the features of the Constitution that we venerate were not thought through but were instead the product of pure compromise, in which the framers took vastly inconsistent positions when necessary in order to secure sufficient support for ratification. So, far from being a philosophically perfect document or system, the Constitution created a cumbersome and inequitable system, one that no other democratic system has chosen to copy since.

The problem with amending the Constitution is that the features Levinson considers most offensive—especially the unequal representation in the Senate—are virtually impossible to change. Article V specifies that no state can be deprived of its equal representation in the Senate without its consent (something that no state could ever be expected to do). The only recourse is a constitutional convention, in which delegates would consider fundamental reform. Levinson regards this as essential in order to allow the national government to respond to the challenge of modern economic and political times.

Eric Lane and Michael Oreskes take the more traditional stance that the Constitution is fine as it is; they argue that it is the people who must change. The key problem is that people do not understand the purpose of checks and balances or other features of the Constitution that frustrate their policy demands. But the Constitution is not just a mechanism for giving each of us what we want: the Constitution, they argue, is a vehicle for protecting liberty and providing the opportunity for individuals to pursue what they want through political and economic freedom. Instead of evaluating our legislators by how well they fulfill their constitutional duties, we base our evaluation on how much pork they can deliver to the folks at home. We are looking for an institutional fix through constitutional change when the problem is that our own fidelity to constitutional principles is waning. Evidence that the Constitution got it right comes from the fact that it produced the richest, freest, and most powerful country that has ever existed.

If there is one area of agreement between Levinson and Lane and Oreskes, it is that democracy is fragile, though they arrive at that conclusion for different reasons: Levinson because government fails to give the public what it wants, Lane and Oreskes because we are using our power to demand the wrong things.

Sanford Levinson

The Ratification Referendum: Sending the Constitution to a New Convention for Repair

The U.S. Constitution is radically defective in a number of important ways. Unfortunately, changing the Constitution is extremely difficult, for both political and constitutional reasons. But the difficulty of the task does not make it any less important that we first become aware of the magnitude of the deficiencies in the current Constitution and then turn our minds, as a community of concerned citizens, to figuring out potential solutions. This [reading] is organized around the conceit that Americans [should] have the opportunity to vote on the following proposal: "Shall Congress call a constitutional convention empowered to consider the adequacy of the Constitution, and, if thought necessary, to draft a new constitution that, upon completion, will be submitted to the electorate for its approval or disapproval by majority vote? Unless and until a new constitution gains popular approval, the current Constitution will continue in place."

Although such a referendum would be unprecedented with regard to the U.S. Constitution, there is certainly nothing "un-American" about such a procedure. As Professor John J. Dinan has noted in his recent comprehensive study of what he terms "the American state constitutional tradition," fourteen American states in their own constitutions explicitly give the people an opportunity "to periodically vote on whether a convention should be called." Article XIX of the New York Constitution, for example, provides that the state electorate be given the opportunity every twenty years to vote on the following question: "Shall there be a convention to revise the constitution and amend the same?" Should the majority answer in the affirmative, then the voters in each senate district will elect three delegates "at the next ensuring general election," while the statewide electorate "shall elect fifteen delegates-at-large." It should occasion no surprise that one author has described such a "mandatory referendum" as a means of "enforcing the people's right to reform their government."

It is no small matter to give people a choice with regard to the mechanisms—as well as the abstract principles—by which they are to be governed. The imagined referendum would allow "We the People of the United States of America," in whose name the document is ostensibly "ordain[ed]," to examine the fit between our national aspirations, set out in the Preamble to the Constitution, and the particular means chosen to realize those goals.

I am assuming that those reading this * * * are fellow Americans united by a deep and common concern about the future of our country. * * * I hope to convince you that, as patriotic Americans truly committed to the deepest principles of the Constitution, we should vote yes and thus trigger a new convention. My task is to persuade you that the Constitution we currently live under is grievously flawed, even in some ways a "clear and present danger" to achieving the laudable and inspiring goals to which this country professes to be committed, including republican self-government.

I believe that the best way to grasp the goals of our common enterprise is to ponder the inspiring words of the Preamble to the Constitution:

> We the People of the United States, in Order to form a more perfect Union, establish Justice, insure domestic tranquility, provide for the common defence, promote the general Welfare, and secure the Blessings of Liberty to ourselves and our Posterity, do ordain and establish this Constitution for the United States of America.

It is regrettable that law professors rarely teach and that courts rarely cite the Preamble, for it is *the single most important part* of the Constitution. The reason is simple: It announces the *point* of the entire enterprise. The 4,500 or so words that followed the Preamble in the original, unamended Constitution were all in effect merely means that were thought to be useful to achieving the great aims set out above. It is indeed the ends articulated in the Preamble that justify the means of our political institutions. And to the extent that the means turn out to be counterproductive, then we should revise them.

It takes no great effort to find elements in the original Constitution that run counter to the Preamble. It is impossible for us today to imagine how its authors squared a commitment to the "Blessings of Liberty" with the toleration and support of chattel slavery that is present in various articles of the Constitution. The most obvious example is the bar placed on Congress's ability to forbid the participation by Americans in the international slave trade until 1808. The most charitable interpretation of the framers, articulated by Frederick Douglass, is that they viewed these compromises with the acknowledged evil of slavery as temporary; the future would see its eradication through peaceful constitutional processes.

One might believe that the Preamble is incomplete because, for example, it lacks a commitment to the notion of equality. Political scientist Mark Graber has suggested that the reference to "*our* Posterity" suggests a potentially unattractive limitation of our concerns *only* to members of the American political community, with no notice taken of the posterity of other societies, whatever their plight. Even if one would prefer a more explicitly cosmopolitan Preamble, I find it hard to imagine rejecting any of the overarching values enunciated there. In any event, I am happy to endorse the Preamble as the equivalent of our creedal summary of America's civil religion.

There are two basic responses to the discovery that ongoing institutional practices are counterproductive with regard to achieving one's announced goals. One is to adjust the practices in ways that would make achievement of the aims more likely. This is, often, when we mean by the very notion of rationality: One does not persist in behaviors that are acknowledged to make more difficult the realization of one's professed hopes. Still, a second response, which has its own rationality, is to adjust the goals to the practices. Sometimes, this makes very good sense if one comes to the justified conclusion that the goals may be utopian. In such cases, it is a sign of maturity to recognize that we will inevitably fall short in our aims and that "the best may be enemy of the good" if we are tempted to throw over quite adequate, albeit imperfect, institutions in an attempt to attain the ideal.

Perhaps one might even wish to defend the framers' compromises with slavery on the ground that they were absolutely necessary to the achievement of the political union of the thirteen states. One must believe that such a union, in turn, was preferable to the likely alternative, which would have been the creation of two or three separate countries along the Atlantic coast. Political scientist David Hendrickson has demonstrated that many of the framers—and many other theorists as well—viewed history as suggesting a high probability that such separate countries would have gone to war with one another and made impossible any significant measure of "domestic tranquility." Hendrickson well describes the Constitution as a "peace pact" designed to prevent the possibility of war. If there is one thing we know, it is that unhappy compromises must often be made when negotiating such pacts. Of course, American slaves—and their descendants— could scarcely be expected to be so complacently accepting of these compromises, nor, of course, should *any* American who takes seriously the proclamation of the Pledge of Allegiance that ours is a system that takes seriously the duty to provide "liberty and justice for all."

Not only must we restrain ourselves from expecting too much of any government; we must also recognize that the Preamble sets out potentially conflicting goals. It is impossible to maximize the achievement of all of the great ends of the Constitution. To take an obvious example, providing for the "common defence" may require on occasion certain incursions into the "Blessings of Liberty." One need only refer to the military draft, which was upheld in 1918 by the Supreme Court against an attack claiming that it constituted the "involuntary servitude"—that is, slavery—prohibited by the Thirteenth Amendment. We also properly accept certain limitations on the freedom of the press with regard, say, to publishing certain information—the standard example is troop movements within a battle zone—deemed to be vital to American defense interests. The year 2005 ended with the beginning of a great national debate about the propriety of warrantless interceptions of telephone calls and other incursions on traditional civil liberties in order, ostensibly, to protect ourselves against potential terrorists.

Even if one concedes the necessity of adjusting aims in light of practical realities, it should also be readily obvious that one can easily go overboard. At the very least, one should always be vigilant in assessing such adjustments lest one find, at the end of the day, that the aims have been reduced to hollow shells. It is also necessary to ask if a rationale supporting a given adjustment that might well have been convincing at time A necessarily continues to be present at time B. Practical exigencies that required certain political compromises in 1787 no longer obtain today. We have long since realized this about slavery. It is time that we apply the same critical eye to the compromise of 1787 that granted all states an equal vote in the Senate.

To criticize that particular compromise—or any of the other features of the Constitution that I shall examine below—is not necessarily to criticize the founders themselves. My project—and, therefore, your own vote for a new convention, should you be persuaded by what follows—requires no denigration of the founders. They were, with some inevitable exceptions, an extraordinary group of men who performed extraordinary deeds, including drafting a Constitution that started a brand-new governmental system. By and large, they deserve the monuments that have been erected in their honor. But they themselves emphasized the importance—indeed, necessity—of learning from experience.

They were, after all, a generation that charted new paths by overturning a centuries-long notion of the British constitutional order because it no longer conformed to their own sense of possibility (and fairness). They also, as it happened, proved ruthlessly willing to ignore the limitations of America's "first constitution," the Articles of Confederation. Although Article XIII of that founding document required unanimous approval by the thirteen state legislatures before any amendment could take effect, Article VII of the Constitution drafted in Philadelphia required the approval of only nine of the thirteen states, and the approval was to be given by state conventions rather than by the legislatures.

The most important legacies handed down by the founding generation were, first, a remarkable willingness to act in bold and daring ways when they believed that the situation demanded it, coupled with the noble visions first of the Declaration of Independence and then of the Preamble. Both are as inspiring—and potentially disruptive—today as when they were written more than two centuries ago. But we should also be inspired by the copious study that Madison and others made of every available history and analysis of political systems ranging from ancient Greece to the Dutch republic and the British constitutional order. We best honor the framers by taking the task of creating a republican political order as seriously as they did and being equally willing to learn from what the history of the past 225 years, both at home and abroad, can teach us about how best to achieve and maintain such an order. At the time of its creation, we could legitimately believe that we were the only country committed to democratic self-governance. That is surely no longer the case, and we might well have lessons to learn from our co-ventures in that enterprise. To the extent that experience teaches us that the Constitution in significant aspects demeans "the consent of the governed" and has become an impediment to achieving the goals of the Preamble, we honor rather than betray the founders by correcting their handiwork.

Overcoming Veneration

* * * I suspect * * * that at least some readers might find it difficult to accept even the possibility that our Constitution is seriously deficient because they

venerate the Constitution and find the notion of seriously criticizing it almost sacrilegious.

In an earlier book, *Constitutional Faith*, I noted the tension between the desire of James Madison that Americans "venerate" their Constitution and the distinctly contrasting views of his good friend Thomas Jefferson that, instead, the citizenry regularly subject it to relentless examination. Thus, whatever may have been Jefferson's insistence on respecting what he called the "chains" of the Constitution, he also emphasized that the "Creator has made the earth for the living, not the dead." It should not be surprising, then, that he wrote to Madison in 1789, "No society can make a perpetual constitution, or even a perpetual law."

Jefferson and Madison might have been good friends and political associates, but they disagreed fundamentally with regard to the wisdom of subjecting the Constitution to critical analysis. Jefferson was fully capable of writing that "[w]e may consider each generation as a distinct nation, with a right, by the will of its majority, to bind themselves, but none to bind the succeeding generation, more than the inhabitants of another country." His ultimate optimism about the Constitution lay precisely in its potential for change: "Happily for us, that when we find our constitutions defective and insufficient to secure the happiness of our people, we can assemble with all the coolness of philosophers, and set it to rights, while every other nation on earth must have recourse to arms to amend or restore their constitutions." * * *

Madison, however, would have none of this. He treated 1787 almost as a miraculous and singular event. Had he been a devotee of astrology, he might have said that the stars were peculiarly and uniquely aligned to allow the drafting of the Constitution and then its ratification. Though Madison was surely too tactful to mention this, part of the alignment was the absence of the famously contentious Jefferson and John Adams. Both were 3,000 miles across the sea, where they were serving as the first ambassadors from the new United States to Paris and London, respectively. Moreover, it certainly did not hurt that Rhode Island had refused to send any delegates at all and therefore had no opportunity to make almost inevitable mischief, not to mention being unable to vote in an institutional structure where the vote of one state could make a big difference. And, if pressed, Madison would presumably have agreed that the Constitutional Convention—and the ratifying conventions thereafter—would never have succeeded had the delegates included American slaves, Native Americans, or women in the spirit of Abigail Adams. She had famously—and altogether unsuccessfully—told her husband that leaders of the new nation should "remember the ladies." One need not see the framers in Philadelphia as an entirely homogeneous group—they were not—in order to realize that the room was devoid of those groups in America that were viewed as merely the *objects*, and not the active *subjects*, of governance.

Madison sets out his views most clearly in the *Federalist*, No. 49, where he explicitly takes issue with Jefferson's proposal for rather frequent constitutional conventions that would consider whether "alter[ation]" of the constitution might be desirable. Madison acknowledges the apparent appeal, in a system where "the people are the only legitimate fountain of power," of "appeal[ing] to the people themselves." However, "there appear to be insuperable objections against the proposed recurrence to the people." Perhaps the key objection is that *"frequent appeal to the people would carry an implication of some defect in the government [and] deprive the government of that veneration which time bestows on every thing, and without which perhaps the wisest and freest governments would not possess the requisite stability."* Only "a nation of philosophers" can forgo this emotion of veneration—and, therefore, feel free of guilt-ridden anxiety about the idea of constitutional change. However, "a nation of philosophers is as little to be expected as the philosophical race of kings wished for by Plato."

Madison is thus fearful of "disturbing the public tranquillity by interesting too strongly the public passions." The success of Americans in replacing a defective Articles of Confederation with a better Constitution does not constitute a precedent for future action. We should "recollect," he says, "that all the existing constitutions were formed in the midst of a danger which repressed the passions most unfriendly to order and concord." Moreover, the people at large possessed "an enthusiastic confidence . . . in their patriotic leaders," which, he says, fortunately "stifled the ordinary diversity of opinions on great national questions." He is extremely skeptical that the "future situations in which we must expect to be usually placed" will "present any equivalent security against the danger" of an excess of public passion, disrespect for leaders, and the full play of diverse opinions. In case there is any doubt, he writes of his fear that the "*passions*, therefore, not the *reasons*, of the public would sit in judgment."

Madison's view of his fellow Americans was far closer to that of Alexander Hamilton, with whom he had coauthored the *Federalist*. One can doubt that Madison expressed any reservations when hearing Hamilton, addressing his fellow delegates to the Philadelphia convention on June 18, 1787, denounce the conceit that "the voice of the people" is "the voice of God." On the contrary, said Hamilton: "The people are turbulent and changing; they seldom judge or determine right." Although Madison was not opposed to constitutional amendment as such, he clearly saw almost no role for a public that would engage in probing questions suggesting that there might be serious "defects" in the Constitution. Only philosophers (like himself?) or, perhaps, "patriotic leaders" could be trusted to engage in dispassionate political dialogue and reasoning. In contrast, the general public should be educated to feel only "veneration" for their Constitution rather than be encouraged to use their critical faculties and actually assess the relationship between the great ends set out in the Preamble and the instruments devised for their realization.

* * *

This is a mistake. To the extent that we continue thoughtlessly to venerate, and therefore not subject to truly critical examination, our Constitution, we are in the position of the battered wife who continues to profess the "essential goodness" of her abusive husband. To stick with the analogy for a moment, it may well be the case that the husband, when sober or not gambling, is a decent, even loving, partner. The problem is that such moments are more than counterbalanced by abusive ones, even if they are relatively rare. And he becomes especially abusive when she suggests the possibility of marital counseling and attendant change. Similarly, that there are good features of our Constitution should not be denied. But there are also significantly abusive ones, and it is time for us to face them rather than remain in a state of denial.

Trapped Inside the Article V Cage

The framers of the Constitution were under no illusion that they had created a perfect document. The best possible proof for this proposition comes from George Washington himself. As he wrote to his nephew Bushrod two months after the conclusion of the Philadelphia convention over which he had presided, *"The warmest friends and the best supporters the Constitution has do not contend that it is free from imperfections*; but they found them unavoidable and are sensible if evil is likely to arise there from, the remedy must come hereafter." Sounding a remarkably Jeffersonian note, Washington noted that the "People (for it is with them to Judge) can, as they will have the advantage of experience on their Side, decide with as much propriety on the alteration[s] and amendment[s] which are necessary." Indeed, wrote the man described as the Father of Our

Country, "I do not think we are more inspired, have more wisdom, or possess more virtue, than those who will come after us."

Article V itself is evidence of the recognition of the possibility—and inevitable reality—of imperfection, else they would have adopted John Locke's suggestion in a constitution that he drafted for the Carolina colonies that would have made the document unamendable. It is an unfortunate reality, though, that Article V, practically speaking, brings us all too close to the Lockean dream (or nightmare) of changeless stasis.

As University of Houston political scientist Donald Lutz has conclusively demonstrated, the U.S. Constitution is the most difficult to amend of any constitution currently existing in the world today. Formal amendment of the U.S. Constitution generally requires the approval of two-thirds of each of the two houses of our national Congress, followed by the approval of three-quarters of the states (which today means thirty-eight of the fifty states). Article V does allow the abstract possibility that amendments could be proposed through the aegis of a constitutional convention called by Congress upon the petition of two-thirds of the states; such proposals, though, would still presumably have to be ratified by the state legislatures or, in the alternative, as was done with regard to the Twenty-first Amendment repealing the prohibition of alcohol required by the Eighteenth Amendment, by conventions in each of the states. As a practical matter, though, Article V makes it next to impossible to amend the Constitution with regard to genuinely controversial issues, even if substantial—and intense—majorities advocate amendment.

As I have written elsewhere, some significant change functionally similar to "amendment" has occurred informally, outside of the procedures set out by Article V. One scholar has aptly described this as a process of "constitutional change off-the-books." Yale law professor Bruce Ackerman has written several brilliant books detailing the process of "non-Article V" amendment, and I warmly commend them to the reader. Yet it is difficult to argue that such informal amendment has occurred, or is likely to occur, with regard to the basic *structural* aspects of the American political system with which this book is primarily concerned.

It is one thing to argue, as Ackerman has done, that the New Deal worked as a functional amendment of the Constitution by giving Congress significant new powers to regulate the national economy. Similarly, one could easily argue that the president, for good or for ill, now possesses powers over the use of armed forces that would have been inconceivable to the generation of the framers. Whatever the text of the Constitution may say about the power of Congress to "declare war" or whatever the original understanding of this clause, it is hard to deny that many presidents throughout our history have successfully chosen to take the country to war without seeking a declaration of war (or, in some cases, even prior congressional approval of any kind). Ackerman and David Golove have also persuasively argued that the Treaty Clause, which requires that two-thirds of the Senate assent to any treaty, has been transformed through the use of "executive agreements." Although such agreements are unmentioned in the text of the Constitution, presidents have frequently avoided the strictures of the Treaty Clause by labeling an "agreement" what earlier would have been viewed as a "treaty." Thus, the North American Free Trade Agreement did not have to leap the hurdles erected by the Treaty Clause; instead, it was validated by majority votes of both the House of Representatives and the Senate.

These developments are undoubtedly important, and any complete analysis of our constitutional system should take account of such flexibility. But we should not overemphasize our system's capacity to change, and it is *constitutional stasis* rather than the potential for adaptation that is my focus.

* * *

* * * One cannot, as a practical matter, litigate the obvious inequality attached to Wyoming's having the same voting power in the Senate as California. Nor can we imagine even President George W. Bush, who has certainly not been a shrinking violet with regard to claims of presidential power, announcing that Justice John Paul Stevens—appointed in 1976 and embarking on this fourth decade of service on the Supreme Court at the age of eighty-six—is simply "too old" or has served "long enough," and that he is therefore nominating, and asking the Senate to confirm, a successor to Justice Stevens in spite of the awkward fact that the justice has not submitted his resignation.

In any event, * * * the Constitution makes it unacceptably difficult to achieve the inspiring goals of the Preamble and, therefore, warrants our disapproval. * * *

Although I am asking you to take part in a hypothetical referendum and to vote no with regard to the present Constitution, I am *not* asking you to imagine simply tearing it up and leaping into the unknown of a fanciful "state of nature." All you must commit yourself to is the proposition that the Constitution is sufficiently flawed to justify calling a new convention authorized to scrutinize all aspects of the Constitution and to suggest such changes as are felt to be desirable. The new convention would be no more able to bring its handiwork into being by fiat than were the framers in Philadelphia. All proposals would require popular approval in a further national referendum. This leaves open the possibility that, even after voting to trigger the convention, you could ultimately decide that the "devil you know" (the present Constitution) is preferable to the "devil you don't" (the proposed replacement). But the important thing, from my perspective, is to recognize that there are indeed "devilish" aspects of our present Constitution that should be confronted and, if at all possible, exorcised. To complete this metaphor, one might also remember that "the devil is in the details." * * *

Eric Lane and Michael Oreskes
We

We live in a remarkable political age. More people than ever before in history, possibly a majority of all the people on earth, live under governments that could reasonably be described as democracies. The enormity of this can only be grasped by going back * * * to that moment in the late 1700s when democracy as we now know it barely existed in the world. Indeed, the word *democracy* was essentially an insult, a synonym for *mob rule*. Yes, there were places where the king had ceded some measure of power to aristocracies or even to semirepresentative parliaments. There were also commercial cities in Europe that had allowed considerable popular participation in decision making.

But nowhere was there anything like what a group of men, desperately trying to save their fledgling country, invented in Philadelphia in the summer of 1787. They wrote "a Constitution which . . . has brought such a happy order out of so gloomy a chaos," James Madison said of his handiwork many years later. They wrote a Constitution that invented a new kind of representative government. It ushered in what we can now see as the Age of Democracy in which "representative government bottomed on the principle of popular sovereignty . . . has become the political norm." In a recent book on the rise of democracy, the British scholar John Dunn finds Madison's pride understandable given the far-reaching effects of his invention: "It secured the new Republic extremely effectively, and, as we now know, for a very long time. In doing so, it turned the United States into the most politically definite, the best consolidated and the most politically self-confident society on earth. It also, over time . . . opened the way for it to become overwhelmingly the most powerful state in human history."

Quite an impressive summer's work.

But where are we in the life span of this invention? The American experiment has now lasted longer than any democracy in history. (Athens, for example, lasted only around 170 years as a democracy.) It has also spawned and inspired many others to pursue democracy. After much spillage of words and blood across the twentieth century, there is no longer even a serious intellectual challenger to representative democracy as the best and most legitimate way to organize government. What a long way we have come from 1787! "The United States is now the oldest enduring republic in world history, with a set of political institutions and traditions that have stood the test of time," wrote the historian Joseph J. Ellis.

The framers would have been stunned by this success. They knew the lessons of history were against them. They had learned from experience that individuals set free pursued their own interests. Large numbers of individuals pursuing their own interests led to chaos. Chaos invited dictators, homegrown or external, to intervene to restore order, snuffing out the very liberty people had fought to establish. They understood this cycle from their reading and, more, from the first eleven years of their own nation, which by 1787 seemed to them to be descending into the gloomy chaos Madison wrote of later.

That is why they saw democracy as "fragile."

Fragile because the framers had come to understand that in pursuit of their self-interests, Americans, like everyone else, would be willing to trample the "democracy" of others thus endangering their own.

Fragile because it was dependent on the broad participation of Americans in the nation's political processes.

Fragile because it was dependent on the willingness of Americans to acquiesce to the results of such a process.

Fragile because of the Constitution's delicate arrangement of checks and balances.

Fragile because it was a system for institutionalizing compromise. There would always be citizens searching for a more perfect system, some system that promised more wealth, or more security, or more equality, or a more glorious future, or just more of whatever it is they particularly wanted.

That was the challenge the framers confronted in 1787. People wanted what they wanted for themselves. The framers' solution, wonderfully modern and, in 1787, totally original, was to adopt a more realistic view of people and adapt their design for government to that view. They enlisted vice "on the side of virtue." They set out to prove how a representative democracy could operate without special public virtue, how "an avaricious society can form a government able to defend itself against the avarice of its members." In other words, this was not a government as good as its people. It was a government designed to produce results better than the desires of each individual person! And that is how the people ensured their own liberty. Out of many one, *E Pluribus Unum*.

To accept democracy as it emerged from Philadelphia meant to accept, as Franklin said, that this was no perfect system, just the closest to perfection a human design could come.

The framers worried that their new democracy would last only a few years. But amazingly it succeeded. Two hundred and twenty years later, the many offshoots of modern representative democracy have triumphed around the world. How ironic, then, that its original American version, with its complicated checks and balances, faces meaningful challenge in the place where it was born.

This is not the first such challenge in American history, of course, and we hope not the last. It won't be if we face it, as previous generations faced their constitutional challenges. The challenge takes new forms each time. But at heart the issue is always the same: We want what we want, and we are convinced that the system that is stopping us is wrong, flawed, broken or outmoded.

This is the essence of our present challenge. The bond between government and governed has become strained. Americans are deeply frustrated with the workings of their government. They see it as unresponsive, unrepresentative, ineffective, crippling. Can you image even a handful of Americans acknowledging today that the purpose of their government is to produce results better than the desires of the people as individuals? Not likely.

We Americans love the framers. We consume books about them and revere their words. But we have lost our connection to what they actually invented and how that invention over time created in us what we have come to call a Constitutional Conscience. We have lost the narrative thread that connects us to the story of our constitutional democracy. That story tells us two things. First, how the framers learned a series of lessons between 1776 and 1787 and used these lessons to craft our government, the blueprint for which became the Constitution. And second, how we, the people, created a Constitutional Conscience from the essential meaning of that Constitution—its freedoms and its processes and tradeoffs—and guided by these principles were then able to adapt time and again through our history to an evolving America.

This narrative thread is vital to us. It is the story that makes us Americans, ties us to our government and ties our government to us. Without it we have begun, without being totally conscious of what we are doing, to drift away from our constitutional system. We are drifting away because our knowledge of our system has grown thin. From the 1960s onward, according to Derek Bok, civic education has been declining and by the 1980s had nearly vanished. "It is striking how little energy is devoted to trying to engage citizens more actively in the affairs of government. Civic education in the public schools has been almost totally eclipsed by a preoccupation with preparing the workforce of a global economy. Most universities no longer treat the preparation of citizens as an explicit goal of their curriculum."

Reports have documented this steady decline in civic understanding. In 1998, the Department of Education found that 75 percent of high school seniors were "not proficient in civics; one third lacked even a basic comprehension of how the government operates, while only 9 percent could give two reasons why citizens should participate in the democratic process." A report in 2002 concluded "that the nation's citizenry is woefully under-educated about the fundamentals of our American Democracy."

This lack of connection is producing a dangerous spiral of frustration and disenchantment. On the one hand, Americans take the existence of our democracy for granted, while, on the other hand, being frustrated with its workings. This produces a dangerous spiral of frustration and disenchantment. Observed Bok: "Americans have expectations for politics and the political process that are often unrealistic. Convinced that presidents can often accomplish more than is humanly possible, that legislators should be able to arrive at sensible decisions without prolonged disagreement or controversy, and that politicians should refrain from pandering to the voters yet still reflect the views of their constituents, the public seems fated to endure repeated disappointment over the government and those who run it."

Some Americans respond to this disappointment by demanding changes in the system, others by distancing themselves from the system, which leaves those who stay engaged more powerful to push for the agenda they want.

Those demands for change come in two basic forms, although proponents of each argue that their proposals would make the system more democratic by shifting power. There are the Lloyd Cutlers, Oliver Norths and Dick Cheneys who want to shift more power to the president so he can either force the rest of the government to respond or just act without being fettered by the process. And there are others who want to shift more power directly to citizens so they can force government to respond, or simply go around the process. That they want such changes is within their rights. But any meaningful argument for them must occur in the context of the lessons the framers learned long ago. Without this context, we risk making changes that dismantle what has been proven right about our system and even endanger the freedoms it was built to guarantee.

It might be helpful to restate those lessons, in a simple form that everyone can paste on their refrigerator.

The framers boiled their experience down to a Constitution. We have boiled their experience down to these five lessons.

1. Everyone is selfish. This is not to say that people cannot act well or perform acts of great nobility. But essentially people act to achieve their own self-interest, particularly at the level at which government operates: regulating conduct and redistributing wealth. People are, however, willing to trade one benefit for another and sometimes even sacrifice a narrow interest for a broader one that they feel will ultimately do them more good. The government's job is to find those areas of common ground. That is where we can build a common good.

2. Government is the steam valve of society. It funnels and relieves the pressures that build from competing interests.

3. Political process is more important than product. Consensus around a flawed plan can still produce great progress. (The Constitution itself is the best example.) But a "perfect plan" without consensus will only produce conflict and deadlock. (The Clinton health care debacle is one example.) Respect for the system is thus a vital prerequisite for progress. When respect is in such short supply, it is no surprise that progress is, as well.

4. The strength of consensus is directly related to the breadth of representation and the depth of deliberation. A sound-bite society where civic education has vanished has little basis for forging strong consensus.

5. Every interest is a special one. The founders would no doubt be amazed by the scale and power of modern corporations and trade unions. But they would have no difficulty at all with the idea that everyone has wants and desires and that these drive their views and their allegiances to

groups and factions. To them, the only meaningful definition of the *common good* would be the agreement that emerged from an inclusive political and legislative process to resolve competing (special) interests.

Our world is very different from that of the framers. People have powers now they could not have dreamed of then. Information, the lifeblood of democracy, moved then at the speed of sail. It moves now at the speed of light.

But there is no evidence that people have changed. Therefore, we see no reason to abandon the lessons the framers formed about people or the system they built from those lessons. Indeed, some of the changes, most particularly the speed with which society can now move, only reinforce the need for care in our political deliberations and for the speed bumps in the process that prevent us from rushing to judgment. That is what the framers built for us.

Recent experience reminds us that we make mistakes as a country when we move away from how our system was built to work. When people say now they wish the Congress and the media had done more to question the march to war in Iraq, they are saying, too, that they wish the leaders of Congress and of the press had done more to assert their authority, and fulfill their responsibilities, under, respectively, Article I and the First Amendment to the Constitution. Even many proponents of the war concede now that the checks and balances did not work well. We believe this failure was due to the weakening of our sense of constitutional roles, of our Constitutional Conscience.

We as Americans need to continue to remind ourselves of the framers' concern that democracy was fragile.

So far, unlike in the past, no one is openly arguing for an abandonment of democracy. Indeed, what many Americans think we need is what they see as more democracy. Both the proponents of strengthened presidential power and the proponents of direct democracy argue that their proposals would make the system more representative of the general public: the president as the only nationally elected official, and direct democracy as the only means to involve Americans more directly in the decision-making processes. Either way, the argument is for a more direct engagement and less entanglement in Washington process. We understand those feelings. They rise historically from a treasured strain of American belief running back to, at least, Tom Paine, the Declaration of Independence, and the Articles of Confederation.

But we must not forget the warning of the framers that the most likely undoing of democracy would be in the name of more democracy.

That thought is why we wrote this book. We wanted to pick up the dropped narrative thread of the American democratic story, to remind ourselves that the democratic thinking of 1776 is only the first half of our legacy. The second half was born of Madison and his colleagues in 1787. The framers in 1787 saw liberty and direct democracy is inadequate on their own to ensure the very democracy they purported to further. For in the real world in which government works, this directly democratic perspective translates into one group getting its way over the interest of other groups or one branch, whether a powerful legislature or monarchical president, getting too much power over everyone else.

The framers' ideas transformed the thirst for liberty into a real nation. Madison and his colleagues invented a form of government whose purpose, as the historian Gordon Wood summed it up, was not to transcend our differences but to reconcile them.

Americans' current frustration and anger with their government is sapping their commitment to the principles that have made the country work. Rather than drift away from the Constitution, we should renew our connection to it. We should remember that consultation and process and debate are good things, even when they slow and complicate decisions. Most of all, we should remind each other that compromise is a show of strength, not weakness. Reaffirming these constitutional principles will actually address our frustration better than inventing something different, or more accurately, returning to what did not work between 1776 and 1787.

People say that what they want is compromise and consensus. The framers believed in that. It is why the most important and radical word in the Constitution was the first word, *We*. The government was the people and is the people. The power of each branch of government is a grant from the people, and each branch to one degree or another is accountable to them. Nothing like this had ever been created before. One British political leader, comparing the evolution of Britain's unwritten constitution to the seemingly overnight drafting of the U.S. Constitution, called the latter "the most wonderful work ever struck off at a given time by the brain and purpose of man."

But Americans in practice, in the grind of life, are no longer seeing it this way. For one thing, they do not connect their desire for consensus with the Constitution's governmental design. For another, they routinely, and predictably, define the consensus they want as the achievement of their own goals, not something larger. Americans' demands on government are today broad and deeply diverse. And when they are in an uncompromising mood, when they are divided fifty-fifty, red from blue, their representative government reflects this division, and it stalls.

The problem is not that government is unrepresentative. The problem, if you want to call it that, is that the government is very representative. The message we are hearing is that our government does not work. The message we should be hearing is that our government is a reflection of our own divisions. What we need is not a new system of government. We need a renewed willingness to work out our differences and find compromises, consensus and that other now-popular phrase, common ground.

The purpose of American-style democracy is not to guarantee each of us what we want individually. It is to give each of us as large an opportunity as possible to pursue what we want within the limits the Constitution and our Constitutional Conscience impose on us. This tension between individual liberty and community restraint has over time produced a great deal of good for a great many people and worked better than any alternative yet tried. It is still the best system for our sprawling, complicated nation.

To say that ours is the best system is not to say that it is a perfect system. It is not and never will be perfect. It can't be. It is composed of we, the people, with all our flaws. That is the point. We make it work. Our drive. Our demands. Our participation! In 1888, the poet and editor James Russell Lowell remarked on the "splendid complacency" he found among his fellow Americans who were "neglectful" of their "political duties." He traced this neglect back to a widespread but mistaken belief that the framers of the Constitution had "invented a machine that would go of itself." Lowell said he admired the ability of Americans to let "confidence in our luck" and "absorption with material interests" subsume attention to the state of our democracy.

* * *

These problems have been building for years. By the end of the 1980s, politicians in Washington were in open despair that the political system was unable to deal with the problems facing the country.

The political deterioration has grown steadily worse. Not surprisingly, since it is our most representative branch of government, the dysfunction is most visible in the Congress. In a nation of citizens so lacking in an understanding of our system, it is hardly surprising that, increasingly, the men and women they send to Washington don't make an adherence to constitutional principles an important part of their daily work. "People revere the Constitution yet know so little about it—and that goes for some of my fellow senators," said the Senate's top institutionalist, Robert Byrd of West Virginia.

The framers counted on a balance of power between Congress and the president. They were, critically, intended to watch each other. But * * * Congress has wavered in the exercise of its constitutional duty.

The weakness of the legislature throws off the whole design of the system. The strong reassertions of presidential prerogatives would not have surprised the framers. They would have expected this, although some may have been surprised at the degree. "You must . . . oblige [the government] to control itself," Madison wrote. The American system counts on each branch asserting its authority, just as it counts on each individual to press his or her wishes. Balance is essential to the framers' design, but to find the right balance each participant has to push and pull. The danger comes when one branch pushes and the other folds.

* * *

The imbalance we refer to here is far more than the common instinct of members of Congress trying to protect a president of the same party. To some extent, this will always happen. But American history is marked with examples of members of Congress of each party asserting their institutional, constitutional role and challenging a president of their own party. Senator Harry S. Truman investigated President Roosevelt's administration, and Senator Lyndon B. Johnson investigated president Truman's administration. It was a Republican senator, Howard Baker, whose incessant questions crystallized the belief that a Republican president knew more about Watergate than he had told. And it was a Democratic senator, Daniel Patrick Moynihan, who blocked the Democratic president and his wife from their plan to overhaul American health care. Moynihan's critique was a classic defense of constitutional process. The Clintons drafted their plan, Moynihan complained, behind closed doors and failed to consult the Congress or build a consensus. And a few Republican legislators had begun challenging President George W. Bush's Iraq policy by the end of 2006.

But over the last few years on Capitol Hill, the Republican leadership seemed to disown the institutional role in the constitutional design. * * * Without amending the Constitution, both Senator Bill Frist and Speaker Dennis Hastert effectively gave President Bush the parliamentary type of system that Lloyd Cutler had so desperately wanted for President Carter. They operated as the president's floor leaders in the Congress, rather than as his separate and coequal partners in government.

Congress of course is not a piece of machinery. It is 535 individual members. They are the ones who decide how assertive to be. The single most important factor in that decision is the question of how assertive American voters expect them to be. Senator Frist and Speaker Hastert followed their path because it was easy, because they did not feel political pressure to assert their institutional roles under the Constitution. We can blame the voters for not pressuring the leaders. Or we can blame the leaders for not leading the citizens. Both are true. If two of the top elected figures in the country have such little regard for the institutional obligations handed down to them, how can we expect ordinary Americans to pay attention to the Constitution? Yet it is also hard to ask politicians to exercise institutional responsibilities that we give them no credit for exercising.

Both sides of the problem are an outgrowth of how far we have fallen away from an intimate knowledge of or connection to our Constitutional Conscience. We judge our politicians heavily by what we want and how well they deliver. We measure them in the present tense alone. We don't praise honest men and women for taking clear stands on constitutional principle or exercising those institutional responsibilities. We want to know what they have done for us lately; not what they have done to faithfully exercise the responsibilities given them by the Constitution. And how could it be otherwise, for we have little idea what those responsibilities are. * * *

The 2006 election sent a message to the incumbents in Congress. In very much the way the Federalists were tossed out in 1800, after President Adams failed to stop a Federalist Congress from plunging forward with the reviled Sedition Act, the Republicans were tossed out of Congress in 2006 for failing to check a Republican president's plunge into an unpopular war. Elections, as vital as they are, are in effect a last resort—the voters passing judgment after the fact. The system was designed to produce better results before the fact, when it is allowed to work. Whether you in the end supported or opposed American entry into Iraq, that decision, and more particularly the decision of the president and Congress, would have been stronger and more effective if it had been subject to more oversight in Congress and more debate in public. Perhaps you think the more effective policy would have been to stay out of war. Or perhaps you wish the war and its aftermath had been more effectively executed. As it turned out, Congress did not watch over the president, and the country got neither peace nor effective war. In both 1800 and 2006, the election produced dramatic shifts because classic checks and balances failed and thus produced policies that angered the voters. The election results were a punishment. But punishment by itself did not correct the more basic reasons the system of checks and balances failed.

The downward spiral will continue unless we get to the root of the problem. And what is the root of the problem? All of us, Americans, and each of us. A public opinion survey once asked Americans to "suppose the President and Congress have to violate a Constitutional principle to pass an important law the public wanted. Would you support them in this action?" Only 49 percent of the public said no. The other half were a mix of yes (22 percent) and undecided or neither (29 percent). Even on a simple statement of a bedrock principle of our system, we are divided. That is a shaky foundation on which to rest the most important government on earth.

Why does our constitutional commitment seem so thin? At one level, we have come to mistake longevity for permanence. We take for granted the existence of what not so long ago was remarkable and revolutionary. We assume that because we have been a free and successful democracy for our lifetimes and our parents' and grandparents' lifetimes that we will remain such for our children's and our children's children's lifetimes, too. That alone would be worrisome. When citizens take their democracy for granted, they undermine its most basic tenet. Democracy dissolves without the commitment to it of its citizens. That loss of commitment is what the framers most feared.

In our own time, the historian Sean Wilentz put it this way: "Democracy is never a gift bestowed by benevolent, far seeing rulers who seek to reinforce their own legitimacy. It must always be fought for, by political coalitions that cut across distinctions of wealth, power, and interest. It succeeds and survives only when it is rooted in the lives and expectations of its citizens and continually reinvigorated in each generation. Democratic successes are never irreversible."

But instead of reinvigorating our representative government, current generations are disparaging it. We are not fighting for it. Instead, we as a people are frustrated with the day-to-day workings of government and restlessly search for some "fix" for the system.

Perhaps our confidence in the permanence of our democracy has left us feeling free to attack its workings. To a point, that is healthy. The system was built for robust debate, and it has survived a great deal of it. But robust debate requires engagement and information. It requires the debaters to have some context, some sense of shared ground.

Where do we find that common ground? By looking behind the trouble signs. We said that taking our democracy for granted while also being frustrated with our government seems almost contradictory. We said "almost" because in fact we believe they rise from the same source.

Americans don't know their own government anymore. They don't know their own history. We take our democracy for granted because we don't understand how hard it was to build it, how much courage (not just on the battlefield) it took to preserve it, and how close it came to failure on several occasions from the Alien and Sedition Acts, through the Civil War to the Great Depression. And we are frustrated with how it works today because no one is explaining that how it works (most of time) is how the framers, benefiting from the real-life experience of the early nation, designed it to work. Defending the system is not a politically popular thing to do. And in our hurry-up society, no one wants to sit still long enough to hear explanations of the system, let alone defenses. This is frightening. The framers expected flaws to emerge in their design. They expected fixes to be needed.

What is dangerous now is that the debate over the system has lost the context of how the system got to be what it is. In an environment where citizens do not particularly understand the system's basic design, many of the fixes are actually challenges to the overall design. Madison and his colleagues envisioned the Senate, with its members chosen for longer terms from entire states, as a balance and a check to the House, with its larger membership with shorter terms from narrower constituencies. Together they would check the president, with a term halfway between that in the House and that in the Senate. Yet today former senator Gravel is running for president on the express platform of creating a national system of referendum to circumvent the Congress. His campaign is welcome to the extent that it encourages a debate that teaches Americans about the design of the Constitution. Americans are free to change that design. But they should understand what they are doing and what they are abandoning if they do.

We hope the result will be an embrace of improvements, rather than a dismantling of constitutional principles. But if only 49 percent of the country is willing to speak up for a fundamental constitutional principle, we are perilously close to undoing the system itself. The wrong crisis at the wrong moment could push us over the edge before we realize what we have done. Indeed, all that protects us in this situation is the framers' prescience in creating a system where a majority of one is not enough to make radical changes. But then of course we become frustrated that we can't get the change we want, and the spiral starts all over again.

Thomas Jefferson said that the tree of liberty needs to be refreshed from time to time with the blood of patriots and tyrants. What a wonderful bit of Jeffersonian poetry. But we think something less dramatic, but perhaps harder in its own way, is needed right now. We as Americans need to tend our own garden. We need to renew not just our faith in but our understanding of the system the framers gave us. That understanding requires more than some sound bites about liberty and freedom. We need to embrace that our liberty and freedom flow directly from less glamorous but still vital ideas, such as compromise, and checks and balances, and representation and process. A dash of humility would not hurt either.

Two of our most important modern presidents, Franklin Roosevelt and Ronald Reagan, each saw the importance of renewing our understanding of American constitutional government.

Roosevelt became president in the middle of the worst crisis of American democracy since the Civil War. The link between the American political system and its economic success had snapped. Around the world, dictatorships of the left and the right were on the rise. There were people who came to FDR—serious, important people—to advise him that he might have to take authoritarian powers himself. Looking back, we came much closer than many people realize to the loss of our democracy. But we did not lose it, thanks to the resolve of FDR and the strength in the American people of what we have come to describe as our Constitutional Conscience. Four years later, Roosevelt, in his first fireside chat of his second term as president, said he hoped the American people had reread their Constitution in the last few weeks. "Like the Bible," he said, "it ought to be read again and again." Ironically, Roosevelt made this remark in a speech in which he argued for a plan to weaken the Supreme Court and strengthen the power of the presidency and the Congress by putting more of his appointees on the Court. It is a testament to the strength of our Constitutional Conscience that Roosevelt's way of arguing for this plan was to present it as a defense of the Constitution, not an infringement of it. The system stopped him anyway, and even without those expanded powers he guided the country out of the Depression. The Court-packing plan he outlined in that fireside chat has vanished into history. It turns out that the more important notion of that speech was Roosevelt's insistence that we reconnect with the Constitution regularly.

Half a century later, Ronald Reagan was saying farewell after eight years as president. He had come to office in the midst of a crisis of confidence. Watergate, stagflation, the Iran hostage crisis, the residue of the 1960s had combined to shake Americans' faith in their country. Reagan had worked with considerable success to rebuild that faith. As he said farewell, he took pride in that accomplishment. But he recognized that the job was only partly done: "This national feeling is good, but it won't count for much and it won't last unless it is grounded in thoughtfulness and knowledge. An informed patriotism is what we want. And are we doing a good enough job teaching our children what America is and what she represents in the long history of the world? Those of us who are over thirty-five or so years of age grew up in a different America. We were taught, very directly, what it means to be an American. And we absorbed, almost in the air, a love of country and an appreciation of its institutions."

But as America prepared to enter the 1990s, Reagan warned, the fashion had changed. "Younger parents aren't sure that an unambivalent appreciation of America is the right thing to teach modern children. And as for those who create the popular culture, well-grounded patriotism is no longer the style. Our spirit is back, but we haven't reinstitutionalized it."

Roosevelt and Reagan are the touchstone presidents of the American Century. In some ways they could not represent more different political moments. The first brought a powerful centralized federal government into our domestic lives. The other drew the line to limit it. Yet across the half century that separated them, they each affirmed the centrality of connecting Americans to their democratic heritage.

"So we've got to teach history based not on what's in fashion but what's important," said Reagan. He concluded: "If we forget what we did, we won't know who we are. Let's start with some basics: more attention to American history and a greater emphasis on civic ritual."

We agree. Indeed, we think we owe it to the framers and all succeeding Americans who have struggled for the Constitution to renew our connection to our own history. But even more, we owe it to the future, which will be shaped by our actions.

There is a strong sense that we have become selfish and self-involved as a people. It is hard to say whether we are more self-interested than Americans at the time the Constitution was written. It was written because the framers thought we were very selfish, and they decided they could not fight human nature, only harness it. That was the genius of their system. It accepted us for who we are and yet still offered the optimistic vision that we could, as a nation, compromise our differences to agree to do great things.

We are all for ideas to make us less selfish or self-interested. But we are with the framers in doubting that human nature can be fundamentally changed.

They were right that our more selfish impulses can be channeled. Americans throughout their history have understood that it was in their own interest, ultimately, to preserve this system that balanced everyone's demands. That understanding is what we mean by our Constitutional Conscience. It is what Sean Wilentz is talking about when he describes coalitions that cut across lines of wealth, power and interest. It is noble to try to make people different. We admire those who try. But politics is the art of the possible. The framers made it possible for us to live together in liberty and community. The 220-year history of our Constitution is a history of Americans repeatedly rekindling their belief that their own interests are served by this system that grants extensive liberty in exchange for a willingness to compromise and tolerate differences. We Americans need to rekindle that belief once more.

If this [reading] has one message, it is that there is nothing about our past success that guarantees our future success. Each generation must do that for itself. Nevertheless, this is a hopeful message, because we are not alone in our struggle. We have been given a great gift and with it a great responsibility. We are the inheritors of the longest democratic tradition in the world. We still hold in great respect the men who began that tradition and the men and women who carried it forth and bequeathed it to us. That respect is a resource for us now. The struggles we are having, the frustrations we are feeling, are exactly the struggles and frustrations the framers anticipated when they designed our democracy. We can lean on them and their experience. By reaching backward to them and their ideas, we can move forward.

DISCUSSION QUESTIONS

1. Most of the time, people become critical of the Constitution when they don't get the policy results they want. When Congress fails to pass legislation because of the power of small-state senators, when the Supreme Court issues a ruling they oppose, when the president makes a decision regarding the use of force that they oppose, the immediate impulse is to blame the system and call for change that would make the preferred policies more likely. Is this a valid reason for wanting the system to change?

2. The Constitution was written over two hundred years ago by a group of white men who had very "unmodern" views about democracy and equality. On what basis should we be bound by the decisions that they made? What is the foundation of constitutional fidelity? What would be the result if each generation were permitted to remake the rules?

3. Often, opinions about the Constitution divide along philosophical lines. On one side are people who believe that the most important purpose of a constitution is to limit government size and power. On the other are people who believe that the Constitution must protect rights and promote equality (which almost always involves expanding the size and power of government). Who has the better case? Why?

3

Federalism: Immigration Reform and State Power

Immigration policy is one of the new areas of conflict in federalism. Who has the power to control the flow of illegal immigrants across borders: the national or state governments? It would seem to be a power of the national government, but what happens when states believe that the national government is not enforcing its own laws? Do states have the right to fill the breech? The recent *Arizona v. United States* case helped answer some of these questions, but left one other important question unanswered, at least for now.

The central constitutional question in this case concerns national supremacy—the pre-emption of state law by federal law when there is a conflict between the two. For example, the clause in the Arizona law that made it a criminal offense for employers to hire illegal immigrants is only a civil violation under national law; it was presumed, then, that the national law would hold, not the state law. Kevin Johnson explains that this well-established principle of federal pre-emption held in three of the four sections of the Arizona law. However, the controversial status check—or "show your papers"—provision of the state law was upheld by the Supreme Court because Arizona was simply enforcing the federal law. Johnson argues that this part of the case could have been decided as a civil rights claim rather than on the basis of federalism and pre-emption. However, he says that the Obama administration did not want to assert that Arizona residents and citizens were being denied equal protection of the laws under the fourteenth Amendment because that argument would have been more difficult to prove than preemption. Johnson also speculates that President Obama may not have wanted to be seen as "playing the race card" during an election year.

The split verdict on different sections of the law meant that reactions to the decision were all over the map, ranging from those who saw it as a reaffirmation of Congress's role in immigration policy to those who thought it was more favorable to the states. Jay Sekulow is clearly in the latter camp, saying, "The Supreme Court's decision in *Arizona v. United States* represents an important victory for Arizona and proponents of the States' authority to protect their borders and citizens when the federal government fails to do so." Sekulow is pleased that the Court did not adopt a simple view of preemption, but rather made a distinction between active enforcement and non-enforcement of laws by the executive branch. States should be allowed to step in to enforce the intent of Congress when the executive branch is not enforcing the law.

On the other hand, Richard Peltz-Steele concludes that the Arizona decision (along with the Supreme Court's decision on the Affordable Care Act) reflect a "dismantling federalism [that] is a shortcut with a steep price." Peltz-Steele is sympathetic to Justice Scalia's dissenting opinion, which argued the majority opinion "deprives States of what most would consider the defining characteristic of sovereignty: the power to exclude from the sovereign's territory people who have no right to be there. Neither the Constitution itself nor even any law passed by Congress supports this result." Peltz-Steele is concerned that state governments are losing too much power to control their own policies.

While this was not a central point of debate between the various authors in this section, it is important to note that other constitutional scholars have reached a very different conclusion than Peltz-Steele concerning the implications of the Supreme Court's decision upholding most of "Obamacare." Rather than seeing this as another blow to federalism, this perspective points out that the Supreme Court may have limited future efforts by Congress to impose broad policy agendas on the states. In striking down the "coercive federalism" basis for the expansion of Medicaid (that is, states would have lost federal support if they did not expand health care for the poor) and in arguing that the commerce clause could not provide the constitutional basis for the individual mandate to buy health insurance, the Court strengthened the position of the states in their future battles with Congress over policy.

Jay Sekulow

State Sovereignty Is the Issue

The Court's decision to uphold the immigration status check provision is a big win for state sovereignty. But in the end, does President Obama's selective enforcement of immigration law win the day? It was a little more than one week ago when President Obama actually changed immigration law by simply issuing a directive—an order to stop deporting many young illegal immigrants who were brought to the United States as children.

The Supreme Court's decision in *Arizona v. United States* represents an important victory for Arizona and proponents of the States' authority to protect their borders and citizens when the federal government fails to do so. Granted, the Court's holding that some of the Arizona law (SB 1070)'s provisions are pre-empted by federal immigration policy is disappointing (for the reasons Justice Scalia explained in his dissenting opinion). But, the Court's holding that the immigration status check provision (Section 2(B)) is not preempted by federal law represents an important rejection of the position that States are powerless to counteract the negative impact that illegal immigration has on their citizens when the President, Attorney General, or other federal Executive Branch actors choose not to enforce, or to otherwise disregard, duly enacted federal immigration laws.

Summary of Section 2(B) and the Court's Decision

Section 2(B) of SB 1070 states that, "[f]or any lawful stop, detention or arrest" made by Arizona law enforcement officers, "where reasonable suspicion exists that the person is an alien and is unlawfully present in the United States, a reasonable attempt shall be made, when practicable, to determine the immigration status of the person." Section 2(B) also states that "[t]he person's immigration status shall be verified with the federal government pursuant to 8 U.S.C. section 1373(c)," which requires the Immigration and Nationalization Service to verify the citizenship or immigration status of any individual when requested to do so by state or local law enforcement agencies.

In addition, if the lawful status of an arrested person cannot be presumed or determined, the status verification must occur "before the person is released." A person is presumed to be lawfully present if he presents a valid Arizona driver's license, tribal identification, or identification from any unit of government in the

United States that requires proof of lawful presence. Section 2(B) expressly states that law enforcement officers "may not consider race, color, or national origin in implementing the requirements of this subsection except to the extent permitted by the United States or Arizona Constitution."

The Department of Justice (DOJ) argued that Section 2(B) conflicted with federal law enforcement objectives for two reasons: 1) The provision requires immigration status checks in some situations that the Attorney General would not likely have the individual removed; and 2) The provision could justify prolonged detentions while status checks are conducted. The Court rejected these arguments, noting that Arizona law enforcement officers generally contact Immigration and Customs Enforcement (ICE), which is required by federal law to respond to requests made by state officials to verify an individual's immigration or citizenship status and operates a support center for this purpose 24 hours a day, 7 days a week. * * * In addition, the Court concluded that hypothetical concerns that prolonged detentions may be authorized under Section 2(B) were premature, as Section 2(B) could be interpreted to avoid those concerns. The Court stated, "[h]owever the law is interpreted, if § 2(B) only requires state officers to conduct a status check during the course of an authorized, lawful detention or after a detainee has been released, the provision likely would survive preemption—at least absent some showing that it has other consequences that are adverse to federal law and its objectives." * * *

Justice Scalia concurred in the decision to uphold Section 2(B) but dissented from the Court's decision to invalidate other provisions of the law. He stated that the majority opinion "deprives States of what most would consider the defining characteristic of sovereignty: the power to exclude from the sovereign's territory people who have no right to be there. Neither the Constitution itself nor even any law passed by Congress supports this result." * * * (Scalia, J., dissenting in part). He said that accusing Arizona of contradicting federal law by enforcing provisions that the President declines to enforce "boggles the mind." * * * Justice Scalia also noted that the States would not have agreed to ratify the Constitution if it included a provision that prevented the States from taking action to defend their borders if the President declined to enforce immigration laws. * * *

Analysis

Scholars, pundits, and politicians from all corners are sure to spin the Court's decision in various ways, but the importance of the Court's holding concerning Section 2(B) cannot be denied. It not only affirms a level of State sovereignty to enact provisions like Section 2(B), but it also (at least indirectly) reestablishes that Congress, not the Executive Branch, is the ultimate source of federal immigration policy.

Opponents of SB 1070 essentially argued that *any* State provision (including the entirety of SB 1070) that seeks to enforce federal immigration law, or to otherwise protect States from the harmful effects of large-scale illegal immigration, is necessarily preempted by federal law. This is especially true if the Attorney General or the Department of Justice claims that the State provision undermines the Executive Branch's decision to under-enforce (or not enforce) federal statutes, even where the State provision is identical to, or otherwise mirrors, federal statutes. Under this view of preemption, the Executive Branch may effectively wrest *de facto* control of immigration law from Congress by both adopting a policy of under-enforcement or non-enforcement of federal statutes and actively fighting any State attempts to pursue Congress's stated goals.

If the Court had adopted this simplistic if–then approach to preemption (if the DOJ opposes a State law that touches upon some immigration matter, citing law enforcement concerns, then it must be preempted), State efforts to mitigate the deleterious effects of the federal government's failure to combat illegal immigration could be ground to a halt. Importantly, the Court's decision upholding Section 2(B) rejected DOJ's claim that a conflict between a State law and *the Attorney General's preferences* is necessarily a conflict *with federal law* for purposes of preemption. This may (and should) have major implications for the inevitable future battles over State provisions that mirror federal statutes that the Executive Branch objects to. As a basis for a preemption argument, the DOJ stated that, under Section 2(B) "the officers must make an inquiry even in cases where it seems unlikely that the Attorney General would have the alien removed. This might be the case, for example, when an alien is an elderly veteran with significant and longstanding ties to the community." The Court responded by stating, "Congress has done nothing to suggest it is inappropriate to communicate with ICE in these situations, however. Indeed, it has encouraged the sharing of information about possible immigration violations. . . . The federal scheme thus leaves room for a policy requiring state officials to contact ICE as a routine matter." In other words, an Executive Branch preference that ICE not be contacted for an immigration status check in certain situations *does not establish a conflict*, for purposes of preemption, between a state law requiring ICE to be contacted and federal statutes encouraging such contacts.

Conclusion

The Court's decision in *Arizona v. United States* is just one chapter (albeit an important one) in the ongoing story of how the federal, state, and local governments wrestle with the hot-button issue of illegal immigration. Importantly, the Court did not carve the States out of the story entirely by adopting a blanket rule that whatever the Executive Branch says in informal memos or court documents about a State provision represents federal "law" with preemptive power.

In light of the Court's decision, States will continue to enact provisions that are designed to remain consistent with federal statutes while mitigating the problems caused by the federal government's failure to adequately address illegal immigration. The Executive Branch will likely continue to attempt to elevate its (often unwritten) policy of under-enforcement or non-enforcement of federal immigration statutes to the level of federal "law" that would create a conflict between state statutes and identical, or nearly identical, federal statutes. The courts will continue to interpret the fine line between federal law that preempts state law and mere Executive Branch preferences that do not. That the States remain major players concerning this issue is a big defeat for the Executive Branch and its attempt to effectively rewrite immigration law through non-enforcement and litigation against the States.

Richard Peltz-Steele

Dismantling Federalism Is a Shortcut With a Very Steep Price

Recent decisions from the Supreme Court delivered a one-two punch to American federalism. While media focus on the political impact of the immigration and healthcare decisions on the elections, our constitutional system is reeling from a blow of greater proportion.

In the first high-profile decision, Arizona substantially lost its battle to maintain a state immigration enforcement system. The dispute arose from the gap between what the Feds say and what they do, specifically the failure to police immigration to the satisfaction of Arizona taxpayers.

The decision in *Arizona v. United States* was mostly about federal preemption of state law. And preemption law is notoriously fuzzy: "eye of the beholder" unfortunately characterizes the Court's approach. The majority saw the Arizona case as an instance of Congress so thoroughly "occupying the field" that no room remained for state law. Justice Thomas, in a concise dissent, reasoned that Congress had not precluded state law such as Arizona's, which merely echoes federal law.

Whatever one thinks of Justice Scalia's dissent, he got the facts right. The difference between majority and dissenter perceptions turns in part on whether the President's *inaction* in enforcing federal immigration law has preemptive significance. And certainly, as Scalia wrote, the framers would have abhorred this result; the states always have cherished their borders. One columnist wryly noted that the framers would not have signed a constitution abolishing slavery.

True, but that deficiency of our Constitution was addressed through amendment. No amendment yet has erased state borders.

Preemption always poses a fuzzy question, but the Court's ruling against Arizona takes a bite out of state power. Expansive federal *inaction* was read to displace a traditionally sound exercise of state police power that only sought to complement federal law—as written. The states now seem more than ever at the mercy of the federal government and its deep pockets to decide what is and is not the province of the state electorate.

So what local policy decisions will next take up residence between Capitol Hill and K Street? Healthcare, it seems. In *NFIB v. Sebelius*, the Court substantially upheld the national healthcare initiative advanced by the President, including the controversial individual mandate.

The Court majority rejected the mandate as an exercise of Commerce Clause power. But leaving academic jaws agape, the majority capitalized on a marginal, throw-it-at-the-wall-and-see-if-it-sticks government argument that the penalty for failure to comply with the mandate was not a penalty at all—rather, a tax within the power of the Taxing Clause (as well as the Sixteenth Amendment, a further flimsy stretch).

The majority's use of the Taxing Clause dealt another blow to federalism. Again pundits derided the dissent, this time for getting hung up on the infamous hypothetical of government-compelled broccoli consumption and stubbornly failing to acknowledge that the individual decision *not* to buy health insurance (*inaction* again) is itself a regulable commercial act.

The problem of federalism can get lost in the shuffle. But in using the Taxing Clause, the Court offered precious little in the way of limiting principles. Indeed, the Taxing Clause now seems poised to become Congress's favorite new toy to run circles around the Commerce Clause and its carefully erected barriers to federal omnipotence. Whatever mandates formerly defied the reach of Congress may now be offered to individuals as a "choice," and persons lacking the wisdom to choose correctly may be "taxed" accordingly. Congress need not even use the word "tax"; the Justices will strain their eyes to find a tax wherever a penalty lies.

Citizens refusing to buy their shares of broccoli admittedly seems far-fetched. Imagine instead a domestic airline industry on the brink of collapse. A federal bailout compels all persons to buy airline tickets—or to invest in troubled banks, or to subscribe to failing newspapers—it's the patriotic choice, after all. Agoraphobic? Prefer to keep money under the mattress and get your news from TV? No problem; the "tax" on non-compliance comes due April 15.

Federalism is not an anachronism. The "United States" has—have—survived because of a well-drawn balance between sovereign states and the federal government. This system of "vertical separation of powers" is one of our essential checks and balances, right along with the three branches of government ("horizontal separation of powers") that kids learn about in grade school. Imbalance in this formula can spell catastrophe; think Civil War or European financial collapse.

Immigration and healthcare are critical public policy problems, but they are not intractable. Congress and the President have ample constitutional power at their disposal to achieve meaningful reforms without running roughshod over the States. Dismantling federalism is a shortcut with a steep price.

Kevin Johnson

The Debate Over Immigration Reform Is Not Over Until It's Over

On one of the last days of the 2011 term, the Supreme Court decided *Arizona v. United States* and determined the constitutionality of four provisions of the controversial Arizona immigration enforcement law known as S.B. 1070. The case had received a great deal of attention from Court watchers—and not just those interested in immigration. Indeed, it had a little something for just about everybody, from federalism to civil rights to election-year politics . . .

The Decision: States Have Some Immigration Enforcement Power

In many respects, the Supreme Court's decision in *Arizona v. United States* will be far from satisfying to many. Unlike lawsuits brought by other plaintiffs challenging S.B. 1070, the U.S. government challenged the Arizona law solely on the ground that it violated the Supremacy Clause of the U.S. Constitution, which makes federal law the "supreme law of the land." The body of law at issue is known as federal preemption doctrine, which is far from scintillating to most law professors, much less the general public.

In addressing the U.S. government's preemption challenge, the U.S. Court of Appeals for the Ninth Circuit had agreed with the district court that four provisions of S.B. 1070 impermissibly intruded on the federal power to regulate immigration law. The four provisions struck down include:

(1) Section 2(B), which requires state and local police to check the immigration status of persons about whom they have a reasonable suspicion of being undocumented;
(2) Section 3, which would have made it a crime not to complete or carry an "alien registration document" (and is directly contrary to the Court's decision in *Hines v. Davidowitz*);
(3) Section 5(C), which *criminalizes* the conduct of undocumented *employees* and goes well beyond the *civil* sanctions that U.S. immigration law allows to be imposed on employers of undocumented workers; and
(4) Section 6, which allows for a warrantless arrest if the "officer has probable cause to believe [that a person] has committed any public offense that makes the person removable from the United States" under federal immigration law.

The Supreme Court, in a majority opinion by Justice Kennedy that was joined by Chief Justice Roberts and Justices Ginsburg, Breyer, and Sotomayor, affirmed the Ninth Circuit's ruling with respect to three of the four provisions. Justice Kagan, the former Solicitor General, took no part in the consideration or decision in the case.

At the outset, the majority emphasized that "[t]he Government of the United States has broad, undoubted power over the subject of immigration and the regulation of aliens" and that "[t]he federal power to determine immigration policy is well settled." After reaffirming federal primacy over immigration, the Court applied conventional federal preemption precedent. It carefully parsed each of the four sections individually, struck down Sections 3, 5(C), and 6, and upheld Section 2(B). In upholding that lone section, the Court found that there were adequate safeguards in place, including the law's ban on racial profiling, which saved it from being invalidated on its face.

It is important to note that, in upholding Section 2(B), the Court emphatically left the door open to future claims challenging its application: "This opinion does not foreclose other preemption and constitutional challenges to the law as interpreted and applied after it goes into effect."

Not even able to agree among themselves, Justices Scalia, Thomas, and Alito all filed separate opinions concurring in part and dissenting in part. Most jarring was Justice Scalia's dissent, which would have upheld S.B. 1070 in its entirety. Besides expressing unhappiness with the Obama Administration's immigration enforcement policies, Justice Scalia contended that the framers of the Constitution understood that the states had sovereign power over immigration. He stated sarcastically that "[i]f securing its territory in this fashion is not within the power of Arizona, we should cease referring to it as a sovereign State."

Avoiding the Civil Rights Concerns

Since the passage of S.B. 1070, Section 2(B) alone generated a firestorm of controversy. It, like many of the other new immigration enforcement laws passed by the States, requires state and local police to verify the immigration status of anyone whom they have a "reasonable suspicion" is undocumented. Critics claimed that S.B. 1070 would increase racial profiling of Latinos in law enforcement, a serious civil rights concern.

The majority's federal preemption analysis in *Arizona* allowed the Court to conveniently side-step this most frequently voiced public concern with the Arizona law. In so doing, the Court was aided by the parties.

Unlike the challenges to the Arizona law brought by civil rights groups, the U.S. government—the only plaintiff whose claims were before the Supreme Court—did not include a claim that S.B. 1070 violated the Equal Protection Clause of the Fourteenth Amendment. The administration consciously wanted to avoid any claim of racial profiling. Indeed, during oral argument, Solicitor General Donald Verrilli unequivocally admitted in response to questioning from the Justices that racial profiling was not at issue in the case. Arizona, of course, would have no reason to disagree. The Justices eagerly seized on the admission that racial profiling was not at issue in the case to duck the race issue and write a treatise-like opinion on federal preemption.

There are at least two possible explanations for the U.S. government's strategy to avoid making the case a racial profiling case:

First, a claim of racial profiling presumably would be based on the Equal Protection Clause of the Fourteenth Amendment. To prevail on an equal protection claim, the U.S. government would have to prove that the state of Arizona acted with a "discriminatory intent" in enacting S.B. 1070. . . . This is a heavy burden, especially in a challenge to the constitutionality of a law on its face as opposed to as it has been applied.

Second, the Obama Administration may have wanted to avoid appearing to play the proverbial "race card" in challenging S.B. 1070 as a form of racial discrimination. Such reluctance would seemingly grow as the 2012 presidential election nears. It was relatively easy to avoid race and civil rights concerns when the parties were willing and when a readily available, and far less contentious, legal argument (federal preemption) was at hand.

In the end, the decision in *Arizona v. United States* centered on the power of the federal vis-à-vis state government over immigration. However, many critics of the state immigration enforcement laws like those in Arizona, Georgia, and South Carolina are less worried about state intrusion on federal power and much more concerned that the laws would encourage discrimination against Latinos, including lawful immigrants and U.S. citizens. Ultimately, a gaping disconnect exists between the Court's resolution of the case on legal technicalities and the civil rights concerns of certain segments of the public.

The Impact of *Arizona v. United States*

Only time will tell on what the real impact will be of the Supreme Court's decision in *Arizona v. United States* on the enforcement of the U.S. immigration laws. Several possibilities come to mind.

The Court's decision would appear to be far from the end of the matter with respect to the lawfulness of Section 2(B) of Arizona's S.B. 1070. We can expect challenges to that section as it is applied by the police, including claims by U.S. citizens of Mexican ancestry who are stopped and questioned about their immigration status by state and local law enforcement authorities. Racial discrimination in the criminal justice system has long been a problem in Arizona. In May, the U.S. Department of Justice brought a civil rights action against the Maricopa County Sheriff's Office, and celebrity Sheriff Joe Arpaio, for allegedly engaging in a "pattern of unlawful discrimination" against Latinos and immigrants.

It does seem clear after *Arizona v. United States* that there is a narrow space for the states to enforce the U.S. immigration laws. The decision may encourage more states to pass laws copycatting Section 2(B) and other lawful provisions of S.B. 1070 and perhaps even attempt to more aggressively "assist" the U.S. government in enforcing the immigration laws.

The Court's decision to uphold Section 2(B) will allow state and local governments on a daily basis to be involved in immigration enforcement as officers enforce the ordinary criminal laws. This will ensure that the decision has a significant impact in Arizona, but also in other states with laws similar in important respects, such as Alabama, Georgia, and South Carolina.

At the same time, the Court's careful review of the specific provisions of S.B. 1070 makes it clear that states do not have a blank check in terms of immigration enforcement. State leaders thinking about their own S.B. 1070 would need to think about the benefits of a largely symbolic—and possibly politically popular—law compared to the costs of enforcement (as well as litigating challenges to the law).

Importantly, nothing in the Court's decision suggests any change in the Court's approach to the run-of-the-mill immigration case, in which it looks to the text of the statute and the reasonableness of the agency's interpretation of the statute. Immigrants in recent years have prevailed in a *majority* of the Court's immigration decisions in the last few years.

Although immigrant rights advocates may be disappointed and restrictionists may be jubilant, it would be hazardous to read too much into *Arizona v. United States*. The newest Justice, Elena Kagan, did not participate in the decision, and future cases will push beyond the boundaries of the decision. For example, Alabama's H.B. 56, which goes further than S.B. 1070 by barring undocumented students from public colleges and universities and requiring school districts to collect immigration status information of K–12 students and parents, touches on education and raises many different legal and civil rights issues. . . .

In conclusion, the Supreme Court has cracked open the door to new state legislation, new claims of racial discrimination, and new lawsuits. States are likely to test the boundaries of *Arizona v. United States* with new, if not improved, immigration enforcement legislation. Litigation over the constitutionality of the laws is likely to continue. The lasting solution to the proliferation of state immigration enforcement laws, which is beyond the power of the Supreme Court, is for Congress to enact comprehensive immigration reform that has the support of the public. Perhaps the publicity over *Arizona v. United States* will prod Congress to act. Until it does, we can expect the status quo to continue.

DISCUSSION QUESTIONS

1. Who do you think should control immigration policy, the national government or the states? What if the executive branch is under-enforcing the law? Should states be able to step in and enforce congressional law?

2. Do you see the Arizona decision as a blow to states' rights, or a reaffirmation of their role in the formation of immigration policy?

3. The Arizona case is known as a "facial test" of the policy rather than an "as applied" test. That is, the law had not been applied yet, so the constitutionality of the law had to be determined "on its face." Once the law is applied, do you think that the "show your papers" part of the law will be upheld?

4

The Constitutional Framework and the Individual—Civil Liberties and Civil Rights: Same-Sex Marriage

One of the most controversial and politically significant civil rights issues in the past few years is same-sex marriage. As of this writing, there are twelve states and the District of Columbia in which same-sex marriage is legal and ten others that recognize same-sex civil unions. In 2012, Maine, Maryland, and Washington became the first states to approve same-sex marriage through a referendum, and voters in Minnesota rejected a constitutional amendment that would have defined marriage as applying only to heterosexual couples.

Marriage has both religious and legal ramifications. As a legal matter, marriage comes with a set of rights and obligations: married couples pay a lower marginal tax rate (though two-income couples can face a "marriage penalty," in which the total tax paid for a couple filing jointly can be more than the sum of the taxes they would have paid if they were single); automatically enjoy insurance and pension benefits that are extended to families; have inheritance rights when one spouse dies; and so on. Apart from the concrete legal benefits, marriage implies a societal recognition of the legitimacy and value of a relationship. There are obligations as well, primarily from the consequences of ending a marriage through divorce.

The main argument against same-sex marriage is that it upends a longstanding and stable institution that has been central to social stability and families. Traditionalists argue that marriage has always involved one man and one woman, an arrangement that is vital for raising children. Woven into this is the view of many that homosexuality is immoral or contrary to religious tenets, and a "slippery slope" argument that recognizing same-sex marriage would inevitably lead to further redefinitions like polygamy. Supporters counter that the definition of marriage has always been evolving, and that the arguments against same-sex marriage are no different than earlier opposition to interracial marriage. Public opinion on the issue is changing rapidly. A number of public opinion polls taken in 2012 show a slight majority in favor of legalizing same-sex marriage, with the percentages supporting it ranging from about 50 percent to 54 percent (as opposed to around 35–45 percent supporting it over the previous decade). There is a huge generational difference in these views. A poll taken for the Pew Forum on Religion and Public Life found that among young people aged 18–29, 62 percent favored gay marriage, as opposed to only 32 percent of those over 65.

Ross Douthat rejects some of the standard arguments against same-sex marriage, but still argues for the ideal of marriage as being between a man and a woman. If society gives up on this ideal, he says, "we're giving up on one of the great ideas of Western civilization: the celebration of lifelong heterosexual monogamy as a unique and indispensable estate. That ideal is still worth honoring, and still worth striving to preserve." Douthat recognizes that our society has already moved away from that ideal with no-fault divorces, out-of-wedlock births, and serial monogamy, yet he believes the ideal is still important.

Justin Raimando offers a libertarian case against same-sex marriage. Libertarians believe in limited government and individual rights. In the extreme, libertarians believe that the government messes up everything that it touches. Raimando argues that same-sex marriage is no different. If the government were to endorse same-sex marriage, he says this "would not only be a setback for liberty but a disaster for those it supposedly benefits: gay people themselves." Raimando is also critical of the shift in the gay rights movement from fighting against the oppressive state, to adopting the approach of the civil rights movement and seeking the protection of the state from private sector discrimination.

Jonathan Rauch suggests two reasons why people are opposed to same-sex marriage: the simple anti-homosexual position and the not-so-simple view based on tradition. The latter is rooted in the gut-level feeling that marriage between two men or two women is simply wrong because marriage has always been between a man and a woman: no law can change this basic institution because it has roots that are deeper and older than any government or law (which comes pretty close to Douthat's view). Rauch situates this argument within the political thought of

F.A. Hayek, one of the great conservative thinkers of the twentieth century. Hayek warns that changing traditions and customs may lead to social chaos. This is precisely one of the arguments made against same-sex marriage: it will undermine the institution of marriage. Rauch replies that other changes have had a far greater impact on undermining the institution of marriage, such as allowing women to own property, the abolition of arranged marriages, legalized contraception, and "no-fault" divorce law. While recognizing the legitimacy of the concerns about same-sex marriage, Rauch concludes that the fears of its negative impact are overstated and the benefits of same-sex marriage for gays and lesbians outweigh the costs for heterosexuals.

Ross Douthat
The Marriage Ideal

Here are some commonplace arguments against gay marriage: Marriage is an ancient institution that has always been defined as the union of one man and one woman, and we meddle with that definition at our peril. Lifelong heterosexual monogamy is natural; gay relationships are not. The nuclear family is the universal, time-tested path to forming families and raising children.

These have been losing arguments for decades now, as the cause of gay marriage has moved from an eccentric-seeming notion to an idea that roughly half the country supports. And they were losing arguments again last week, when California's Judge Vaughn Walker ruled that laws defining marriage as a heterosexual union are unconstitutional, irrational, and unjust.

These arguments have lost because they're wrong. What we think of as "traditional marriage" is not universal. The default family arrangement in many cultures, modern as well as ancient, has been polygamy, not monogamy. The default mode of child-rearing is often communal, rather than two parents nurturing their biological children.

Nor is lifelong heterosexual monogamy obviously natural in the way that most Americans understand the term. If "natural" is defined to mean "congruent with our biological instincts," it's arguably one of the more unnatural arrangements imaginable. In crudely Darwinian terms, it cuts against both the male impulse toward promiscuity and the female interest in mating with the highest-status male available. Hence the historic prevalence of polygamy. And hence many societies' tolerance for more flexible alternatives, from concubinage and prostitution to temporary arrangements like the "traveler's marriages" sanctioned in some parts of the Islamic world.

So what are gay marriage's opponents really defending, if not some universal, biologically inevitable institution? It's a particular vision of marriage, rooted in a particular tradition, that establishes a particular sexual ideal.

This ideal holds up the commitment to lifelong fidelity and support by two sexually different human beings—a commitment that involves the mutual surrender, arguably, of their reproductive self-interest—as a uniquely admirable kind of relationship. It holds up the domestic life that can be created only by such unions, in which children grow up in intimate contact with both of their biological parents, as a uniquely admirable approach to child-rearing. And recognizing the difficulty of achieving these goals, it surrounds wedlock with a distinctive set of rituals, sanctions, and taboos.

The point of this ideal is not that other relationships have no value, or that only nuclear families can rear children successfully. Rather, it's that lifelong heterosexual monogamy at its best can offer something distinctive and remarkable—a microcosm of civilization, and an organic connection between human generations—that makes it worthy of distinctive recognition and support.

Again, this is not how many cultures approach marriage. It's a particularly Western understanding, derived from Jewish and Christian beliefs about the order of creation, and supplemented by later ideas about romantic love, the rights of children, and the equality of the sexes.

Or at least, it *was* the Western understanding. Lately, it has come to co-exist with a less idealistic, more accommodating approach, defined by no-fault divorce, frequent out-of-wedlock births, and serial monogamy.

In this landscape, gay-marriage critics who fret about a slippery slope to polygamy miss the point. Americans already have a kind of postmodern polygamy available to them. It's just spread over the course of a lifetime, rather than concentrated in a "Big Love"-style menage.

If this newer order completely vanquishes the older marital ideal, then gay marriage will become not only acceptable but morally necessary. The lifelong commitment of a gay couple is more impressive than the serial monogamy of straights. And a culture in which weddings are optional celebrations of romantic love, only tangentially connected to procreation, has no business discriminating against the love of homosexuals.

But if we just accept this shift, we're giving up on one of the great ideas of Western civilization: the celebration of lifelong heterosexual monogamy as a unique and indispensable estate. That ideal is still worth honoring, and still worth striving to preserve. And preserving it ultimately requires some public acknowledgment that heterosexual unions and gay relationships are different: similar in emotional commitment, but distinct both in their challenges and their potential fruit.

But based on Judge Walker's logic—which suggests that any such distinction is bigoted and un-American—I don't think a society that declares gay marriage to be a fundamental right will be capable of even entertaining this idea.

Justin Raimondo

The Libertarian Case Against Gay Marriage

Opponents of same-sex marriage have marshaled all sorts of arguments to make their case, from the rather alarmist view that it would de-sanctify and ultimately destroy heterosexual marriage to the assertion that it would logically lead to polygamy and the downfall of Western civilization. None of these arguments—to my mind, at least—make the least amount of sense, and they have all been singularly ineffective in beating back the rising tide of sentiment in favor of allowing same-sex couples the "right" to marry.

The problem with these arguments is that they are all rooted in religion or in some secular concept of morality alien to American culture in the 21st century—a culture that is characterized by relativism, impiety, and a preoccupation with other matters that make this issue less pressing than it otherwise might be. Yet there is an effective conservative—or rather libertarian—case to be made against legalizing gay marriage, one that can be summarized by the old aphorism: be careful what you ask for because you just might get it.

The imposition of a legal framework on the intricate web of relationships that have previously existed in the realm of freedom—that is, outside the law and entirely dependent on the trust and compliance of the individuals involved—would not only be a setback for liberty but a disaster for those it supposedly benefits: gay people themselves.

Of course, we already have gay marriages. Just as heterosexual marriage, as an institution, preceded the invention of the state, so the homosexual version existed long before anyone thought to give it legal sanction. Extending the authority of the state into territory previously untouched by its tender ministrations, legalizing relationships that had developed and been found rewarding entirely without this imprimatur, would wreak havoc where harmony once prevailed. Imagine a relationship of some duration in which one partner, the breadwinner, had supported his or her partner without much thought about the economics of the matter: one had stayed home and tended the house, while the other had been in the workforce, bringing home the bacon. This division of labor had prevailed for many years, not requiring any written contract or threat of legal action to enforce its provisions.

Then, suddenly, they are legally married—or, in certain states, considered married under the common law. This changes the relationship, and not for the better. For now the property of the breadwinner is not his or her own: half of it belongs to the stay-at-home. Before when they argued, money was never an issue: now, when the going gets rough, the threat of divorce—and the specter of alimony—hangs over the relationship, and the mere possibility casts its dark shadow over what had once been a sunlit field.

If and when gay marriage comes to pass, its advocates will have a much harder time convincing their fellow homosexuals to exercise their "right" than they did in persuading the rest of the country to grant it. That's because they have never explained—and never could explain—why it would make sense for gays to entangle themselves in a regulatory web and risk getting into legal disputes over divorce, alimony, and the division of property.

Marriage evolved because of the existence of children: without them, the institution loses its biological, economic, and historical basis, its very reason for being. This is not to say childless couples—including gay couples—are any less worthy (or less married) than others. It means only that they are not bound by necessity to a mutual commitment involving the ongoing investment of considerable resources.

From two sets of given circumstances, two parallel traditions have evolved: one, centered around the rearing of children, is heterosexual marriage, the habits and rules of which have been recognized and formalized by the state. The reason for this recognition is simple: the welfare of the children, who must be protected from neglect and abuse.

The various childless unions and alternative relationships that are an increasing factor in modern society have evolved informally, with minimal state intervention. Rather than anchored by necessity, they are governed by the centrality of freedom.

The prospect of freedom—not only from traditional moral restraints but from legal burdens and responsibilities—is part of what made homosexuality appealing in the early days of the gay liberation movement. At any rate, society's lack of interest in formalizing the love lives of the nation's homosexuals did not result in any decrease in homosexuality or make it any less visible. Indeed, if the experience of the past thirty years means anything, quite the opposite is the case. By superimposing the legal and social constraints of heterosexual marriage on gay relationships, we will succeed only in de-eroticizing them. Are gay marriage advocates trying to take the gayness out of homosexuality?

The gay rights movement took its cues from the civil rights movement, modeling its grievances on those advanced by the moderate wing led by Dr. Martin Luther King and crafting a legislative agenda borrowed from the NAACP and allied organizations: the passage of anti-discrimination laws—covering housing, employment, and public accommodations—at the local and national level. Efforts to institutionalize gay marriage have followed this course, with "equality" as the goal.

But the civil rights paradigm never really fit: unlike most African Americans, lesbians and gay men can render their minority status invisible. Furthermore, their economic status is not analogous—indeed, there are studies that show gay men, at least, are economically better off on average than heterosexuals. They tend to be better educated, have better jobs, and these days are not at all what one could call an oppressed minority. According to GayAgenda.com, "studies show that [gay] Americans are twice as likely to have graduated from college, twice as likely to have an individual income over $60,000 and twice as likely to have a household income of $250,000 or more."

Gays an oppressed minority group? I don't think so.

The gay liberation movement started as a protest against state oppression. The earliest gay rights organizations, such as the Mattachine Society and the Daughters of Bilitis, sought to legalize homosexual activity, then illegal per se. The movement was radicalized in the 1960s over police harassment. A gay bar on New York City's Christopher Street, known as the Stonewall, was the scene of a three-day riot provoked by a police raid. Tired of being subjected to continual assault by the boys in blue, gay people fought back—and won. At the time, gay bars were under general attack from the New York State Liquor Authority, which pulled licenses as soon as a bar's reputation as a gay gathering place became apparent. Activists of that era concentrated their fire on the issues that really mattered to the gay person in the street: the legalization of homosexual conduct and the protection of gay institutions.

As gay activists grew older, however, and began to channel their political energy into the Democratic Party, they entered a new and more "moderate" phase. Instead of celebrating their unique identity and history, they undertook the arid quest for equality—which meant, in practice, battling "discrimination" in employment and housing, a marginal issue for most gay people—and finally taking up the crusade for gay marriage.

Instead of battling the state, they began to use the state against their perceived enemies. As it became fashionable and politically correct to be "pro-gay," a propaganda campaign was undertaken in the public schools, epitomized by the infamous "Rainbow Curriculum" and the equally notorious tome for tots *Heather Has Two Mommies*. For liberals, who see the state not as Nietzsche's "cold monster" but as a warm and caring therapist who is there to help, this was only natural. The Therapeutic State, after all, is meant to transform society into a liberal Utopia where no one judges anyone and everyone listens to NPR.

These legislative efforts are largely educational: once enacted, anti-discrimination ordinances in housing, for example, are meant to show that the state is taking a side and indirectly teaching citizens a lesson—that it's wrong to discriminate against gays. The reality on the ground, however, is a different matter: since there's no way to know if one is being discriminated against on account of one's presumed sexuality—and since gays have the choice not to divulge that information—it is impossible to be sure if such discrimination has occurred, short of a "No Gays Need Apply" sign on the door. Moreover, landlords, even the bigots among them, are hardly upset when a couple of gays move in, fix up the place to look like something out of *House & Garden*, and pay the rent on time. The homosexual agenda of today has little relevance to the way gay people actually live their lives.

But the legislative agenda of the modern gay rights movement is not meant to be useful to the gay person in the street: it is meant to garner support from heterosexual liberals and others with access to power. It is meant to assure the careers of aspiring gay politicos and boost the fortunes of the left wing of the Democratic Party. The gay marriage campaign is the culmination of this distancing trend, the *reductio ad absurdum* of the civil rights paradigm.

The modern gay-rights movement is all about securing the symbols of societal acceptance. It is a defensive strategy, one that attempts to define homosexuals as an officially sanctioned victim group afflicted with an inherent disability, a disadvantage that must be compensated for legislatively. But if "gay pride" means anything, it means not wanting, needing, or seeking any sort of acceptance but self-acceptance. Marriage is a social institution designed by heterosexuals for heterosexuals: Why should gay people settle for their cast-off hand-me-downs?

Jonathan Rauch

Objections to These Unions

There are only two objections to same-sex marriage that are intellectually honest and internally consistent. One is the simple anti-gay position: "It is the law's job to stigmatize and disadvantage homosexuals, and the marriage ban is a means to that end." The other is the argument from tradition—which turns out, on inspection, not to be so simple.

Many Americans may agree that there are plausible, even compelling, reasons to allow same-sex marriage, and that many of the objections to such unions are overwrought, unfair, or misguided. And yet they draw back. They have reservations that are hard to pin down but that seem not a whit less powerful for that. They may cite religion or culture, but the roots of their misgivings go even deeper. Press them, and they might say something like this:

"I understand how hard it must be to live a marriageless life, or at least I try to understand. I see that some of the objections to same-sex marriage are more about excluding gays than about defending marriage. Believe me, I am no homophobe; I want gay people to have joy and comfort. I respect their relationships and their love, even if they are not what I would want for myself.

"But look. No matter how I come at this question, I keep bumping into the same wall. For the entire history of civilization, marriage has been between men and women. In every religion, every culture, every society—maybe with some minor and rare exceptions, none of them part of our own heritage—marriage has been reserved for the union of male and female. All the words in the world cannot change that. Same-sex marriage would not be an incremental tweak but a radical reform, a break with all of Western history.

"I'm sorry. I am not prepared to take that step, not when we are talking about civilization's bedrock institution. I don't know that I can even give you good reasons. It is just that what you are asking for is too much."

Perhaps it doesn't matter what marriage is for, or perhaps we can't know exactly what marriage is for. Perhaps it is enough simply to say that marriage is as it is, and you can't just make it something else. I call this the Hayekian argument, for Friedrich August von Hayek, one of the 20th century's great economists and philosophers.

Hayek the Conservative?

Hayek—Austrian by birth, British by adoption, winner of the 1974 Nobel Memorial Prize in Economic Sciences—is generally known as one of the leading theoreticians of free market economics and, more broadly, of libertarian (he always said "liberal") social thought. He was eloquent in his defense of the dynamic change that markets bring, but many people are less aware of a deeply traditionalist, conservative strand in his thinking, a strand that traces its lineage back at least to Edmund Burke, the 18th-century English philosopher and politician. Burke famously poured scorn on the French Revolution and its claims to be inventing a new and enlightened social order. The attempt to reinvent society on abstract principles would result not in Utopia, he contended, but in tyranny. For Burke, the existing order might be flawed, even in some respects evil, but it had an organic sense to it; throwing the whole system out the window would bring greater flaws and larger evils.

Outside Britain and America, few people listened. The French Revo-lution inspired generations of reformers to propose their own Utopian social experiments. Communism was one such, fascism another; today, radical Islamism (the political philosophy, not the religion) is yet one more. "The attempt to make heaven on earth invariably produces hell," wrote Karl Popper, another great Austrian-British philosopher, in 1945, when the totalitarian night looked darkest. He and Hayek came of age in the same intellectual climate, when not only Marxists and fascists but many mainstream Western intellectuals took for granted that a handful of smart people could make better social decisions than could chaotic markets, blind traditions, or crude majorities.

It was in opposition to this "fatal conceit," as he called it, that Hayek organized much of his career. He vigorously argued the case for the dynamism and "spontaneous order" of free markets, but he asserted just as vigorously that the dynamism and freedom of constant change were possible only within a restraining framework of rules and customs and institutions that, for the most part, do not change, or change at a speed they themselves set. No expert or political leader can possibly have enough knowledge to get up every morning and order the world from scratch; decide whether to wear clothing, which side of the street to drive on, what counts as mine and what as yours. "Every man growing up in a given culture will find in himself rules, or may discover that he acts in accordance with rules and will similarly recognize the actions of others as conforming or not conforming to various rules," Hayek wrote in *Law, Legislation, and Liberty*. The rules, he added, are not necessarily innate or unchangeable, but "they are part of a cultural heritage which is likely to be fairly constant, especially so long as they are not articulated in words and therefore also are not discussed or consciously examined."

Tradition Over Reason

Hayek the economist is famous for the insight that, in a market system, the prices generated by impersonal forces may not make sense from any one person's point of view, but they encode far more economic information than even the cleverest person or the most powerful computer could ever hope to organize. In a similar fashion, Hayek the social philosopher wrote that human societies' complicated web of culture, traditions, and institutions embodies far more cultural knowledge than any one person could master. Like prices, the customs generated by societies over time may seem irrational or arbitrary. But the very fact that these customs have evolved and survived to come down to us implies that a practical logic may be embedded in them that might not be apparent from even a sophisticated analysis. And the web of custom cannot be torn apart and reordered at will, because once its internal logic is violated it may fall apart.

It was on this point that Hayek was particularly outspoken: Intellectuals and visionaries who seek to deconstruct and rationally rebuild social traditions will produce not a better order but chaos. In his 1952 book *The Counter-Revolution of Science: Studies in the Abuse of Reason*, Hayek made a statement that demands to be quoted in full and read at least twice:

> It may indeed prove to be far the most difficult and not the least important task for human reason rationally to comprehend its own limitations. It is essential for the growth of reason that as individuals we should bow to forces and obey principles which we cannot hope fully to understand, yet on which the advance and even the preservation of civilization depends. Historically this has been achieved by the influence of the various religious creeds and by traditions and superstitions which made man submit to those forces by an appeal to his emotions rather than to his reason. The most dangerous stage in the growth of civilization may well be that in which man has come

to regard all these beliefs as superstitions and refuses to accept or to submit to anything which he does not rationally understand. The rationalist whose reason is not sufficient to teach him those limitations of the powers of conscious reason, and who despises all the institutions and customs which have not been consciously designed, would thus become the destroyer of the civilization built upon them. This may well prove a hurdle which man will repeatedly reach, only to be thrown back into barbarism.

For secular intellectuals who are unhappy with the evolved framework of marriage and who are excluded from it—in other words, for people like me—the Hayekian argument is very challenging. The age-old stigmas attached to illegitimacy and out-of-wedlock pregnancy were crude and unfair to women and children. On the male side, shotgun marriages were coercive and intrusive and often made poor matches. The shame associated with divorce seemed to make no sense at all. But when modern societies abolished the stigmas on illegitimacy, divorce, and all the rest, whole portions of the social structure just caved in.

Not long ago I had dinner with a friend who is a devout Christian. He has a heart of gold, knows and likes gay people, and has warmed to the idea of civil unions. But when I asked him about gay marriage, he replied with a firm no. I asked if he imagined there was anything I could say that might budge him. He thought for a moment and then said no again. Why? Because, he said, male-female marriage is a sacrament from God. It predates the Constitution and every other law of man. We could not, in that sense, change it even if we wanted to. I asked if it might alter his conclusion to reflect that legal marriage is a secular institution, that the separation of church and state requires us to distinguish God's law from civil law, and that we must refrain from using law to impose one group's religious precepts on the rest of society. He shook his head. No, he said. This is bigger than that.

I felt he had not answered my argument. His God is not mine, and in a secular country, law can and should be influenced by religious teachings but must not enforce them. Yet in a deeper way, it was I who had not answered his argument. No doubt the government has the right to set the law of marriage without kowtowing to, say, the Vatican. But that does not make it wise for the government to disregard the centuries of tradition—of accumulated social knowledge—that the teachings of the world's great religions embody. None of those religions sanctions same-sex marriage.

My friend understood the church-state distinction perfectly well. He was saying there are traditions and traditions. Male-female marriage is one of the most hallowed. Whether you call it a sacrament from God or part of Western civilization's cultural DNA, you are saying essentially the same thing: that for many people a same-sex union, whatever else it may be, can never be a marriage, and that no judge or legislature can change this fact.

Here the advocates of same-sex marriage face peril coming from two directions. On the one side, the Hayekian argument warns of unintended and perhaps grave social consequences if, thinking we're smarter than our customs, we decide to rearrange the core elements of marriage. The current rules for marriage may not be the best ones, and they may even be unfair. But they are all we have, and you cannot reengineer the formula without causing unforeseen results, possibly including the implosion of the institution itself. On the other side, political realism warns that we could do serious damage to the legitimacy of marital law if we rewrote it with disregard for what a large share of Americans recognize as marriage.

If some state passed a law allowing you to marry a Volkswagen, the result would be to make a joke of the law. Certainly legal gay marriage would not seem so silly, but people who found it offensive or illegitimate might just ignore it or, in effect, boycott it. Civil and social marriage would fall out of step. That might not be the end of the world—the vast majority of marriages would be just as they were before—but it could not do marriage, or the law any good either. In such an environment, same-sex marriage would offer little beyond legal arrangements that could be provided just as well through civil unions, and it would come at a price in diminished respect for the law.

Call those, then, the problem of unintended consequences and the problem of legitimacy. They are the toughest problems same-sex marriage has to contend with. But they are not intractable.

The Decoy of Traditional Marriage

The Hayekian position really comes in two quite different versions, one much more sweeping than the other. In its strong version, the Hayekian argument implies that no reforms of longstanding institutions or customs should ever be undertaken, because any legal or political meddling would interfere with the natural evolution of social mores. One would thus have had to say, a century and a half ago, that slavery should not be abolished, because it was customary in almost all human societies. More recently, one would have had to say that the federal government was wrong to step in and end racial segregation instead of letting it evolve at its own pace.

Obviously, neither Hayek nor any reputable follower of his would defend every cultural practice simply on the grounds that it must exist for a reason. Hayekians would point out that slavery violated a fundamental tenet of justice and was intolerably cruel. In calling for slavery's abolition, they would do what they must do to be human: They would establish a moral standpoint from which to judge social rules and reforms. They thus would acknowledge that sometimes society must make changes in the name of fairness or decency, even if there are bound to be hidden costs.

If the ban on same-sex marriage were only mildly unfair or if the costs of lifting it were certain to be catastrophic, then the ban could stand on Hayekian grounds. But if there is any social policy today that has a claim to being scaldingly inhumane, it is the ban on gay marriage. Marriage, after all, is the most fundamental institution of society and, for most people, an indispensable element of the pursuit of happiness. For the same reason that tinkering with marriage should not be undertaken lightly (marriage is important to personal and social well-being), barring a whole class of people from marrying imposes an extraordinary deprivation. Not so long ago, it was illegal in certain parts of the United States for blacks to marry whites; no one would call this a trivial disfranchisement. For many years, the champions of women's suffrage were patted on the head and told, "Your rallies and petitions are all very charming, but you don't really need to vote, do you?" It didn't wash. The strong Hayekian argument has traction only against a weak moral claim.

To rule out a moral and emotional claim as powerful as the right to marry for love, saying that bad things might happen is not enough. Bad things always might happen. People predicted that bad things would happen if contraception became legal and widespread, and indeed bad things did happen, but that did not make legalizing contraception the wrong thing to do; and, in any case, good things happened too. Unintended consequences can also be positive, after all.

Besides, by now the traditional understanding of marriage, however you define it, has been tampered with in all kinds of ways, some of them more consequential than gay marriage is likely to be. No-fault divorce dealt a severe blow to, "till death do us part," which was certainly an essential element of the traditional meaning of marriage.

It is hard to think of a bigger affront to tradition than allowing married women to own property independently of their husbands. In *What Is Marriage For?*, her history of marriage, the journalist E. J. Graff quotes a 19th-century New York legislator as saying that allowing wives to own property would affront both God and nature, "degrading the holy bonds of matrimony [and] striking at the root of those divinely ordained principles upon which is built the superstructure of our society." In 1844 a New York legislative committee said that permitting married women to control their own property would lead to "infidelity in the marriage bed, a high rate of divorce, and increased female criminality" and would turn marriage "from its high and holy purpose" into something arranged for "convenience and sensuality." A British parliamentarian denounced the proposal as "contrary not only to the law of England but to the law of God."

Graff assembles other quotations in the same vein, and goes on to add, wryly, "The funny thing, of course, is that those jeremiads were right." Allowing married women to control their economic destinies did indeed open the door to today's high divorce rates; but it also transformed marriage into something less like servitude for women and more in keeping with liberal principles of equality in personhood and citizenship.

An off-the-cuff list of fundamental changes to marriage would include not only divorce and property reform but also the abolition of polygamy, the fading of dowries, the abolition of childhood betrothals, the elimination of parents' right to choose mates for their children or to veto their children's choices, the legalization of interracial marriage, the legalization of contraception, the criminalization of marital rape (an offense that wasn't even recognized until recently), and of course the very concept of civil marriage. Surely it is unfair to say that marriage may be reformed for the sake of anyone and everyone except homosexuals, who must respect the dictates of tradition.

Some people will argue that permitting same-sex marriage would be a more fundamental change than any of the earlier ones. Perhaps so; but equally possible is that we forget today just how unnatural and destabilizing and contrary to the meaning of marriage it once seemed, for example, to put the wife on a par, legally, with the husband. Anyway, even if it is true that gay marriage constitutes a more radical definitional change than earlier innovations, in an important respect it stands out as one of the narrowest of reforms. All the earlier alterations directly affected many or all married couples, whereas same-sex marriage would directly pertain to only a small minority. It isn't certain that allowing same-sex couples to marry would have any noticeable effect on heterosexual marriage at all.

True, you never know what might happen when you tinker with tradition. A catastrophe cannot be ruled out. It is worth bearing in mind, though, that predictions of disaster if open homosexuals are integrated into traditionally straight institutions have a perfect track record: They are always wrong. When openly gay couples began making homes together in suburban neighborhoods, the result was not Sodom on every street corner; when openly gay executives began turning up in corporate jobs, stud collars did not replace neckties. I vividly remember, when I lived in London in 1995, the forecasts of morale and unit cohesion crumbling if open homosexuals were allowed to serve in the British armed forces. But when integration came (under court order), the whole thing turned out to be a nonevent. Again and again, the homosexual threat turns out to be imaginary; straights have far less to fear from gay inclusion than gays do from exclusion.

Jeopardizing Marriage's Universality

So the extreme Hayekian position—never reform anything—is untenable. And that point was made resoundingly by no less an authority than F. A. Hayek himself. In a 1960 essay called "Why I Am Not a Conservative," he took pains to argue that his position was as far from that of reactionary traditionalists as from that of utopian rationalists. "Though there is a need for a 'brake on the vehicle of progress,' " he said, "I personally cannot be content with simply helping to apply the brake." Classical liberalism, he writes, "has never been a backward-looking doctrine." To the contrary, it recognizes, as reactionary conservatism often fails to, that change is a constant and the world cannot be stopped in its tracks.

His own liberalism, Hayek wrote, "shares with conservatism a distrust of reason to the extent that the liberal is very much aware that we do not know all the answers," but the liberal, unlike the reactionary conservative, does not imagine that simply clinging to the past or "claiming the authority of supernatural sources of knowledge" is any kind of answer. We must move ahead, but humbly and with respect for our own fallibility.

And there are times, Hayek said (in *Law, Legislation, and Liberty*), when what he called "grown law" requires correction by legislation. "It may be due simply to the recognition that some past development was based on error or that it produced consequences later recognized as unjust," he wrote. "But the most frequent cause is probably that the development of the law has lain in the hands of members of a particular class whose traditional views made them regard as just what could not meet the more general requirements of justice. . . . Such occasions when it is recognized that some hereto accepted rules are unjust in the light of more general principles of justice may well require the revision not only of single rules but of whole sections of the established system of case law."

That passage, I think, could have been written with gay marriage in mind. The old view that homosexuals were heterosexuals who needed punishment or prayer or treatment has been exposed as an error. What homosexuals need is the love of another homosexual. The ban on same-sex marriage, hallowed though it is, no longer accords with liberal justice or the meaning of marriage as it is practiced today. Something has to give. Standing still is not an option.

Hayek himself, then, was a partisan of the milder version of Hayekianism. This version is not so much a prescription as an attitude. Respect tradition. Reject utopianism. Plan for mistakes rather than for perfection. If reform is needed, look for paths that follow the terrain of custom, if possible. If someone promises to remake society on rational or supernatural or theological principles, run in the opposite direction. In sum: Move ahead, but be careful.

Good advice. But not advice, particularly, against gay marriage. Remember Hayek's admonition against dogmatic conservatism. In a shifting current, holding your course can be just as dangerous as oversteering. Conservatives, in their panic to stop same-sex marriage, jeopardize marriage's universality and ultimately its legitimacy. They are taking risks, and big ones, and unnecessary ones. The liberal tradition and the *Declaration of Independence* are not currents you want to set marriage against.

It is worth recalling that Burke, the patron saint of social conservatism and the scourge of the French Revolution, supported the American Revolution. He distinguished between a revolt that aimed to overthrow established rights and principles and a revolt that aimed to restore them. Many of the American founders, incidentally, made exactly the same distinction. Whatever else they may have been, they were not Utopian social engineers. Whether a modern-day Burke or Jefferson would support gay marriage, I cannot begin to say; but I am confident they would, at least, have understood and carefully weighed the possibility that to preserve the liberal foundation of civil marriage, we may find it necessary to adjust its boundaries.

DISCUSSION QUESTIONS

1. What do you make of the "slippery slope" argument that if we expand the definition of marriage beyond one man and one woman, there is no principled way to oppose further redefinition to include polygamy or other forms of marriage? Or is Douthat correct that we're already there, having replaced traditional marriage with "serial monogamy?"

2. To what extent should laws reflect a particular view of morality? Are there concrete reasons to oppose same-sex marriage, or are they rooted primarily in a moral view about what is proper?

3. If same-sex marriage becomes legal, should it be done through the courts (which would presumably invalidate state statutes or override state constitutional prohibitions as invalid under the U.S. Constitution), or through legislatures or initiatives?

4. Do you agree with Raimondo's argument that state recognition of same-sex marriage would actually make gay people worse off? If this libertarian argument is correct, should it be applied to heterosexual marriage as well?

5

Congress: Pork-Barrel Politics

In an era of enormous budget deficits, federal spending is under intense scrutiny. One type of spending—"pork-barrel" policies that are targeted to a specific district or project—is especially controversial because it raises questions about the capacity of Congress to deal effectively with national problems and priorities. However, the debate over pork-barrel politics illustrates the difficulties of defining national interests as opposed to parochial, or local, interests and the role of Congress in policy making.

Pork may take many forms. The most common legislative vehicle for distributing pork is the "earmark," which identifies specific, targeted spending, usually as part of a larger bill. Transportation bills and water projects are two of the traditional outlets for pork-barrel spending, but in recent years even bills funding the war against terrorism, homeland security, and the wars in Iraq and Afghanistan have been full of pork. A moratorium was placed on this type of pork in both the House and Senate starting in 2011. But Citizens Against Government Waste, the leading watchdog group on this topic, identified 152 earmarks worth $3.3 billion in the 2012 fiscal year. An article in the Capitol Hill newspaper *Roll Call* entitled "Working Around Earmark Ban" explained how members continue to "bring home the bacon" to their district. Another study uncovered "stealth pork" in which members of Congress did not require spending in an earmark but "asked for it nicely," with the same effect. Finally, the compromise that led to the resolution of the "fis-cal cliff' early in 2013 included billions of dollars in tax expenditures targeted at specific industries, another favorite technique of delivering benefits to constitu-ents. Suffice it to say, member of Congress will continue to find ways to deliver benefits to their constituents and claim credit for them, despite the moratorium on earmarks.

The Cato Institute is a libertarian think tank that is highly critical of wasteful government spending. The selection from the Cato Handbook provides a general example of how special interests win over the general interests, specific instances of pork in recent years (including grants for the Shedd Aquarium in Chicago and the Rock and Roll Hall of Fame in Cleveland), and the broader implications of pork for the policy-making process. Cato's overall critique of pork is that the American taxpayer should not be funding these programs. Rather, the private sector should provide funding (if any). Pork contributes to the ballooning federal deficit and debt and is the "currency of corruption." The selection ends with a call for more trans-parency in pork spending and its eventual elimination (which would go beyond the current ban on earmarks).

Where Cato sees waste and abuse of the nation's resources, however, James Inhofe, a Republican senator from Oklahoma, and Jonathan Rauch see many posi-tive virtues. In an interview with Brian Friel, Inhofe characterizes earmark reform as a phony issue. Inhofe sees earmarks as maintaining Congress's control over spending. Otherwise, the power to decide which projects get funded would shift to unelected bureaucrats. Also, Inhofe argues that national interests can be served by allowing local interests to dip into the pork barrel.

Rauch agrees that the power of the purse should remain with Congress rather than the executive branch, but also points out that a recent bill that was criticized as being "full of pork" had less than 2 percent of the offending spending. (Overall, pork accounts for less than 1 percent of federal spending.) Furthermore, much of the accountability and transparency Cato calls for is already in place: it isn't that easy to get an earmark, and earmark sponsors are made public. Other supporters of pork have called it the "glue" of legislating. If it takes a little pork for the home district or state to get important legislation through Congress, so be it. Also, one person's pork could be another person's essential spending. Members of Con-gress are best able to determine that need.

Cato Handbook for Policymakers

Corporate Welfare and Earmarks

When considering budget issues, federal policymakers are supposed to have the broad public interest in mind. Unfortunately, that is not how the federal budget process usually works in practice. Many federal programs are sustained by special-interest groups working with policymakers seeking narrow benefits at the expense of taxpayers and the general public.

* * *

How can special interests regularly triumph over the broad public interest in our democracy? For one thing, recipients of federal handouts have a strong incentive to create organizations to lobby Congress to keep the federal gravy train flowing. By contrast, average citizens have no strong incentive to lobby against any particular subsidy program because each program costs just a small portion of their total tax bill.

When average citizens do speak out against particular programs, they are usually outgunned by the professionals who are paid to support programs. Those professionals have an informational advantage over citizens because the workings of most federal programs are complex. The lobby groups that defend subsidy programs are staffed by top program experts, and they are skilled at generating media support. One typical gambit is to cloak the narrow private interests of subsidy recipients in public interest clothing, and proclaim that the nation's future depends on increased funding.

TABLE 1
Majority Voting Does Not Ensure That a Project's Benefits Outweigh Costs

Legislator	Vote	Benefits Received by Constituents	Taxes Paid by Constituents
Clinton	Yea	$12	$10
Cochran	Yea	$12	$10
Collins	Yea	$12	$10
Carper	Nay	$2	$10
Coburn	Nay	$2	$10
Total	Pass	$40	$50

Another reason it is hard to challenge spending programs is that lobby groups, congressional supporters, and federal agencies rarely admit that any program is a failure. Washington insiders become vested in the continued funding of programs because their careers, pride, and reputations are on the line, and they will battle against any cuts or reforms.

How do dubious spending programs get enacted in the first place? Table 1 shows how Congress can pass special-interest legislation in which the costs outweigh the benefits. The table assumes that legislators vote in the narrow interest of their districts. The hypothetical project shown creates benefits of $40 and costs taxpayers $50, and is thus a loser for the nation. Nonetheless, the project gains a majority vote. The program's benefits are more concentrated than its costs, and that is the key to gaining political support.

The pro-spending bias of Congress is strengthened by the complex web of vote trading, or logrolling, that often occurs. Table 2 shows that because of logrolling, projects that are net losers to society can pass even if they do not have majority support. Because Projects A and B would fail with stand alone votes, Clinton, Cochran, and Collins enter an agreement to mutually support the two projects. That is, they logroll. The result is that the two projects get approved, even though each imposes net costs on society and benefits only a minority of voters.

The popularity of logrolling means that programs that make no economic sense and have only minimal public support are enacted all the time.

* * *

TABLE 2

Logrolling Allows Passage of Subsidies That Benefit Minorities of Constituents

	Project A		Project B		Vote on a Bill Including Projects A and B
Legislator	Benefits Received by Constituents	Taxes Paid by Constituents	Benefits Received by Constituents	Taxes Paid by Constituents	
Clinton	$15	$10	$8	$10	Yea
Cochran	$15	$10	$8	$10	Yea
Collins	$4	$10	$20	$10	Yea
Carper	$3	$10	$2	$10	Nay
Coburn	$3	$10	$2	$10	Nay
Total	$40	$50	$40	$50	Pass

Earmarks

The federal budget practice of "earmarking" has exploded during the last fifteen years. Earmarks are line items in spending bills inserted by legislators for specific projects in their home states. Some infamous earmarks funded a $50 million indoor rain forest in Iowa and a $223 million "bridge to nowhere" in Alaska. Earmarks can provide recipients with federal grant money, contracts, loans, or other types of benefits. Earmarks are often referred to as "pork" spending.

* * * [T]he number of pork projects increased from fewer than 2,000 annually in the mid-1990s to almost 14,000 in 2005. Various scandals and the switch to Democratic control of Congress then slowed the pace of earmarking for a couple of years. But earmarking is on the rise again. The fiscal year 2008 omnibus appropriations bill was bloated with 11,610 spending projects inserted by members of Congress for their states and districts.

Earmarked projects are generally those that have not been requested by the president and have not been subject to expert review or competitive bidding. Thus, if the government had $1 billion to spend on bioterrorism research, it might be earmarked to go to laboratories in the districts of important politicians, rather than to labs chosen by a panel of scientists. Earmarking has soared in most areas of the budget, including defense, education, housing, scientific research, and transportation.

The main problem with earmarking is that most spending projects chosen by earmark are properly the responsibility of state and local governments or the private sector, not the federal government. The rise in earmarks is one manifestation of Congress's growing intrusion into state affairs, . . . Consider these earmarks from the FY08 omnibus appropriations bill:

1. $1,648,850 for the private Shedd Aquarium in Chicago, which is also awash with corporate funding;
2. $787,200 for "green design" changes at the Museum of Natural History in Minneapolis;
3. $492,000 for the Rocky Flats Cold War Museum in Arvada, Colorado;
4. $1,950,000 for a library and archives at the Charles B. Rangel Center for Public Service at the City College of New York;
5. $2,400,000 for renovations to Haddad Riverfront Park in Charleston;
6. $500,000 for upgrades to Barracks Row, a swank Capitol Hill neighborhood;

7. $742,764 for fruit fly research, partly conducted in France;
8. $188,000 for the Lobster Institute in Maine; and
9. $492,000 for fuel cell research for Rolls-Royce Group of Canton, Ohio.

Projects 1 to 3 give taxpayer money to groups that should be funding their own activities from admissions fees and charitable contributions. Interestingly, the nonprofit Shedd Aquarium has spent hundreds of thousands of dollars on lobbyists to secure federal earmarks, and its chief executive earned a huge $600,000 salary in 2006. Or consider that the Rock and Roll Hall of Fame in Cleveland has received federal grants, even though there are thousands of music industry millionaires who should be footing the bill.

Projects 4 to 6 are examples of items that state and local governments should fund locally. Unfortunately, state and local officials are increasingly asking Washington for handouts, and lobby groups such as Cassidy and Associates are helping them "mine" the federal budget for grants.

Projects 7 to 9 fund activities that should be left to the private sector. Industries should fund their own research, which is likely to be more cost-effective than government efforts. Besides, successful research leads to higher profits for private businesses, and it makes no sense for taxpayers to foot the bill for such private gains.

Earmarks' Erosion of Fiscal Responsibility

Defenders of earmarks argue that they are no big deal since they represent just a small share of overall federal spending. The problem is that earmarking has contributed to the general erosion in fiscal responsibility in Washington. Earmarks have exacerbated the parochial mindset of most members, who spend their time appeasing state and local interest groups rather than tackling issues of broad national concern. Many politicians complain about the soaring federal deficit, yet their own staff members spend most of their time trying to secure earmarks in spending bills.

The rise in earmarking has encouraged a general spendthrift attitude in Congress. Why should rank-and-file members restrain themselves when their own leaders are usually big recipients of pork? Sen. Tom Coburn (R-OK) is right that the problem with earmarks is "the hidden cost of perpetuating a culture of fiscal irresponsibility. When politicians fund pork projects they sacrifice the authority to seek cuts in any other program." Similarly, Rep. Jeff Flake

(R-AZ) concludes that "earmarking . . . has become the currency of corruption in Congress. . . . Earmarks are used as inducements to get members to sign on to large spending measures."

Reforms to Increase Transparency and Downsize the Government

A first step toward eliminating earmarks, corporate welfare, and other special-interest spending is to further increase transparency in the congressional and agency spending processes. Under pressure from reformers, the government has set up a searchable database of federal grants and contracts at www.usaspending .gov. A second step is for citizens to use this website and other tools to research federal spending, and then to call their members of Congress and tell them what programs should be cut.

Citizens should also ask their members to support reforms to the budget process. One idea for cutting corporate welfare is to set up a commission akin to the successful military base–closing commissions of the 1990s. It would draw up a list of current subsidies and present it to Congress, which would vote on the cuts as a package without amendment. To make the package a political winner, all budget savings would go toward immediate tax cuts for families.

Ultimately, earmarking and corporate welfare should be abolished, and spending on activities that are legitimate federal functions should be determined by a system of competitive bidding and expert review. Of course, it will not be easy to reform the spending practices of Congress. Members often feel committed to expanding spending in their districts and on their favored programs. But taxpayers fund all those programs, and they need to do a better job of convincing their members to cut unneeded programs and pass much leaner federal budgets.

—Prepared by Chris Edwards and Jeff Patch

Brian Friel

Inhofe: Earmarks Are Good for Us

Sen. James Inhofe, R-Okla., the ranking member on the Senate Environment and Public Works Committee, spent the past eight years battling liberals over climate change and arguing that predictions of catastrophic global warming are a "hoax." Now Inhofe is taking on what he describes as another "phony" issue—earmark reform. But this crusade puts him at odds with fellow conservatives in his own party.

In recent years, taxpayer watchdog groups and anti-pork-barrel lawmakers—including Sens. John McCain, R-Ariz.; Jim DeMint, R-S.C.; and Inhofe's home-state colleague and fellow Republican, Tom Coburn—have turned earmarks into a dirty word. They contend that lawmakers' long-standing practice of earmarking funding for pet projects promotes waste, big spending, and corruption. The Senate foes regularly offer floor amendments attempting to strip earmarks from legislation.

Inhofe, who ranked as the most conservative senator in *National Journal's* 2009 vote ratings, launched a campaign this week to recast earmarks as a tool that conservatives should embrace, not deride. He noted that most people took global warming as a fact eight years ago, and he contended that he has effectively shown that it is not. His earmark battle is aimed at showing that what everyone believes about earmarks is also untrue, he said.

"They're winning on the phrase," Inhofe said of anti-earmarkers, in an interview. "It's fraudulent."

Elected to the House in 1986 and to the Senate in 1994, Inhofe says that his efforts on global warming ultimately led to the recent demise of cap-and-trade climate-change legislation. To environmentalists and many congressional Democrats, he is a villain. Dan Lashof, the climate center director of the Natural Resources Defense Council, calls Inhofe "the Senate's chief spokesman for climate deniers." But the Oklahoman has become a star in conservative circles for his outspoken and often lonely fight on the issue.

Armed with those bona fides, Inhofe is planning to take his pro-earmark campaign to rank-and-file conservatives. He said he was inspired, in part, by a column that Jonathan Rauch wrote in this magazine. . . . Inhofe is slated to speak to a "tea party" group in Jacksonville, Fla., later this month, where he expects to test-drive his message. He has drafted an op-ed outlining his views on the "phony issue of earmarks." He also hopes to convince conservative talk-radio hosts that their frequent earmark-bashing misses the more important goal: reducing overall spending to ensure greater fiscal responsibility in Washington.

"You don't save anything by cutting earmarks," Inhofe said. He maintained that eliminating lawmakers' earmarks doesn't shrink the over-all budget; it just leaves it to federal agencies—currently controlled by the Democratic Obama administration—to decide how to distribute the money. "These nonelected bureaucrats are the ones who are making the decisions."

As an example, Inhofe pointed to a transportation program that pays for low-budget initiatives such as bike trails, streetscapes, and congestion mitigation. In 2008, Congress distributed the millions of dollars in program funding through earmarks that boosted 102 projects in 35 states. The year before, when no earmarks were permitted, the Transportation Department funded projects through a grant competition in just five big cities—Miami, Minneapolis-St. Paul, New York City, San Francisco, and Seattle.

Inhofe argues that earmarks have funded many programs that conservatives support, particularly in national defense. As the second-ranking Republican on the Armed Services Committee, behind McCain, Inhofe notes that Congress has used earmarks to keep several military programs chugging along despite executive branch objections, including additional C-17 cargo planes that President Obama fought against last year. McCain offered an amendment to the Defense appropriations bill that would have nixed the funds for the extra planes, but Inhofe and 63 other senators defeated it.

Instead of imposing an earmark moratorium, Inhofe proposes a freeze in nonsecurity appropriations at fiscal 2008 levels, a move that he says would save $600 billion more than Obama's proposal in February to freeze such spending at fiscal 2010 levels. He also maintains that individual projects should be assessed on their merits, not on whether they are deemed to be earmarks.

Opponents counter, though, that earmarked congressional projects have become a symbol of what is wrong with Washington.

"I think there is a justifiable argument for earmarks, that we as legislators probably know better in some instances than bureaucrats in Washington about how money should be spent," Sen. George LeMieux, R-Fla., conceded. "But earmarks are, unfortunately, the engine that drives the train that gets us into these huge spending problems. If I put an earmark in a particular appropriations bill, and then that appropriations bill is 15 percent more than it was last year, and I say I can't support that, they'll say, well, your earmark is in there. So the earmark is what buys you into bigger spending."

While not naming names, Inhofe argues that some Republican senators use their anti-earmark credentials as a fig leaf to cover their votes to authorize massive spending programs. As examples, he cited the $700 billion bank bailout in October 2008; the Fannie Mae and Freddie Mac takeover in July 2008; and a bill the same month to increase funding for HIV/AIDS programs in Africa from $15 billion to $50 billion.

"If you look at those three things, you're well over a trillion dollars," he said. "And you look at the Republicans who voted for them. They've been able to use earmarks to distract people."

DeMint voted with Inhofe against all three measures. McCain voted for the bank bailout; and Coburn voted for both the bank bill and the AIDS legislation. DeMint, McCain, and Coburn are among the sponsors of earmark-moratorium legislation introduced last month.

Inhofe said that if Congress bans earmarks, his fallback position is that they should be defined only as projects that receive appropriations without having been previously authorized by Congress. Inhofe is a chief authorizer—for transportation programs at the Environment and Public Works Committee and for military programs at the Armed Services Committee. He and other authorizers regularly struggle for power with appropriators, who often have their own ideas about which projects to fund in their annual spending bills.

In a brief interview, McCain defended his anti-earmark stance. "My record is very clear," he said. "For 20 years I've fought against ear-marks and their corruption. They breed corruption, and they've bred corruption."

McCain said he believes that the root of the problem is unauthorized appropriations. "You've got to get the definition of an earmark: that is, an unauthorized appropriation. If you authorize it, even if I disagree with it, that's the right process," he said. "What [earmarks] have done is totally circumvent what we should be doing: that is, authorizing and *then* appropriating."

Sen. Saxby Chambliss, R-Ga.—the ranking member on the Senate Agriculture, Nutrition, and Forestry Committee, another key authorizing panel—said that giving authorizers more power to say where money should be spent could be one part of earmark reform. He is a co-sponsor of the earmark moratorium. "I hope we get some sort of meaningful earmark reform as a result of continuing to stir that issue up," Chambliss said.

Inhofe's pro-earmark campaign will certainly cause a stir among his colleagues. Some House and Senate Republicans have urged the party to unilaterally adopt an earmark moratorium to paint a strong contrast to the Democrats. Inhofe counters that doing so would simply give more money to Obama to spend on liberal-supported projects and that it would distract attention from the core issues that the GOP can ride to victory in November.

"The Republican Party has the greatest issues ever in the history of politics in America—health care, cap-and-trade, closing Gitmo—that's terrorists coming into the United States, and the deficit, and the debt," Inhofe said. "Making an issue out of earmarks serves to only mislead voters by providing cover for big spenders. Railing against earmarks helps those who vote for the billion-dollar spending bills seem more conservative than they really are."

Jonathan Rauch
Earmarks Are a Model, Not a Menace

Naturally, when a gigantic omnibus appropriations bill came to the Senate floor last week, 98 percent of it got almost no attention. "Member projects—aka earmarks or 'pork'—account for less than 2 percent of spending in the $410 billion omnibus bill on the floor of the Senate this week, but they're drawing most of the opposition fire," *The Christian Science Monitor* reported. Less than 2 percent! Of course, this orgy of waste offended me for the same reason it offended everyone else: I was not getting an earmark.

I decided to get an earmark. Seemed easy enough. Just call someone in a congressional office, make a silly request—propose converting pig vomit into drywall, that sort of thing—and voila, I would have my very own "pet project."

So I called my congressman, Rep. Jim Moran, D-Va., who, handily enough, is a member of the Appropriations Committee. Imagine my shock when I got a staffer who insisted that I would have to *apply*.

Apply? For a *pet project*? Right. There was a form. As in, paperwork. The exact form would depend on which Appropriations subcommittee has jurisdiction. And I would need to meet with legislative aides to explain why my project deserved funding. And they would probably vet my request with the relevant federal agency.

Oh. But then I'm in, right?

Not quite. Moran told me he will get a thousand earmark applications this year. "It actually goes up every year." He will accept only the best hundred or so.

But *then* I'm in?

No, then the relevant Appropriations subcommittee further whittles the list. About three dozen of Moran's earmarks will get funded, he figures.

So my chances of scoring boodle were on the order of only 3 percent. I didn't fill out the form, even though it was only a page long. Down in Norfolk, Rep. Bobby Scott, D-Va., requires earmark applicants to fill out a seven-page form that looks like my tax return—and I itemize. "Please check *all* that apply:. . . This project is largely for EPA consent decree. . . . Preliminary planning and engineering design is completed." Really, it takes all the thrill out of pet projects.

Beating up on earmarks is fun. But if you interrupt the joy long enough to take a closer look, you may discover that the case against earmarks has pretty much evaporated over the past few years. In fact, reformers seem to want to hound out of existence a system that actually works better than much of what Washington does.

When former Rep. Jim Kolbe, R-Ariz., entered Congress in 1985, "there were no earmarks," he told me recently. Perhaps, you say, this was because appropriators were indifferent to how much federal money flowed to their districts? Sorry, bad guess.

In those days, according to Kolbe (an Appropriations Committee member who retired in 2007), appropriators felt little need to write earmarks into law. Instead, subcommittee chairmen and ranking members just dropped money into program accounts. Then they called up executive branch bureaucrats with advice on how to spend it.

"Most agencies didn't need to be threatened if the chairman of their subcommittee called," says Scott Lilly, a former House Appropriations Committee staff director and now a senior fellow with the Center for American Progress. Sometimes, Lilly says, "you'd increase the entire national program in order that it would have a better chance that it would spill into your state."

In the 1980s and 1990s, the once-sequestered system cracked open. The number of earmarks increased by a factor of 25 between 1991 and 2005. Earmarks were often invisible, at least until after they were enacted. "The bill would be passed before people even started digging into what was in there," Lilly says. Public outrage swelled.

On its heels, however, came reform, notably in the last couple of years. Every earmark request now must be made public before Congress votes on it. The sponsoring member, the amount and nature of the request, and the name and address of the beneficiary must all be disclosed. You can find all this stuff online. As I was miffed to discover, many congressional offices have formalized the application procedure. Getting an earmark now is a lot like applying for a grant.

As transparency has taken over, the case against earmarks has melted away. Their budgetary impact is trivial in comparison with entitlements and other large programs. Obsessing about earmarks, indeed, has the perverse, if convenient, effect of distracting the country from its real spending problems, thus substituting indignation for discipline.

Earmarks are often criticized for rewarding political clout rather than merit. If earmarks were merit-based, says Steve Ellis of the watchdog group Taxpayers for Common Sense, you wouldn't see them flowing disproportionately to Appropriations Committee members. And earmarks, he adds, reflect parochial rather than national priorities. "There's no way the Appropriations Committee is able to vet the thousands of earmarks worth billions of dollars."

Fair enough. But if you think that executive branch decisions are strictly apolitical and merit-based, I have two words for you: Karl Rove. "The idea that the only politicians in the government are in the Congress is just false," Lilly says. If you think that executive branch decision-making is transparent, I have two more words for you: Dick Cheney.

And if you think Congress is parochial, take it up with Mr. Madison. He wrote the Constitution, which says, in terms that leave no room for quibbling, that the power of the purse belongs to Congress. The Founders' notion was that accountability to local voters was the best safeguard for the people's money. "The idea that unless something is in the president's budget Congress shouldn't consider it turns the Constitution on its head," Kolbe says.

"The problem with a lot of federal programs is that they have to take a cookie-cutter approach," Moran says. Big, conventionally authorized programs, with their funding formulas and contracting rules and national purview, may be too slow to meet urgent local needs, too rigid to support innovation, too formulaic to finance a one-shot project.

Kolbe recalls an earmark that sped up an approved but languishing highway project in Arizona. "It was desperately needed; there were huge backups on the interstate," he says. "Seeing the growing need, not anticipated at the time of its initial approval, we simply jumped it up on the priority list."

Political discretion can be abused, and one would certainly not want most federal spending to be subject to it. But, provided that transparency is assured, shouldn't there be a place in government for elected officials to exercise judgment in the use of taxpayer money? In fact, if you wanted to create a nonbureaucratic, transparent system of rapid-response grants for pressing local concerns, you would come up with something very much like today's earmarking system (and you'd call it "reinventing government").

Some earmark spending is silly, but then so is some non-earmark spending, and there is a lot more of the latter. Competition for funding, combined with flexibility and local knowledge, makes earmarks "often some of the best expenditures the federal government makes in a particular area," Lilly says. "I would say, on the whole, earmarks probably provide as much value-added as non-earmarked federal spending."

And earmark spending today is, if anything, more transparent, more accountable, and more promptly disclosed than is non-earmark spending. Indeed, executive agencies could stand to emulate some of the online disclosure rules that apply to earmarks.

These days, the problem is not so much with earmarking as with Congress's and the public's obsession with it. "It just takes too damn much time," Lilly says. "Congress is spending an inordinate amount of time on 1 percent of the budget and giving the executive branch much too free a rein on the other 99 percent."

Reformers who want to ban earmarking might think again. "You're never going to abolish earmarks," Moran says. "What you'll wind up abolishing is the transparency, the accountability." If unable to earmark, legislators will inveigle executive agencies behind the scenes, fry bureaucrats at hearings, and expand or rewrite entire programs to serve parochial needs. This, of course, is the way things worked in the bad old days. "I think you'll wind up going back to that system," Kolbe cautions.

A better approach is to improve transparency and further routinize the earmarking process, as President Obama proposed on Wednesday when he signed the omnibus spending bill. But here is a reform that would help much more: Declare earmarking an ex-problem and move on. Next time you come across someone who looks at a giant federal spending bill and sees only the 2 percent that happens to be earmarked, tell that person to get over it.

DISCUSSION QUESTIONS

1. How would you define pork-barrel projects? Are all pork projects contrary to the national interest? How do we distinguish between local projects that are in the national interest and those that are not?

2. Consider Cato's list of examples of pork. If you were a member of Congress, which of these would you clearly support? Which would you clearly oppose? Which would you want to find out more about before deciding?

3. Members of Congress face strong incentives to serve constituent needs and claim credit for delivering federal dollars. Pork-barrel projects provide the means to do just that. What changes in Congress or the political process might be made to alter legislative behavior, or to change the incentives legislators face when securing re-election? Do we want members of Congress to be focused primarily on broad national issues rather than local priorities?

6

The Presidency: Prospects, Possibilities and Perils in Obama's Second Term

After a rocky first term, with both major policy success and major controversies (at times on the same issue), Obama was reelected by a comfortable 51–47 percent margin. He became the third consecutive two-term president. What are the prospects for Obama's second term? What issues will he push, and how likely is he to succeed? Or is he destined for failure, like so many other second-term presidents?

Conventional wisdom holds that second terms are fraught with peril, a view confirmed by scandals and crises in earlier presidencies: George W. Bush suffered from extremely low popularity stemming from the Iraq War, lost control of Congress, and had no success pushing Social Security reform. Clinton was impeached, Reagan suffered through Iran-Contra, and Nixon resigned over Watergate. Is this just a sequence of coincidences, or is there a reason why presidents seem to stumble in their second terms?

There are a number of possible explanations (assuming, of course, that the underlying pattern of failure is actually true): lame-duck status, departure of key personnel after the first term, reliance on second-tier policy ideas not pushed in the first term, congressional resistance, and public weariness, to name a few.

The readings here offer different perspectives on Obama's second term. Clymer, writing in the *New York Times*, notes the pattern of second term failures (going back to FDR's disastrous proposal to pack the Supreme Court), but also points out that not all presidents suffer. Eisenhower had some notable second-term successes, particularly (in Clymer's view) his decision to send the U.S. military into Little Rock, Arkansas, to enforce a school desegregation order. Reagan got a major tax reform law passed in 1986. Clinton, who was the first Democratic president since Truman to face a Republican Congress, nevertheless achieved some notable policy successes prior to his impeachment. Even George W. Bush pushed through the Troubled Asset Relief Program in the fall of 2008.

Cavanaugh, writing in the libertarian journal *Reason*, is worried that Obama's popular-vote majority will embolden the president to push aggressively in a second term. Freed from the fear of electoral repudiation, Obama can to pursue an even grander agenda, with the result that we will have more government and less freedom.

Amar takes a middle position, arguing that second terms hold both peril and promise, and that presidents must deal with long-term shifts in public attitudes that they cannot control. He provides some basic guidelines for a second-termer—designate a successor, don't be afraid to "go bold," and seek structural reforms that make it more difficult to obstruct your agenda.

Adam Clymer

Triumphant Obama Faces New Foe in 'Second-Term Curse'

Now that President Obama has overcome Mitt Romney, "super PACs" and a sluggish economy, he faces a challenge with deep roots in political history: what historians and commentators call the "second-term curse."

It is almost a truism that second terms are less successful than first terms, especially domestically. Franklin Delano Roosevelt lost his hold on Congress with his 1937 plan to pack the Supreme Court. Ronald Reagan faced the 1986 Iran-contra scandal. Bill Clinton was impeached in 1998. Richard Nixon resigned to avoid that fate in 1974.

Even George Washington had angry mobs surrounding his house in Philadelphia to denounce him for the Jay Treaty with Britain dealing with the aftermath of the Revolutionary War; they wanted him to side with France.

But despite these and other failures, most second-term presidents also have accomplishments to be proud of, though perhaps shadowed by a tinge of failure.

Stephen Hess, a scholar at the Brookings Institution and a veteran of the Eisenhower, Nixon, Ford and Carter administrations, said there were several explanations for the second-term curse.

One is that presidents try to push their best ideas when they first take office, often leaving them, he said, without "a whole new set of ideas" for the second.

Presidents also select the best members of the White House staff or cabinet when they first take office. When the pressure cooker of Washington or better jobs lead those first choices away, their successors are often not their equals.

Roosevelt may have had the most accursed second term. The biographer Jean Edward Smith called it "a disaster." After the 1936 death of Louis Howe, his closest adviser for years, he had no one to tell him what a bad idea the court-packing scheme was. It split his party. Conservative Democrats deserted him and allied with Republicans to deny him almost all domestic legislation.

And while that hurt Roosevelt politically—Mr. Smith said he "shot himself in the foot"—he followed with an even worse decision, cutting federal spending in the belief that the Depression was conquered. That brought on a deep recession. With that decision, Mr. Smith wrote, Roosevelt "shot the country in the foot."

Overwhelming victory can often lead to second-term hubris, persuading a president that the country thinks he can do no wrong. As Lou Cannon, the Reagan biographer and Washington Post White House reporter, observed: "Landslides are dangerous to the victor." Roosevelt lost only two states in 1936; Nixon lost only Massachusetts and the District of Columbia in 1972.

Reagan lost only one state in 1984, and the next two years were "the least successful of Reagan's 16 years in office," including his years as governor of California, Mr. Cannon said. Even a narrow victory can create overconfidence. In 2004, George W. Bush won 50.7 percent of the vote, which was no landslide (even compared with his 48.3 percent share four years earlier). But he treated the victory as a huge mandate, and plunged ahead with a plan to privatize Social Security in 2005, as he had promised during his re-election campaign.

But the Social Security plan went nowhere. Republicans cringed, and Democrats eagerly united in opposition.

Second-term presidents are also lame ducks, parrying ambitious would-be successors in the opposition and in their own party. Dwight Eisenhower often complained of the recently enacted 22nd Amendment, limiting presidents to two terms. But earlier presidents faced the same problem, because tradition back to George Washington had established the same term limit, until Roosevelt ran for his third term.

But are second terms inevitably cursed?

Richard Norton Smith, a presidential scholar at George Mason University, argues for a more nuanced approach to measuring them.

Eisenhower, who easily won re-election, is his prime example. He lacked new ideas, and he lost key cabinet officers and his chief of staff, Sherman Adams. He was embarrassed when a U-2 spy plane was shot down over the Soviet Union in 1960 and Nikita Khrushchev scuttled a Paris summit meeting in response.

But Eisenhower sent troops to Little Rock in 1957 to keep Gov. Orval Faubus of Arkansas from thwarting court-ordered school desegregation. And his 1961 farewell address classically warned, "We must guard against the acquisition of unwarranted influence, whether sought or unsought, by the military industrial complex."

Most important, Eisenhower kept the peace with the Soviet Union, an accomplishment hardly predictable in the '50s.

For President Clinton, there was the first balanced budget in decades, achieved in 1997 because Republicans wanted an accomplishment that they, too, could claim. And Mr. Clinton gained international respect for forcing the Serbs to halt a genocidal campaign in Kosovo without putting NATO troops on the ground. But impeachment was a grave scar, not only for him, but for his accusers as well. Months of debate over the issue led to Democratic gains in the House in the midterm 1998 elections.

Roosevelt accomplished little domestically in his second term, beyond the appointments of Supreme Court justices who shaped the law for many years. But his oratory and cunning moved an isolationist nation and Congress to side with Britain and France against Germany. And he began rebuilding the nation's military as World War II loomed. He also made a brilliant personnel choice, bypassing senior generals to elevate Gen. George C. Marshall to the post of Army chief of staff.

President Bush failed to achieve many legislative goals—privatizing Social Security, liberalizing immigration and overhauling the tax code. But he did win a vast increase in spending on AIDS treatment and prevention in Africa and a modest stimulus measure in 2008. And his most substantial achievement was the Troubled Assets Relief Program, a $700 billion program to rescue banks caught in the subprime mortgage mess.

Nixon achieved little domestically in his foreshortened second term. But after the Paris Peace Accords were signed just after his second inauguration in

1973, American troops were withdrawn from Vietnam and prisoners of war were released. In the Middle East, Secretary of State Henry Kissinger's shuttle diplomacy that fall ended the Arab-Israeli war. Nixon also believed that the role of the United States in overthrowing President Salvador Allende of Chile was a signal success, though today it seems a grave mistake.

For Reagan, the troubles of his second term were offset by the 1986 tax law, which closed loopholes and used the savings to lower tax rates, and his arms control agreements with Mikhail S. Gorbachev of the Soviet Union.

Presidents cannot control everything in their second terms, and President Obama has a few obstacles that are special to him. The president and Congress must be willing to work together, which in a deeply partisan Washington may be difficult to accomplish in the next four years. And like other modern presidents, Mr. Obama must cope with a "snarky" news media, said Mr. Smith, the George Mason University scholar, which glare at a president, magnifying anything that looks like success, or, especially, failure.

Tim Cavanaugh

Beware Obama's Big Ideas

The way President Barack Obama's acolytes are calling for bold action in his second term, you'd think he had been some kind of prudent Calvin Coolidge in his first.

"A strategic second term would begin by identifying a list of necessary and achievable goals, and then pursuing them with the unyielding manipulative skill of a Lyndon Johnson," *Washington Post* columnist David Ignatius wrote after Obama's decisive victory over hapless challenger Mitt Romney in November. "Think big. Take risks. Get it done."

"Take this second chance to get it right on housing," wrote Tracy Van Slyke, director of something called the New Bottom Line, at *The Huffington Post*, "and use your mandate to help the millions of underwater homeowners across this country." *Atlantic* Associate Editor Matthew O'Brien didn't even wait for the election results to come in, calling on the president in October to unveil a bold second-term agenda that would embrace the "vision thing" by resurrecting his deep-sixed American Jobs Act.

Given that Obama won re-election largely by not talking about his record, it's probably not surprising that so many people don't seem to have noticed what happened from 2009 through 2012. To recap, Obama rammed through a massive overhaul of medical care in the Patient Protection and Affordable Care Act, a.k.a. ObamaCare. He piled another $830 billion or so onto the national debt with his American Recovery and Reinvestment Act, a.k.a. the stimulus. He also managed to push total debt over $16 trillion.

When the Affordable Care Act's most radical component, the requirement that every American be forced to purchase health insurance, came up for Supreme Court review, the president's bumbling attorneys lucked into a tortured decision in their favor, and the law was upheld by a 5-to-4 margin. Capitalizing on (though not actually solving) the financial crisis that helped him gain office, Obama in 2010 signed the Dodd-Frank Wall Street Reform and Consumer Protection Act, bringing a massive new cudgel to the financial industry (which had hardly been free of Washington oversight and protection prior to that) and creating a federal "consumer" agency whose scope is still not well understood.

Unfazed by a public rebuke in the 2010 midterm elections, Obama continued his mission through a daunting new strategy of regulatory rule making, executive orders, administration through "White House liaison officers," and recess appointments of congressionally unpopular nominees. (These last have been carried out even when Congress was not in recess.) Such tactics are necessary to patch a weakness Obama has discovered in American government: the foundational structure of checks and balances.

"When Congress refuses to act, and as a result, hurts our economy and puts our people at risk, then I have an obligation as president to do what I can without them," the president told a crowd in Shaker Heights, Ohio, in January 2011. "I've got an obligation to act on behalf of the American people. And I'm not going to stand by while a minority in the Senate puts party ideology ahead of the people that we were elected to serve. Not with so much at stake, not at this make-or-break moment for middle-class Americans. We're not going to let that happen."

Following that bold conviction, Obama launched a war in Libya without even the almost-constitutional fig leaf of a congressional authorization vote (thus making him even less deferential to Congress' war-making power than George W. Bush). This "kinetic action" seemed to be a rousing success until the U.S. ambassador was killed by terrorists in September—an episode the administration has worked tirelessly to obscure.

Obama has also claimed powers of life and death beyond Bush's wildest ambitions, granting to himself a new presidential authority to kill citizens and noncitizens alike, both on U.S. soil and abroad, while asserting that an Oval Office discussion with advisers qualifies as constitutional due process.

After all that, what would Obama fans consider an ambitious second-term agenda? I guess mandatory self-esteem boosts, universal health care for cats, and a global war on melancholy haven't been tried yet. But Obama's penchant for intervening in all aspects of American life (according to the U.S. Chamber of Commerce, he added 11,327 pages to the Code of Federal Regulations, a 7.4 percent increase, in his first three years) while overlooking constitutional niceties has produced a consistent pattern: As you get more regulation, you get less law.

For some of us, this is a problem. Law is big and clear. It applies equally to the great and small. You can usually be confident that a law has passed at least some level of civic scrutiny. Regulation, by contrast, is small and stifling. It places burdens primarily on individuals and small companies that don't have sufficient lawyerly infrastructure.

And there's no way to know which White House czar or career apparatchik composed any particular regulation. For example, who at Eric Holder's Department of Justice (DOJ) decided in 2011 that the Americans with Disabilities Act requires hotels, restaurants, and airlines to accommodate "pygmy ponies" as service animals. (And should we be glad the DOJ is mandating horse fairness instead of giving more guns to Mexican drug cartels?)

"The best is yet to come," Obama promised in his November victory speech. And the election result gave him some justification for that promise. He won a lopsided electoral victory and, rare in modern presidential races, a popular majority. This is what makes the second term such a matter of concern. Nearly 61 million voters have gotten to know Obama's mix of soaring rhetoric and bureaucratic reality, messianic claims and crushing mandates, cultish iconography and lawless actions, grand hopes and bland changes. And they decided they wanted more of it.

I don't expect that avoiding the "fiscal cliff" will be reward enough for those folks. Obama came into office with talk of reversing the tides, healing the earth, and "fundamentally transforming the United States of America." He has hinted at delivering big things in the security of a second term. If the first act was any indication, those things are going to suck.

Akhil Reed Amar

"Second Chances"

Second terms in the White House have, in many cases, ranged from the disappointing to the disastrous. Sick of the political infighting that intensified after his reelection, George Washington could hardly wait to retire to Mount Vernon. Ulysses S. Grant's second term was plagued by political scandal and economic panic. Woodrow Wilson left office a broken man, having suffered a massive stroke during his failed crusade to persuade America to join the League of Nations. Republican Dwight D. Eisenhower was routed in his last political battle, leaving Democrats in control of the presidency, the House, the Senate, and the Supreme Court for nearly the rest of his life. More recently, Richard Nixon resigned in disgrace; Ronald Reagan was tarred by the Iran-Contra scandal; Bill Clinton was impeached; and George W. Bush watched helplessly as his opponents surged into both houses of Congress and then the White House.

Hence the legendary "second-term curse." In the early days of the republic, second-termers were by tradition discouraged from seeking another term, and nowadays, presidents are legally barred from a third term, thanks to the Twenty-Second Amendment. Popular wisdom has it that second-termers are therefore lame ducks. Unable to run again, how can a term-limited president reward his allies or restrain his adversaries? If he is seen as a fading force, won't his allies hitch themselves to the next rising star? Won't his adversaries attack relentlessly?

Fortunately for Barack Obama, the situation is not that bleak. For one thing, the idea of a second-term curse fails to account for basic probability. Most presidents fail in one way or another, and many nose-dive so fast that they never get a second term. Perhaps the "curse" is actually an example of what statisticians call "regression to the mean": those presidents who beat the political odds in term one usually cannot maintain their lucky streak in term two. Nor does the curse account for several exceptional presidents whose authority *increased* following reelection. By looking at these two-term stars more closely, we can see how and why Obama might be more blessed than cursed.

From our nation's founding to the present, politics has followed a tidal pattern. Once a party devises a new and successful electoral formula—a workable coalition that can consistently outnumber the opposition—that party tends to win, and keep winning, until eventually, the tide changes and the other party takes the lead. So far, U.S. history has seen four such reversals, each of which coincided with the election, and reelection, of an exceptional president. Yes, each of the four figures who presided over these great shifts—Thomas Jefferson, Abraham Lincoln, Franklin Roosevelt, and Ronald Reagan—had his share of second-term tribulations and catastrophes. (Lincoln, of course, died weeks after delivering his epic second inaugural address, and only days after Lee's surrender.) But thanks to his own exceptional skills, as well as the fragility of the opposition party, each man forged a new electoral coalition that kept winning long after he left office.

The first turning of the political tide occurred shortly after George Washington's death. In 1800, Jefferson's triumph over John Adams marked the beginning of the end of the Federalist era. In 1804, Jefferson won a second term, and in 1808 he transferred power to his political lieutenant. James Madison. Jefferson and Madison's Democratic-Republican Party (later renamed the Democratic Party) remained America's dominant presidential party until the Civil War era, when the tide turned a second time. Lincoln, a Republican, won, won again, and (in the election following his assassination) was succeeded by a political heir, Ulysses Grant. Republicans dominated the presidency until the Great Depression—and FDR's election and reelections—marked a third tidal shift. The Democrats' resulting New Deal/Great Society coalition generally held until it was ripped apart by the Vietnam War and the migration of white southern Democrats to the GOP. Enter Ronald Reagan, whose two terms marked a fourth turning of the electoral tide.

We have been living in the Reagan era ever since. But now, inexorable forces—the changing voting habits of women and young adults, the rising political power of nonwhites and immigrants—mean that the Reagan electoral formula, with its reliance on southern whites, tax-averse businessmen, evangelicals, and Catholics, no longer yields a working majority. The tide may be turning back to the Democrats. Obama's reelection is particularly historic given modern Democratic presidents' track record of failing to win the popular vote. He is only the second Democratic president since the Civil War to win two popular majorities—the other was FDR (who, of course, won four). Since Lincoln, in fact, only four Democrats have won even one popular-vote majority—and that tally includes Jimmy Carter, with 50.1 percent of the vote. Bill Clinton never had a popular majority.

So what lessons might Obama borrow from his successful two-term predecessors to avoid being perceived as a lame duck? First, though he cannot succeed himself in 2016, he can designate a proxy to replace him—a loyal lieutenant willing to help his friends, smite his foes, and keep his secrets long after he leaves office. Reagan fared as well as he did in part because he had designated George H. W. Bush as his wingman, and in effect won a third term when Bush became "Bush 41." By contrast, Eisenhower kept his vice president, Richard Nixon, at a distance. (When asked during the 1960 general election whether his administration had adopted any major ideas of Nixon's, Ike replied, "If you give me a week. I might think of one.") The Lewinsky scandal drove a wedge between Clinton and his wingman, Al Gore. A successor—or the lack of one—can shape not just a president's performance, but also his legacy. When George W. Bush's time was up, his party tapped John McCain, a White House outsider whose relationship with the president was feisty and rivalrous.

Second, Obama should take advantage of his relative youth, which gives him a distinct edge over most of his predecessors: Until recently, most second-term presidents were well past their prime, both physically and mentally. At age 51, Obama can remain a potent political force even in retirement; he should exploit this fact to enhance his current clout. (Only Grant and Clinton were younger than Obama at the start of their second terms—and think of how Clinton has remained relevant in recent years.)

If he's to beat the second-term curse, Obama will also need to go bold and big. Just as FDR's New Deal programs and Reagan's tax cuts won over whole generations of voters, Obama must find ways to entrench his own legacy—and in the process, his new base. Immigration reform, for example, could draw the kind of young, highly skilled workers who might be able to pay for Social Security benefits for retiring Baby Boomers. Election reform might restore the luster of American democracy—while making it easier for Democratic voters to cast ballots.

One caveat: big changes like these can't succeed unless another big change comes early in term two—Senate filibuster reform. The signature accomplishment of Obama's first term, Obamacare, crowded out other reforms because Senate Democrats had to scrape together 60 votes to avoid a filibuster, rather than the simple majority the Constitution requires for passage of a law. If Senate reformers can tame the filibuster early in Obama's second term—and it appears that Democratic leaders are indeed serious about changing the Senate's rules this January, using a party-line vote to limit the minority party's power to slow or stop legislation—then the political picture will change dramatically.

Without filibuster reform, the 45 Republicans in the Senate can quietly block up-or-down votes, with the result being that individual senators from moderate states don't have to visibly go on record voting against popular Obama agenda items. But if the filibuster were blunted, and only 51 senators' votes were needed, many key bills would pass with or without the GOP, and some savvy Republicans would choose to swim with the larger electoral tide. Americans would begin to see Republicans and Democrats working together again in the Senate— and this could change dynamics in the House.

And if not, there's always 2014. When it comes to midterm elections, lameness, handled deftly, can be a source of strength. In 2008, Obama ran as a uniter; had he campaigned aggressively against House Republicans in either 2010 or 2012, he might have tarnished his image, and imperiled his own reelection prospects. But this time around, there's nothing to stop him from going after those who obstruct his agenda. Beware the lame duck: he can bite hard.

By then, in any case, most eyes will be turning to the 2016 campaign trail. Which brings us back to our first lesson—possibly the most important one: each previous tide-turning president was succeeded in the next presidential election by a handpicked ally. Like Reagan, Obama has a possible wingman in his vice president. Joe Biden could dutifully offer to replace him, thus safeguarding Obama's power throughout his second term and beyond. But Obama has at least one other outstanding option: just as Jefferson handed presidential power to his talented secretary of state, James Madison, Obama could do the same with Hillary Clinton.

Ultimately, nothing succeeds like succession.

DISCUSSION QUESTIONS

1. Is the "second term" curse real, or just (as Amar argues) a matter of probability? Do we remember failures more easily than we recall successes? Do you agree with the descriptions of second term failures and successes?

2. Is the political advice in these readings particular to Obama or is it broadly true for all presidents? Do you think Obama's second term will be more or less successful than his first? Why?

3. Was the Twenty-Second Amendment (which imposes a two-term limit) a mistake? How would presidents behave differently if they were eligible for additional terms?

7

Bureaucracy: Privatization of Government Activity

Public organizations (meaning governments) have different incentives and performance measures than private organizations (meaning, in this context, private sector businesses). Another way to say this is that governments tend to be much less efficient than businesses, but this does not mean that government can be run like a business.

Nevertheless, governments today at all levels face pressure to transfer functions to the private sector, either by spinning off government functions entirely (privatization) or by contracting with private firms to provide services once provided by government employees (outsourcing). Turning over the air traffic control system or the postal service to private companies—leaving them to provide services and collect fees in a profitmaking venture—would be examples of privatization. In 2006, the state of Indiana, sold the rights to the state's major highway to a private company. For $3.8 billion, the company leased the highway for 75 years, and the rights to all tolls collected over that period. In return, the company took responsibility for maintaining the road.

Using contractors to deliver services once provided by government—food service at national museums or military bases; private security forces instead of military personnel in Iraq—are examples of outsourcing.

Both outsourcing and privatization have advantages, at least as far as some see it: smaller government or more efficient government. Yet they also have some disadvantages compared to using government agencies to provide services. Compared to private firms, governments are more sensitive to problems of equity and accountability. For example, one reason the Postal Service is inefficient is that *legislators* created laws that require it to serve remote areas of the country and maintain post offices in small towns. A private company (say, something like FedEx or UPS) would most likely not find it profitable to do the same thing, and would either not provide service or charge more for it. We would purchase efficiency at the cost of equity (and your views of whether that trade-off is worth making probably depends heavily on whether you are a beneficiary of those inefficient services).

But, as the controversy over earmarks demonstrated, disputes over whether the government does something well or not is often a policy dispute about whether the government should be doing something at all. The debate here involves some of the same issues. "Privatization" was written by authors at the Cato Institute, a libertarian think tank. Cato supports a significantly smaller government, and here the authors propose privatizing a wide range of government functions: the post office, air traffic control, airports, public lands, etc. They argue that these are not core government functions and could be provided more efficiently by private companies. Shedding these functions would also make financial sense, since private companies would be willing to pay enormous sums of money for them (think of the billions of dollars the federal government earns by auctioning off portions of the electromagnetic spectrum for telecom services).

Not so fast, argues Wedel, who is critical of contracting out government functions. Wedel argues that using contractors to provide crucial government functions—intelligence, security, information technology—has a number of negative consequences, including reduced accountability, loss of vital institutional expertise, and poor supervision. The result is that the federal government has abdicated responsibility for important functions, and has substituted profit-seeking for the more difficult (but still vital) task of allocating resources in a way that meets public demands.

Janine R. Wedel

Federalist No. 70: Where Does the Public Service Begin and End?

Without revolution, public debate, or even much public awareness, a giant work-force has invaded Washington, D.C.—one that can undermine the public and national interest from the inside. This workforce consists of government contrac-tors, specifically those who perform "inherently governmental" functions that the government deems so integral to its work that only federal employees should carry them out. Today, many federal government functions are conducted, and many public priorities and decisions are driven, by private companies and players instead of government agencies and officials who are duty-bound to answer to citizens and sworn to uphold the national interest.

It is hard to imagine that the founding fathers would have embraced this state of affairs. Acting as a nation—defending its security and providing for the safety of its citizens—is a bedrock concept in some of the *Federalist Papers*. For instance, John Jay writes in *Federalist* No. 2,

> As a nation we have made peace and war; as a nation we have vanquished our common enemies; as a nation we have formed alliances, and made trea-ties, and entered into various compacts and conventions with foreign states.
>
> A strong sense of the value and blessings of union induced the people, at a very early period, to institute a federal government to preserve and perpetu-ate it.

James Madison lays out a forceful case for the separation and distribution of government powers. He cautions against "a tyrannical concentration of all the powers of government in the same hands" and outlines the importance of maintaining boundaries among the divisions of government (see *Federalist* No. 47, 48, 51). I argue that the considerable contracting out of government func-tions is counter to the vision espoused by these statesmen. Such contracting out potentially erodes the government's ability to operate in the public and national interest. It also creates the conditions for the intertwining of state and private power and the concentration of power in just a few hands—about which Madi-son warned.

The Indispensable Hand

Once, government contractors primarily sold military parts, prepared food, or printed government reports. Today, contractors routinely perform "inherently governmental" functions—activities that involve "the exercise of sovereign government authority or the establishment of procedures and processes related to the oversight of monetary transactions or entitlements." The 20 "inherently governmental" functions on the books include "command of military forces, especially the leadership of military personnel who are members of the combat, combat support, or combat service support role"; "the conduct of foreign relations and the determination of foreign policy"; "the determination of agency policy, such as determining the content and application of regulations"; "the determination of Federal program priorities or budget requests"; "the direction and control of Federal employees"; "the direction and control of intelligence and counter-intelligence operations; the selection or nonselection of individuals for Federal Government employment, including the interviewing of individuals for employment"; and "the approval of position descriptions and performance standards for Federal employees."

Government contractors are involved in many, if not all, of these arenas of government work. Consider, for instance, that contractors perform the following tasks:

• Run intelligence operations: Contractors from private security companies have been hired to help track and kill suspected militants in Afghanistan and Pakistan. At the National Security Agency (NSA), the number of contractor facilities approved for classified work jumped from 41 in 2002 to 1,265 in 2006. A full 95 percent of the workers at the very secret National Reconnaissance Office (one of the 16 intelligence agencies), which runs U.S. spy satellites and analyzes the information that they produce, are full-time contractors. In more than half of the 117 contracts let by three big agencies of the U.S. Department of Homeland Security (DHS)—the Coast Guard, Transportation Security Administration, and Office of Procurement Operations— the Government Accountability Office (GAO) found that contractors did inherently governmental work. One company, for instance, was awarded $42.4 million to develop budget and policies for the DHS, as well as to support its information analysis, procurement operations, and infrastructure protection.

- Manage—and more—federal taxpayer monies doled out under the stimulus plans and bailouts: The government enlisted money manager BlackRock to help advise it and manage the unsuccessful attempt to rescue Bear Stearns, as well as to save AIG and Citigroup. BlackRock also won a bid to help the Federal Reserve evaluate hard-to-price assets of Freddie Mac and Fannie Mae. * * * With regard to the $700 billion bailout in the fall of 2008, known as the Troubled Asset Relief Program, the U.S. Treasury Department hired several contractors to set up a process to disburse the funds.

- Control crucial databases: In a mega-contract awarded by the DHS in 2004, Accenture LLP was granted up to $10 billion to supervise and enlarge a mammoth U.S. government project to track citizens of foreign countries as they enter and exit the United States. As the undersecretary for border and transportation security at the DHS at the time remarked, "I don't think you could overstate the impact of this responsibility in terms of the security of our nation."

- Choose other contractors: The Pentagon has employed contractors to counsel it on selecting other contractors. The General Services Administration enlisted CACI, a company based in Arlington, Virginia—some of whose employees were among those allegedly involved in the Abu Ghraib prisoner abuse scandal in Iraq, according to U.S. Department of the Army—to help the government suspend and debar other contractors. . . . (CACI itself later became the subject of possible suspension or debarment from federal contracts.)

- Oversee other contractors: The DHS is among the federal agencies that have hired contractors to select and supervise other contractors. Some of these contractors set policy and business goals and plan reorganizations. And, in the National Clandestine Service, an integral part of the Central Intelligence Agency (CIA), contractors are sometimes in charge of other contractors.

- Execute military and occupying operations: The Department of Defense is ever more dependent on contractors to supply a host of "mission-critical services," including "information technology systems, interpreters, intelligence analysts, as well as weapons system maintenance and base operation support." U.S. efforts in Afghanistan and Iraq illustrate this reliance. As of September 2009, U.S.-paid contractors far outnumbered U.S. military personnel in Afghanistan, composing nearly two-thirds of the combined contractor and military personnel workforce (approximately 104,000 Defense Department contractors compared with 64,000 uniformed personnel). In Iraq, contractors made up nearly half of the combined contractor and military personnel workforce (roughly 114,000 Defense Department contractors compared with 130,000 uniformed personnel). These proportions are in sharp contrast to the 1991 Persian Gulf War: The 540,000 military personnel deployed in that effort greatly outnumbered the 9,200 contractors on the scene.

• Draft official documents: Contractors have prepared congressional testimony for the secretary of energy. Websites of contractors working for the Department of Defense also have posted announcements of job openings for analysts to perform functions such as preparing the defense budget. One contractor boasted of having written the U.S. Army's Field Manual on "Contractors on the Battlefield."

In short, the outsourcing of many inherently governmental functions is now routine. The government is utterly dependent on private contractors to carry out many such functions. As the Acquisition Advisory Panel, a government-mandated, typically contractor-friendly task force made up of representatives from industry, government, and academe, acknowledged in a 2007 report that "[m]any federal agencies rely extensively on contractors in the performance of their basic missions. In some cases, contractors are solely or predominantly responsible for the performance of mission-critical functions that were traditionally performed by civil servants." This trend, the report concluded, "poses a threat to the government's long-term ability to perform its mission" and could "undermine the integrity of the government's decision making."

Contractor officials and employees are interdependent with government, involved in all aspects of governing and negotiating "over policy making, implementation, and enforcement," as one legal scholar has noted. Contractor and government employees work side by side in what has come to be called the "blended" or "embedded" workforce, often sitting next to each other in cubicles or sharing an office and doing the same or similar work (but typically with markedly different pay). When the GAO looked into the setup of Defense Department offices, its investigation established that, in some, the percentage of contractors was in the 80s.

Yet contractors' imperatives are not necessarily the same as the government's imperatives. Contractor companies are responsible for making a profit for their shareholders; government is supposedly answerable to the public in a democracy.

Amid this environment, which is complicated by mixed motives, contractors are positioned to influence policy to their liking on even the most sensitive, mission-critical government functions, such as fighting wars, guarding against terrorism, and shaping economic policy. Government investigators looking into intelligence, defense, homeland security, energy, and other arenas have raised questions about who drives policy—government or contractors—and whether government has the information, expertise, institutional memory, and personnel to manage contractors—or is it the other way around? And in three government agencies that the GAO investigated, including the DOD and DHS, the GAO found that "sensitive information is not fully safeguarded and thus may remain at risk of unauthorized disclosure or misuse." The result of all of this is that the nation's safety, security, and sovereignty may be jeopardized, along with the very core of democratic society—citizens' ability to hold their government accountable and have a say in public decisions. This seems far afield from the concept of the nation expressed by, say, John Jay.

Enabling Big Government

How did this state of affairs come to be?

Ironically, the perennial American predilection to rail against "big government" is partly to blame for the creation of still bigger government—the "shadow government" of companies, consulting firms, nonprofits, think tanks, and other nongovernmental entities that contract with the government to do so much of its work. This is government for sure, but often of a less visible and accountable kind.

The necessity of making government *look* small—or at least contained—has fueled the rise of this shadow government. In an ostensible effort to limit government, caps have been put on how many civil servants government can hire. But citizens still expect government to supply all manner of services—from Medicare and Social Security to interstate highways to national defense. To avoid this conundrum, both Democratic and Republican administrations over the years have been busily enlisting more and more contractors (who, in turn, often hire subcontractors) to do the work of government. Because they are not counted as part of the federal workforce, it can appear as if the size of government is being kept in check. Like the Potemkin village of Russia, constructed to make the ruler or the foreigner think that things are rosy, the public is led to believe they have something they do not.

* * *

Where federal employees once executed most government work, today, upwards of three-quarters of the work of federal government, measured in terms of jobs, is contracted out. Many of the most dramatic alterations have occurred since the end of the Cold War. Contracting out accelerated and assumed new incarnations during and after the Bill Clinton administration. The advent of ever more complex technologies, which gave birth to information technologies on which society now relies and which the U.S. government largely outsources, tipped the balance even further. The shadow government, which devises and implements so much policy and forms the core of governance, is the elephant in the room.

The shadow government encompasses all of the entities that swell the ranks of contractors and entire bastions of outsourcing—neighborhoods whose high-rise office buildings house an army of contractors and "Beltway Bandits." Largely out of sight except to Washington-area dwellers, contractors and the companies they work for do not appear in government phone books. They are less likely to be dragged before congressional committees for hostile questioning. They function with less visibility and scrutiny on a regular basis than government employees would face. Most important, they are not counted as government employees, and so the fiction of limited government can be upheld, while the reality is an expanding sprawl of entities that are the government in practice.

The Elephant in the Room

While it may be the elephant in the room, we know little about the nature of the beast. A key barometer of the growth of the shadow government, driven in part by an increase in demand for military, nation-building, and homeland security services after 9/11, is the number of government employees versus contractors. Government scholar Paul C. Light has compiled the most reliable figures on contractors. The number of contract workers—compared with civil servants, uniformed military personnel, and postal service employees—increased steadily over the last two decades. In 1990, roughly three out of every five employees in the total federal labor force worked indirectly for government—in jobs created by contracts and grants, as opposed to jobs performed by civil servants, uniformed military personnel, and postal service workers. By 2002, two out of every three employees in the federal labor force worked indirectly for government, and, by 2008, the number was three out of four.

In the DHS—the mega-bureaucracy established in 2003 through the merger of 180,000 employees and 22 agencies, the creation of which entailed the largest reorganization of the federal government in more than half a century—contractors are more numerous than federal employees. The DHS estimates that it employs 188,000 workers, compared with 200,000 contractors.

In some arenas of government, contractors virtually *are* the government. The DHS, which includes the Customs Service, Coast Guard, and Transportation Security Administration, has relied substantially on contractors to fill new security needs and shore up gaps. In nine cases examined by the GAO, "decisions to contract for . . . services were largely driven by the need for staff and expertise to get DHS programs and operations up and running quickly".

* * *

Meanwhile, about 70 percent of the budget of the U.S. intelligence community is devoted to contracts, according to the Office of the Director of National Intelligence, which was created in 2005 and supervises 16 federal agencies. Contract employees make up an estimated one-quarter of the country's core intelligence workforce, according to the same office. The director both heads the U.S. intelligence community and serves as the main advisor to the president on national security matters.

Contractors are plentiful in other arenas of government that directly affect national and homeland security, not only the departments of defense and homeland security. For instance, nearly 90 percent of the budgets of the Department of Energy and NASA go to contracts.

Information technology (IT), which touches practically every area of government operations, is largely contracted out. Upwards of three-quarters of governmental IT is estimated to have been outsourced even before the major Iraq War-related push to contract out. For companies in search of federal business, IT is the "the new frontier," according to Thomas Burlin, who is in charge of IBM Business Consulting Services' federal practice. With ever more complex technologies always on the horizon, the outsourcing of IT only stands to grow. Although contracting out computer network services may be unproblematic or even desirable, many IT functions cannot be separated from vital operations such as logistics that are integral to an agency's mission. * * *

Contractors are so integrated into the federal workforce that proponents of insourcing acknowledge that they face an uphill battle. Yet the proliferation of contracting widens the de facto base of government in which new forms of unaccountable governance can flourish. It makes government more vulnerable to operations that fall short of the public and national interest.

Swiss-Cheese Government

In theory, contracts and contractors are overseen by government employees who would guard against abuse. But that has become less and less true as the capacity of government oversight has diminished—a lessening that seems to flow directly from the need to maintain the facade of small government. A look at trend lines is illuminating. The number of civil servants who potentially could oversee contractors fell during the Clinton administration and continued to drop during the George W. Bush administration. The contracting business boomed under Bush, while the acquisition workforce—government workers charged with the conceptualization, design, awarding, use, or quality control of contracts and contractors—remained virtually constant. * * *

The result is that government sometimes lacks the information it needs to monitor the entities that work for it. A top GAO official reported that in many cases, government decision makers scarcely supervise the companies on their payrolls. As a result, she observed, they are unable to answer simple questions about what the firms are doing, whether they have performed well or not, and whether their performance has been cost-effective.

* * *

A paucity of oversight is one factor that has led the GAO to identify large procurement operations as "high risk" because of "their greater susceptibility to fraud, waste, abuse, and mismanagement." The list of high-risk areas has, since 1990 or 1992 (depending on the specific area), included the large procurement operations of the Departments of Defense and Energy, as well as NASA. The DHS has been on the high-risk list since its creation in 2003, and it has been faulted for a lack of oversight in procurement. As comptroller general of the United States, David M. Walker (2003) said that he is "not confident that [high-risk] agencies have the ability to effectively manage cost, quality, and performance in contracts." He added that the current challenges to contract oversight are "unprecedented."

* * *

When the number of civil servants available to supervise government contracts and contractors proportionately falls, thus decreasing the government's oversight capacity, and when crucial governmental functions are outsourced, government begins to resemble Swiss cheese—full of holes. Contractors are plugging these holes. As a consequence, contractors have become the home for much information, legitimacy, expertise, institutional memory, and leadership that once resided in government.

* * *

Concentrating Powers

Swiss-cheese government lends itself to the kind of concentration of powers that Madison warned about. Over the past decade and a half, new institutional forms of governing have gathered force as contractors perform inherently governmental functions beyond the capacity of government to manage them; as government and contractor officials interact (or do not) in the course of projects; as chains of command among contractors and the agencies they supposedly work for have become ever more convoluted; and as contractors standing in for government are not subject to the same rules that apply to government officials. The result is that new forms of governing join the state and the private, often most visibly in intelligence, defense, and homeland security enterprises, where so much has taken place since 9/11.

Incentive structures that encourage government executives (notably intelligence and military professionals) to move to the private sector, as well as new contracting practices and a limited number of government contracting firms, are among the factors that facilitate the intertwining of state and private power. With regard to the former, not only are salaries and perks for comparable jobs typically greater in the private sector, but often, so is prestige. Many government executives, retirees, and other employees follow the money by moving to the private sector. But the landing spots that supply the big bucks—and with them, influence and stature—are often those held by former government executives. Although there are rules to address the revolving door syndrome, companies with significant government contracts often are headed by former senior officials of intelligence- and defense-related government agencies. * * *

When government contractors hire former directors of intelligence- and defense-related government agencies, they are banking on "coincidences" of interest between their hires and their hires' former (government) employers. (A coincidence of interest occurs when a player crafts an array of overlapping roles across organizations to serve his own agenda—or that of his network—above that of those of the organizations for which he works.) The result of such coincidences in the intelligence arena is that "the Intelligence Community and the contractors are so tightly intertwined at the leadership level that their interests, practically speaking, are identical," as one intelligence expert said.

Also potentially facilitating the fusion of state and private power are changes in contracting practices and the dearth of competition among and consolidation of government contracting firms, which has led to government dependence on a limited number of firms. The Clinton administration transformed contracting rules with regard to oversight, competition, and transparency under the rubric of "reinventing government." As a result, small contracts often have been replaced by bigger, and frequently open-ended, multiyear, multimillion- and even billion-dollar and potentially much more lucrative contracts with a "limited pool of contractors," as the Acquisition Advisory Panel put it. Today, most federal procurement contracts are conferred either without competition or to a limited set of contractors. A Barack Obama White House memo noted the "significant increase in the dollars awarded without full and open competition" during the period 2001–2008. Moreover, industry consolidation (defense is a case in point) has produced fewer and larger firms. * * *

The routine outsourcing of government functions, the structures of incentives, and new contracting rules and practices encourage new forms of governing in which state and private power are joined. These forms seem very far afield indeed from Madison's vision of a nation in which government powers cannot be concentrated.

Reclaiming the Soul of Government

Some authorities have sounded alarm bells about the present state of affairs. In 2007, David M. Walker, the comptroller general of the United States and long-time head of the GAO, called for "a fundamental reexamination of when and under what circumstances we should use contractors versus civil servants or military personnel," And President Obama acknowledged the problem. Early in his term, Obama announced plans to "insource" certain jobs—transferring work back to the government—and expressed concern about the outsourcing of inherently governmental functions. While the administration has proposed some insourcing and efforts to push back or review the ever upward spiral of outsourcing, the current state of affairs cannot simply be rolled back.

It is not just that government is utterly dependent on private companies to do much of its work. The United States faces an entrenched problem that cannot be fixed simply by insourcing jobs or by hiring more government employees to oversee contractors, as some observers have suggested. A top-to-bottom rethinking of how government makes use of contractors is necessary. One particularly important issue that deserves attention is how to rebuild capacity that has been lost with the privatization of information, expertise, and institutional memory. Another set of challenges lies in reforming the contract laws and regulations that have been changed over the past decade and a half—and that have made the contracting system less transparent and accountable and more vulnerable to the influence of private and corporate agendas.

The changes that have taken place are so systemic and sweeping that a new system, in effect, is now in place. It is the ground on which any future changes will occur. A fundamental redesign of the system is necessary. In that redesign, we would do well to pay attention to the vision of the founding fathers regarding the security of the nation and safety of its citizens, as well as the dangers inherent in the consolidation of powers.

But reclaiming government is not merely a design challenge. Government must take its soul back. While it may be strange to mention "soul" and government in the same breath, linking the quintessentially personal with the quintessentially bureaucratic and impersonal, a government procurement lawyer described the current state of affairs as the "ebbing away of the soul of government." When an institution is drained of expertise, information, and institutional memory, it not only loses its edge, but also its essence.

* * *

Cato Handbook for Policymakers

Privatization

In recent decides, governments on every continent have sold state-owned assets, such as airports, railroads, and energy utilities. The privatization revolution has overthrown the belief widely held in the 20th century that governments should own the most important industries in the economy. Privatization has generally led to reduced costs, higher-quality services, and increased innovation in formerly moribund government industries.

The presumption that government should own industry was challenged in the 1980s by British Prime Minister Margaret Thatcher and by President

Ronald Reagan, who established a Commission on Privatization. But while Thatcher made enormous reforms in Britain, only a few major federal assets have been privatized in this country. Conrail, a freight railroad, was privatized in 1987 for $1.7 billion. The Alaska Power Administration was privatized in 1996. The federal helium reserve was privatized in 1996 for $1.8 billion. The Elk Hills Petroleum Reserve was sold in 1997 for $3.7 billion. The U.S. Enrichment Corporation, which provides enriched uranium to the nuclear industry, was privatized in 1998 for $3.1 billion.

There remain many federal assets that should be privatized, including businesses such as Amtrak and infrastructure such as the air traffic control system. The government also holds billions of dollars of real estate that should be sold off. The benefits to the federal budget of privatization would be modest, but the benefits to the economy would be large as newly private businesses would improve their performance and innovate.

The Office of Management and Budget has calculated that about half of all federal employees perform tasks that are not "inherently governmental." The Bush administration attempted to contract some of those activities to outside vendors, but such "competitive sourcing" is not privatization. Privatization makes an activity entirely private, with the effect of getting spending completely off the government's books, allowing for greater innovation, and preventing corruption, which is a serious pitfall of government contracting.

Privatization of federal assets makes sense for many reasons. First, sales of federal assets would cut the budget deficit. Second, privatization would reduce the responsibilities of the government so that policymakers could better focus on their core responsibilities, such as national security. Third, there is vast foreign privatization experience that could be drawn on in pursuing U.S. reforms. Fourth, privatization would spur economic growth by opening new markets to entrepreneurs. For example, repeal of the postal monopoly could bring major innovation to the mail industry, just as the 1980s' breakup of AT&T brought innovation to the telecommunications industry.

Some policymakers think that certain activities, such as air traffic control, are "too important" to leave to the private sector. But the reality is just the opposite. The government has shown itself to be a failure at providing efficiency and high quality in services such as air traffic control. Such industries are too important to miss out on the innovations that private entrepreneurs could bring to them.

Stand-Alone Businesses

The federal government operates numerous business enterprises that should be converted into publicly traded corporations, including the U.S. Postal Service, Amtrak, and a number of electric utilities.

- **Postal services.** The mammoth 685,000-person U.S. Postal Service is facing declining mail volume and rising costs. The way ahead is to privatize the USPS and repeal the company's legal monopoly over first-class mail. Reforms in other countries show that there is no good reason for the current mail monopoly. Since 1998, New Zealand's postal market has been open to private competition, with the result that postage rates have fallen and labor productivity at New Zealand Post has risen. Germany's Deutsche Post was partly privatized in 2000, and the company has improved productivity and expanded into new businesses. Postal services have also been privatized or opened to competition in Belgium, Britain, Denmark, Finland, the Netherlands, and Sweden. Japan is moving ahead with postal service privatization, and the European Union is planning to open postal services to competition in all its 27 member nations.
- **Passenger rail.** Subsidies to Amtrak were supposed to be temporary after it was created in 1970. That has not occurred, and Amtrak has provided second-rate rail service for more than 30 years while consuming more than $30 billion in federal subsidies. It has a poor on-time record, and its infrastructure is in bad shape. Reforms elsewhere show that private passenger rail can work. Full or partial rail privatization has occurred in Argentina, Australia, Britain, Germany, Japan, New Zealand, and other countries. Privatization would allow Amtrak greater flexibility in its finances, its capital budget, and the operation of its services—free from costly meddling by Congress.

* * *

Infrastructure

Before the 20th century, transportation infrastructure was often financed and built by the private sector. For example, there were more than 2,000 companies that built private toll roads in America in the 18th and 19th centuries. Most of those roads were put out of business by the spread of the railroads. Then, during the 20th century, roads and other infrastructure came to be thought of as government activities. By the 1980s, that started to change, and governments around the world began selling off airports, highways, bridges, and other facilities.

Any service that can be supported by consumer fees can be privatized. A big advantage of privatized airports, air traffic control, highways, and other activities is that private companies can freely tap debt and equity markets for capital expansion to meet rising demand. By contrast, modernization of government infrastructure is subject to the politics and uncertainties of government budgeting processes. As a consequence, government infrastructure is often old, congested, and poorly maintained.

- **Air traffic control.** The Federal Aviation Administration has been mismanaged for decades and provides Americans with second-rate air traffic control. The FAA has struggled to expand capacity and modernize its technology, and its upgrade efforts have often fallen behind schedule and gone over budget. For example, the Government Accountability Office found one FAA technology upgrade project that was started in 1983 and was to be completed by 1996 for $2.5 billion, but the project was years late and ended up costing $7.6 billion. The GAO has had the FAA on its watch list of wasteful "high-risk" agencies for years. Air traffic control (ATC) is far too important for such government mismanagement and should be privatized.

  The good news is that a number of countries have privatized their ATC and provide good models for U.S. reforms. Canada privatized its ATC system in 1996. It set up a private, nonprofit ATC corporation, Nav Canada, which is self-supporting from charges on aviation users. The Canadian system has received high marks for sound finances, solid management, and investment in new technologies.

- **Highways.** A number of states are moving ahead with privately financed and operated highways. The Dulles Greenway in Northern Virginia is a 14-mile private highway opened in 1995 that was financed by private bond and equity issues. In the same region, Fluor-Transurban is building and mainly funding high-occupancy toll lanes on a 14-mile stretch of the Capital Beltway. Drivers will pay to use the lanes with electronic tolling, which will recoup the company's roughly $1 billion investment. Fluor-Transurban is also financing and building toll lanes running south from Washington along Interstate 95. Similar private highway projects have been completed, or are being pursued, in California, Maryland, Minnesota, North Carolina, South Carolina, and Texas. Private-sector highway funding and operation can help pave the way toward reducing the nation's traffic congestion.

- **Airports.** Nearly all major U.S. airports are owned by state and local governments, with the federal government subsidizing airport renovation and expansion. By contrast, airports have been fully or partly privatized in many foreign cities, including Athens, Auckland, Brussels, Copenhagen, Frankfurt, London, Melbourne, Naples, Rome, Sydney, and Vienna. Britain led the way with the 1987 privatization of British Airports Authority, which owns Heathrow and other airports. To proceed with reforms in the United States, Congress should take the lead because numerous federal roadblocks make cities hesitant to privatize. For example, government-owned airports can issue tax-exempt debt, which gives them a financial advantage over potential private airports.

* * *

- **Army Corps of Engineers.** The Corps of Engineers is a federal agency that builds and maintains infrastructure for ports and waterways. Most of the agency's $5 billion annual budget goes toward dredging harbors and investing in locks and channels on rivers, such as the Mississippi. In addition, the corps is the largest owner of hydroelectric power plants in the country, manages 4,300 recreational areas, funds beach replenishment, and upgrades local water and sewer systems.

  Congress has used the corps as a pork barrel spending machine for decades. Funds are earmarked for low-value projects in the districts of important members of Congress, while higher-value projects go unfunded. Further, the corps has a history of scandals, including the levee failures in New Orleans and bogus economic studies to justify expensive projects.

  To solve these problems, the civilian activities of the corps should be transferred to state, local, or private ownership. A rough framework for reform would be to privatize port dredging, hydroelectric dams, beach replenishment, and other activities that could be supported by user fees and charges. Levees, municipal water and sewer projects, recreational areas, locks, and other waterway infrastructure could be transferred to state governments.

Federal Assets

At the end of fiscal year 2007, the federal government held $1.2 trillion in buildings and equipment, $277 billion in inventory, $919 billion in land, and $392 billion in mineral rights. The federal government owns about one-fourth of the land in the United States.

Many government assets are neglected and abused, and would likely be better cared for in the private sector. It is common to see government property in poor shape, with public housing being perhaps the most infamous government eyesore. The GAO has found that "many assets are in an alarming state of deterioration" and the watchdog agency has put federal property holdings on its list of activities at high risk for waste.

The GAO also notes that the federal government has "many assets it does not need," including billions of dollars worth of excess and vacant buildings. The federal government spends billions of dollars each year maintaining excess facilities of the Departments of Defense, Energy, and Veterans Affairs.

The solution is to sell federal assets that are excess to public needs and to better manage the smaller set of remaining holdings. For example, there are substantial maintenance backlogs on facilities of the Forest Service, Park Service, and Fish and Wildlife Service. The solution is not a larger maintenance budget, but trimming asset holdings to fit limited taxpayer resources. Another part of the solution is to scrap the Davis-Bacon rules, which require that artificially high wages be paid on federal contracts, including maintenance contracts.

Federal asset sales would help reduce the federal deficit and create budget room for improved maintenance of remaining assets. Perhaps more important, economic efficiency and growth would increase as underused assets were put into more productive private hands.

DISCUSSION QUESTIONS

1. What is an "inherently governmental function?" The current definition in federal law is "a function so intimately related to the public interest as to require performance by Federal Government employees." But this actually provides very little useful guidance, since it is a tautology: work that must be performed by federal government employees is defined as work so important that it must be performed by federal employees. Is there an alternative definition that is both meaningful and precise? What might that be?

2. When the government outsources, is it possible to specify contractually the correct accountability and equity incentives that would apply if the functions were performed by government agencies? Can we even identify precisely what those incentives are for *government* employees?

8

The Judiciary: Interpreting the Constitution— Originalism or Living Constitution?

Debates over the federal judiciary's role in the political process often focus on the question of how judges should interpret the Constitution. Should judges apply the document's original meaning as stated by the Framers, or should they use a framework that incorporates shifting interpretations across time? This debate intensified during Earl Warren's tenure as Chief Justice (1953–69) because of Court decisions that expanded the scope of civil liberties and criminal rights far beyond what "originalists" thought the Constitution's language authorized. The debate continues in the current, more conservative Court. The two readings in this section offer contrasting viewpoints from two sitting Supreme Court justices.

Antonin Scalia, the intellectual force behind the conservative wing of the Court, argues that justices must be bound by the original meaning of the document, because that is the only neutral principle that allows the judiciary to function as a legal body instead of a political one. The alternative is to embrace an evolving or "Living Constitution," which Scalia criticizes as allowing judges to decide cases on the basis of what seems right at the moment. He says that this "evolutionary" approach does not have any overall guiding principle and therefore "is simply not a practicable constitutional philosophy." He provides several examples of how the Living Constitution approach had produced decisions that stray from the meaning of the Constitution in the areas of abortion rights, gay rights, the right to counsel, and the right to confront one's accuser. This last example is especially provocative, given that it concerned the right of an accused child molester to confront the child who accused him of the crime. Scalia argues that there is no coherent alternative to originalism and forcefully concludes, "The worst thing about the Living Constitution is that it will destroy the Constitution."

Stephen Breyer argues for the Living Constitution approach, and places it within a broader constitutional and theoretical framework. He argues for a "consequentialist" approach that is rooted in basic constitutional purposes, the most important of which is "active liberty," which he defines as "an active and constant participation in collective power." Breyer applies this framework to a range of difficult constitutional issues, including freedom of speech in the context of campaign finance and privacy rights in the context of rapidly evolving technology. He argues that the plain language of the Constitution does not provide enough guidance to answer these difficult questions. He turns the tables on Scalia, arguing that it is the literalist or originalist position that will, ironically, lead justices to rely too heavily on their own personal views, whereas his consequentialist position is actually the view that is more likely to produce judicial restraint. Breyer goes on to criticize the originalist position as fraught with inconsistencies. It is inherently subjective, despite its attempt to emphasize the "objective" words of the Constitution. By relying on the consequentialist perspective, which emphasizes democratic participation and active liberty, justices are more likely to reach limited conclusions that apply to the facts at hand, while maximizing the positive implications for democracy.

Linda Greenhouse, an observer of the Supreme Court, summarized the debate between Scalia and Breyer in these terms: "It is a debate over text versus context. For Justice Scalia, who focuses on text, language is supreme, and the court's job is to derive and apply rules from the words chosen by the Constitution's framers or a statute's drafters. For Justice Breyer, who looks to context, language is only a starting point to an inquiry in which a law's purpose and a decision's likely consequences are the more important elements."

Antonin Scalia

Constitutional Interpretation the Old-Fashioned Way

It's a pizzazzy topic: Constitutional Interpretation. It is, however, an important one. I was vividly reminded how important it was last week when the Court came out with a controversial decision in the *Roper* case. And I watched one television commentary on the case in which the host had one person defending the opinion on the ground that people should not be subjected to capital punishment for crimes they commit when they are younger than eighteen, and the other person attacked the opinion on the ground that a jury should be able to decide that a person, despite the fact he was under eighteen, given the crime, given the person involved, should be subjected to capital punishment. And it struck me how irrelevant it was, how much the point had been missed. The question wasn't whether the call was right or wrong. The important question was who should make the call. And that is essentially what I am addressing today.

I am one of a small number of judges, small number of anybody—judges, professors, lawyers—who are known as originalists. Our manner of interpreting the Constitution is to begin with the text, and to give that text the meaning that it bore when it was adopted by the people. I'm not a "strict constructionist," despite the introduction. I don't like the term "strict construction." I do not think the Constitution, or any text, should be interpreted either strictly or sloppily; it should be interpreted reasonably. Many of my interpretations do not deserve the description "strict." I do believe, however, that you give the text the meaning it had when it was adopted.

This is such a minority position in modern academia and in modern legal circles that on occasion I'm asked when I've given a talk like this a question from the back of the room—"Justice Scalia, when did you first become an originalist?"—as though it is some kind of weird affliction that seizes some people—"When did you first start eating human flesh?"

Although it is a minority view now, the reality is that, not very long ago, originalism was orthodoxy. Everybody at least *purported* to be an originalist. If you go back and read the commentaries on the Constitution by Joseph Story, he didn't think the Constitution evolved or changed. He said it means and will always mean what it meant when it was adopted.

Or consider the opinions of John Marshall in the Federal Bank case, where he says, we must not, we must always remember it is a constitution we are expounding. And since it's a constitution, he says, you have to give its provisions expansive meaning so that they will accommodate events that you do not know of which will happen in the future.

Well, if it is a constitution that changes, you wouldn't have to give it an expansive meaning. You can give it whatever meaning you want and, when future necessity arises, you simply change the meaning. But anyway, that is no longer the orthodoxy.

Oh, one other example about how not just the judges and scholars believed in originalism, but even the American people. Consider the 19th Amendment, which is the amendment that gave women the vote. It was adopted by the American people in 1920. Why did we adopt a constitutional amendment for that purpose? The Equal Protection Clause existed in 1920; it was adopted right after the Civil War. And you know that if the issue of the franchise for women came up today, we would not have to have a constitutional amendment. Someone would come to the Supreme Court and say, "Your Honors, in a democracy, what could be a greater denial of equal protection than denial of the franchise?" And the Court would say, "Yes! Even though it never meant it before, the Equal Protection Clause means that women have to have the vote." But that's not how the American people thought in 1920. In 1920, they looked at the Equal Protection Clause and said, "What does it mean?" Well, it clearly doesn't mean that you can't discriminate in the franchise—not only on the basis of sex, but on the basis of property ownership, on the basis of literacy. None of that is unconstitutional. And therefore, since it wasn't unconstitutional, and we wanted it to be, we did things the good old-fashioned way and adopted an amendment.

Now, in asserting that originalism used to be orthodoxy, I do not mean to imply that judges did not distort the Constitution now and then; of course they did. We had willful judges then, and we will have willful judges until the end of time. But the difference is that prior to the last fifty years or so, prior to the advent of the "Living Constitution," judges did their distortions the good old-fashioned way, the honest way—they lied about it. They said the Constitution means such and such, when it never meant such and such.

It's a big difference that you now no longer have to lie about it, because we are in the era of the evolving Constitution. And the judge can simply say, "Oh yes, the Constitution didn't used to mean that, but it does now." We are in the age in which not only judges, not only lawyers, but even school children have come to learn the Constitution changes. I have grammar school students come into the Court now and then, and they recite very proudly what they have been taught: "The Constitution is a living document." You know, it morphs.

Well, let me first tell you how we got to the "Living Constitution." You don't have to be a lawyer to understand it. The road is not that complicated. Initially, the Court began giving terms in the text of the Constitution a meaning they didn't have when they were adopted. For example, the First Amendment, which forbids Congress to abridge the freedom of speech. What does the freedom of speech mean? Well, it clearly did not mean that Congress or government could not impose any restrictions upon speech. Libel laws, for example, were clearly constitutional. Nobody thought the First Amendment was *carte blanche* to libel someone. But in the famous case of *New York Times v. Sullivan*, the Supreme Court said, "But the First Amendment does prevent you from suing for libel if you are a public figure and if the libel was not malicious"—that is, the person, a member of the press or otherwise, thought that what the person said was true. Well, that had never been the law. I mean, it might be a good law. And some states could amend their libel law.

It's one thing for a state to amend its libel law and say, "We think that public figures shouldn't be able to sue." That's fine. But the courts have said that the First Amendment, which never meant this before, now means that if you are a public figure, that you can't sue for libel unless it's intentional, malicious. So that's one way to do it.

Another example is the Constitution guarantees the right to be represented by counsel. That never meant the state had to pay for your counsel. But you can reinterpret it to mean that.

That was step one. Step two, I mean, that will only get you so far. There is no text in the Constitution that you could reinterpret to create a right to abortion, for example. So you need something else. The something else is called the doctrine of "Substantive Due Process." Only lawyers can walk around talking about substantive process, inasmuch as it's a contradiction in terms. If you referred to substantive process or procedural substance at a cocktail party, people would look at you funny. But, lawyers talk this way all the time.

What substantive due process is is quite simple—the Constitution has a Due Process Clause, which says that no person shall be deprived of life, liberty, or property without due process of law. Now, what does this guarantee? Does it guarantee life, liberty, or property? No, indeed! All three can be taken away. You can be fined, you can be incarcerated, you can even be executed, but not without due process of law. It's a procedural guarantee. But the Court said, and this goes way back, in the 1920s at least—in fact the first case to do it was *Dred Scott*. But it became more popular in the 1920s. The Court said there are some liberties that are so important, that no process will suffice to take them away. Hence, substantive due process.

Now, what liberties are they? The Court will tell you. Be patient. When the doctrine of substantive due process was initially announced, it was limited in this way: the Court said it embraces only those liberties that are fundamental to a democratic society and rooted in the traditions of the American people.

Then we come to step three. Step three: that limitation is eliminated. Within the last twenty years, we have found to be covered by due process the right to abortion, which was so little rooted in the traditions of the American people that it was criminal for 200 years; the right to homosexual sodomy, which was so little rooted in the traditions of the American people that it was criminal for 200 years. So it is literally true, and I don't think this is an exaggeration, that the Court has essentially liberated itself from the text of the Constitution, from the text and even from the traditions of the American people. It is up to the Court to say what is covered by substantive due process.

What are the arguments usually made in favor of the Living Constitution? As the name of it suggests, it is a very attractive philosophy, and it's hard to talk people out of it—the notion that the Constitution grows. The major argument is the Constitution is a living organism; it has to grow with the society that it governs or it will become brittle and snap.

This is the equivalent of, an anthropomorphism equivalent to, what you hear from your stockbroker, when he tells you that the stock market is resting for an assault on the 11,000 level. The stock market panting at some base camp. The stock market is not a mountain climber and the Constitution is not a living organism, for Pete's sake; it's a legal document, and like all legal documents, it says some things, and it doesn't say other things. And if you think that the aficionados of the Living Constitution want to bring you flexibility, think again.

My Constitution is a very flexible Constitution. You think the death penalty is a good idea—persuade your fellow citizens and adopt it. You think it's a bad idea—persuade them the other way and eliminate it. You want a right to abortion—create it the way most rights are created in a democratic society: persuade your fellow citizens it's a good idea and enact it. You want the opposite—persuade them the other way. That's flexibility. But to read either result into the Constitution is not to produce flexibility, it is to produce what a constitution is designed to produce—rigidity. Abortion, for example, is offstage, it is off the democratic stage; it is no use debating it; it is unconstitutional. I mean prohibiting it is unconstitutional; I mean it's no use debating it anymore—now and forever, coast to coast, I guess until we amend the Constitution, which is a difficult thing. So, for whatever reason you might like the Living Constitution, don't like it because it provides flexibility.

That's not the name of the game. Some people also seem to like it because they think it's a good liberal thing—that somehow this is a conservative/liberal battle, and conservatives like the old-fashioned originalist Constitution and liberals ought to like the Living Constitution. That's not true either. The dividing line between those who believe in the Living Constitution and those who don't is not the dividing line between conservatives and liberals.

Conservatives are willing to grow the Constitution to cover their favorite causes just as liberals are, and the best example of that is two cases we announced some years ago on the same day, the same morning. One case was *Romer v. Evans*, in which the people of Colorado had enacted an amendment to the state constitution by plebiscite, which said that neither the state nor any subdivision of the state would add to the protected statuses against which private individuals cannot discriminate. The usual ones are race, religion, age, sex, disability and so forth. Would not add sexual preference—somebody thought that was a terrible idea, and, since it was a terrible idea, it must be unconstitutional. Brought a lawsuit, it came to the Supreme Court. And the Supreme Court said, "Yes, it is unconstitutional." On the basis of—I don't know. The Sexual Preference Clause of the Bill of Rights, presumably. And the liberals loved it, and the conservatives gnashed their teeth.

The very next case we announced is a case called *BMW v. Gore*. Not the Gore you think; this is another Gore. Mr. Gore had bought a BMW, which is a car supposedly advertised at least as having a superb finish, baked seven times in ovens deep in the Alps, by dwarfs. And his BMW apparently had gotten scratched on the way over. They did not send it back to the Alps, they took a can of spray paint and fixed it. And he found out about this and was furious, and he brought a lawsuit. He got his compensatory damages, a couple of hundred dollars—the difference between a car with a better paint job and a worse paint job—plus $2 million against BMW for punitive damages for being a bad actor, which is absurd of course, so it must be unconstitutional. BMW appealed to my Court, and my Court said, "Yes, it's unconstitutional." In violation of, I assume, the Excessive Damages Clause of the Bill of Rights. And if excessive punitive damages are unconstitutional, why aren't excessive compensatory damages unconstitutional? So you have a federal question whenever you get a judgment in a civil case. Well, that one the conservatives liked, because conservatives don't like punitive damages, and the liberals gnashed their teeth.

I dissented in both cases because I say, "A pox on both their houses." It has nothing to do with what your policy preferences are; it has to do with what you think the Constitution is.

Some people are in favor of the Living Constitution because they think it always leads to greater freedom—there's just nothing to lose, the evolving Constitution will always provide greater and greater freedom, more and more rights. Why would you think that? It's a two-way street. And indeed, under the aegis of the Living Constitution, some freedoms have been taken away.

Recently, last term, we reversed a 15-year-old decision of the Court, which had held that the Confrontation Clause—which couldn't be clearer, it says, "In all criminal prosecutions, the accused shall enjoy the right . . . to be confronted with the witness against him." But a Living Constitution Court held that all that was necessary to comply with the Confrontation Clause was that the hearsay evidence which is introduced—hearsay evidence means you can't cross-examine the person who said it because he's not in the court—the hearsay evidence has to bear indicia of reliability. I'm happy to say that we reversed it last term with the votes of the two originalists on the Court. And the opinion said that the only indicium of reliability that the Confrontation Clause acknowledges is confrontation. You bring the witness in to testify and to be cross-examined. That's just one example; there are others, of eliminating liberties.

So, I think another example is the right to jury trial. In a series of cases, the Court had seemingly acknowledged that you didn't have to have trial by jury of the facts that increase your sentence. You can make the increased sentence a "sentencing factor"—you get thirty years for burglary, but if the burglary is committed with a gun, as a sentencing factor the judge can give you another ten years. And the judge will decide whether you used a gun. And he will decide it, not beyond a reasonable doubt, but whether it's more likely than not. Well, we held recently, I'm happy to say, that this violates the right to a trial by jury. The Living Constitution would not have produced that result. The Living Constitution, like the legislatures that enacted these laws, would have allowed sentencing factors to be determined by the judge because all the Living Constitution assures you is that what will happen is what the majority wants to happen. And that's not the purpose of constitutional guarantees.

Well, I've talked about some of the false virtues of the Living Constitution; let me tell you what I consider its principle vices are. Surely the greatest—you should always begin with principle—its greatest vice is its illegitimacy. The only reason federal courts sit in judgment of the constitutionality of federal legislation is not because they are explicitly authorized to do so in the Constitution. Some modern constitutions give the constitutional court explicit authority to review German legislation or French legislation for its constitutionality; our Constitution doesn't say anything like that. But John Marshall says in *Marbury v. Madison*: Look, this is lawyers' work. What you have here is an apparent conflict between the Constitution and the statute. And, all the time, lawyers and judges have to reconcile these conflicts—they try to read the two to comport with each other. If they can't, it's judges' work to decide which ones prevail. When there are two statutes, the more recent one prevails. It implicitly repeals the older one. But when the Constitution is at issue, the Constitution prevails because it is a "super-statute." I mean, that's what Marshall says: It's judges' work.

If you believe, however, that the Constitution is not a legal text, like the texts involved when judges reconcile or decide which of two statutes prevail; if you think the Constitution is some exhortation to give effect to the most fundamental values of the society as those values change from year to year; if you think that it is meant to reflect, as some of the Supreme Court cases say, particularly those involving the Eighth Amendment, if you think it is simply meant to reflect the evolving standards of decency that mark the progress of a maturing society—if that is what you think it is, then why in the world would you have it interpreted by nine lawyers? What do I know about the evolving standards of decency of American society? I'm afraid to ask.

If that is what you think the Constitution is, then *Marbury v. Madison* is wrong. It shouldn't be up to the judges, it should be up to the legislature. We should have a system like the English—whatever the legislature thinks is constitutional is constitutional. They know the evolving standards of American society, I don't. So in principle, it's incompatible with the legal regime that America has established.

Secondly, and this is the killer argument—I mean, it's the best debaters' argument—they say in politics you can't beat somebody with nobody. It's the same thing with principles of legal interpretation. If you don't believe in originalism, then you need some other principle of interpretation. Being a non-originalist is not enough. You see, I have my rules that confine me. I know what I'm looking for. When I find it—the original meaning of the Constitution—I am handcuffed. If I believe that the First Amendment meant when it was adopted that you are entitled to burn the American flag, I have to come out that way even though I don't like to come out that way. When I find that the original meaning of the jury trial guarantee is that any additional time you spend in prison which depends upon a fact must depend upon a fact found by a jury—once I find that's what the jury trial guarantee means, I am handcuffed. Though I'm a law-and-order type, I cannot do all the mean conservative things I would like to do to this society. You got me.

Now, if you're not going to control your judges that way, what other criterion are you going to place before them? What is the criterion that governs the Living Constitutional judge? What can you possibly use, besides original meaning? Think about that. Natural law? We all agree on that, don't we? The philosophy of John Rawls? That's easy. There really is nothing else. You either tell your judges, "Look, this is a law, like all laws; give it the meaning it had when it was adopted." Or, you tell your judges, "Govern us. You tell us whether people under eighteen, who committed their crimes when they were under eighteen, should be executed. You tell us whether there ought to be an unlimited right to abortion or a partial right to abortion. You make these decisions for us." I have put this question—you know I speak at law schools with some frequency just to make trouble—and I put this question to the faculty all the time, or incite the students to ask their Living Constitutional professors: "Okay professor, you are not an originalist, what is your criterion?" There is none other.

And finally, this is what I will conclude with although it is not on a happy note. The worst thing about the Living Constitution is that it will destroy the Constitution. You heard in the introduction that I was confirmed, close to nineteen years ago now, by a vote of ninety-eight to nothing. The two missing were Barry Goldwater and Jake Games, so make it one hundred. I was known at that time to be, in my political and social views, fairly conservative. But still, I was known to be a good lawyer, an honest man—somebody who could read a text and give it its fair meaning—had judicial impartiality and so forth. And so I was unanimously confirmed. Today, barely twenty years later, it is difficult to get someone confirmed to the Court of Appeals. What has happened? The American people have figured out what is going on. If we are selecting lawyers, if we are selecting people to read a text and give it the fair meaning it had when it was adopted, yes, the most important thing to do is to get a good lawyer. If on the other hand, we're picking people to draw out of their own conscience and experience a new constitution with all sorts of new values to govern our society, then we should not look principally for good lawyers. We should look principally for people who agree with us, the majority, as to whether there ought to be this right, that right and the other right. We want to pick people that would write the new constitution that we would want.

And that is why you hear in the discourse on this subject, people talking about moderate—we want moderate judges. What is a moderate interpretation of the text? Halfway between what it really means and what you'd like it to mean? There is no such thing as a moderate interpretation of the text. Would you ask a lawyer, "Draw me a moderate contract?" The only way the word has any meaning is if you are looking for someone to write a law, to write a constitution, rather than to interpret one. The moderate judge is the one who will devise the new constitution that most people would approve of. So, for example, we had a suicide case some terms ago, and the Court refused to hold that there is a constitutional right to assisted suicide. We said, "We're not yet ready to say that. Stay tuned, in a few years, the time may come, but we're not yet ready." And that was a moderate decision, because I think most people would not want—if we had gone, looked into that and created a national right to assisted suicide—that would have been an immoderate and extremist decision.

I think the very terminology suggests where we have arrived—at the point of selecting people to write a constitution, rather than people to give us the fair meaning of one that has been democratically adopted. And when that happens, when the Senate interrogates nominees to the Supreme Court, or to the lower courts—you know, "Judge so-and-so, do you think there is a right to this in the Constitution? You don't? Well, my constituents think there ought to be, and I'm not going to appoint to the court someone who is not going to find that"—when we are in that mode, you realize, we have rendered the Constitution useless, because the Constitution will mean what the majority wants it to mean. The senators are representing the majority, and they will be selecting justices who will devise a constitution that the majority wants. And that, of course, deprives the Constitution of its principle utility. The Bill of Rights is devised to protect you and me against, who do you think? The majority. My most important function on the Supreme Court is to tell the majority to take a walk. And the notion that the justices ought to be selected because of the positions that they will take, that are favored by the majority, is a recipe for destruction of what we have had for 200 years.

To come back to the beginning, this is new—fifty years old or so—the Living Constitution stuff. We have not yet seen what the end of the road is. I think we are beginning to see. And what it is should really be troublesome to Americans who care about a Constitution that can provide protections against majoritarian rule. Thank you.

Stephen Breyer
Our Democratic Constitution

I shall focus upon several contemporary problems that call for govern- mental action and potential judicial reaction. In each instance I shall argue that, when judges interpret the Constitution, they should place greater emphasis upon the "ancient liberty," i.e., the people's right to "an active and constant participation in collective power." I believe that increased emphasis upon this active liberty will lead to better constitutional law, a law that will promote governmental solutions consistent with individual dignity and community need.

At the same time, my discussion will illustrate an approach to constitutional interpretation that places considerable weight upon consequences—consequences valued in terms of basic constitutional purposes. It disavows a contrary consti- tutional approach, a more "legalistic" approach that places too much weight upon language, history, tradition, and precedent alone while understating the importance of consequences. If the discussion helps to convince you that the more "consequential" approach has virtue, so much the better.

Three basic views underlie my discussion. First, the Constitution, considered as a whole, creates a framework for a certain kind of government. Its general objectives can be described abstractly as including (1) democratic self-government, (2) dispersion of power (avoiding concentration of too much power in too few hands), (3) individual dignity (through protection of individual liberties), (4) equality before the law (through equal protection of the law), and (5) the rule of law itself.

The Constitution embodies these general objectives in particular provisions. In respect to self-government, for example, Article IV guarantees a "republican Form of Government;" Article I insists that Congress meet at least once a year, that elections take place every two (or six) years, that a census take place every decade; the Fifteenth, Nineteenth, Twenty-fourth, and Twenty-sixth Amendments secure a virtually universal adult suffrage. But a general constitutional objective such as self-government plays a constitutional role beyond the interpretation of an individual provision that refers to it directly. That is because constitutional courts must consider the relation of one phrase to another. They must consider the document as a whole. And consequently the document's handful of general purposes will inform judicial interpretation of many individual provisions that do not refer directly to the general objective in question. My examples seek to show how that is so. And, as I have said, they will suggest a need for judges to pay greater attention to one of those general objectives, namely participatory democratic self-government.

Second, the Court, while always respecting language, tradition, and precedent, nonetheless has emphasized different general constitutional objectives at different periods in its history. Thus one can characterize the early nineteenth century as a period during which the Court helped to establish the authority of the federal government, including the federal judiciary. During the late nineteenth and early twentieth centuries, the Court underemphasized the Constitution's efforts to secure participation by black citizens in representative government— efforts related to the participatory "active" liberty of the ancients. At the same time, it overemphasized protection of property rights, such as an individual's freedom to contract without government interference, to the point where President Franklin Roosevelt commented that the Court's Lochner-era decisions had created a legal "no-man's land" that neither state nor federal regulatory authority had the power to enter.

The New Deal Court and the Warren Court in part reemphasized "active liberty." The former did so by dismantling various Lochner-era distinctions, thereby expanding the scope of democratic self-government. The latter did so by interpreting the Civil War Amendments in light of their purposes and to mean what they say, thereby helping African-Americans become members of the nation's community of self-governing citizens—a community that the Court expanded further in its "one person, one vote" decisions.

More recently, in my view, the Court has again underemphasized the importance of the citizen's active liberty. I will argue for a contemporary reemphasis that better combines "the liberty of the ancients" with that "freedom of governmental restraint" that Constant called "modern."

Third, the real-world consequences of a particular interpretive decision, valued in terms of basic constitutional purposes, play an important role in constitutional decision-making. To that extent, my approach differs from that of judges who would place nearly exclusive interpretive weight upon language, history, tradition and precedent. In truth, the difference is one of degree. Virtually all judges, when interpreting a constitution or a statute, refer at one time or another to language, to history, to tradition, to precedent, to purpose, and to consequences. Even those who take a more literal approach to constitutional interpretation sometimes find consequences and general purposes relevant. But the more "literalist" judge tends to ask those who cannot find an interpretive answer in language, history, tradition, and precedent alone to rethink the problem several times, before making consequences determinative. The more literal judges may hope to find in language, history, tradition, and precedent objective interpretive standards; they may seek to avoid an interpretive subjectivity that could confuse a judge's personal idea of what is good for that which the Constitution demands; and they may believe that these more "original" sources will more readily yield rules that can guide other institutions, including lower courts. These objectives are desirable, but I do not think the literal approach will achieve them, and, in any event, the constitutional price is too high. I hope that my examples will help to show you why that is so, as well as to persuade some of you why it is important to place greater weight upon constitutionally valued consequences, my consequential focus in this lecture being the effect of a court's decisions upon active liberty.

To recall the fate of Socrates is to understand that the "liberty of the ancients" is not a sufficient condition for human liberty. Nor can (or should) we replicate today the ideal represented by the Athenian agora or the New England town meeting. Nonetheless, today's citizen does participate in democratic self-governing processes. And the "active" liberty to which I refer consists of the Constitution's efforts to secure the citizen's right to do so.

To focus upon that active liberty, to understand it as one of the Constitution's handful of general objectives, will lead judges to consider the constitutionality of statutes with a certain modesty. That modesty embodies an understanding of the judges' own expertise compared, for example, with that of a legislature. It reflects the concern that a judiciary too ready to "correct" legislative error may deprive "the people" of "the political experience and the moral education that come from . . . correcting their own errors." It encompasses that doubt, caution, prudence, and concern—that state of not being "too sure" of oneself—that Learned Hand described as the "spirit of liberty." In a word, it argues for traditional "judicial restraint."

But active liberty argues for more than that. I shall suggest that increased recognition of the Constitution's general democratic participatory objectives can help courts deal more effectively with a range of specific constitutional issues. To show this I shall use examples drawn from the areas of free speech, federalism, privacy, equal protection and statutory interpretation. In each instance, I shall refer to an important modern problem of government that calls for a democratic response. I shall then describe related constitutional implications. I want to draw a picture of some of the different ways that increased judicial focus upon the Constitution's participatory objectives can have a positive effect.

* * *

I begin with free speech and campaign finance reform. The campaign finance problem arises out of the recent explosion in campaign costs along with a vast disparity among potential givers. * * * The upshot is a concern by some that the matter is out of hand—that too few individuals contribute too much money and that, even though money is not the only way to obtain influence, those who give large amounts of money do obtain, or appear to obtain, too much influence. The end result is a marked inequality of participation. That is one important reason why legislatures have sought to regulate the size of campaign contributions.

The basic constitutional question, as you all know, is not the desirability of reform legislation but whether, how, or the extent to which, the First Amendment permits the legislature to impose limitations or ceilings on the amounts individuals or organizations or parties can contribute to a campaign or the kinds of contributions they can make. * * *

One cannot (or, at least, I cannot) find an easy answer to the constitutional questions in language, history, or tradition. The First Amendment's language says that Congress shall not abridge "the freedom of speech." But it does not define "the freedom of speech" in any detail. The nation's Founders did not speak directly about campaign contributions. Madison, who decried faction, thought that members of Congress would fairly represent all their constituents, in part because the "electors" would not be the "rich" any "more than the poor." But this kind of statement, while modestly helpful to the campaign reform cause, is hardly determinative.

Neither can I find answers in purely conceptual arguments. Some argue, for example, that "money is speech"; others say "money is not speech." But neither contention helps much. Money is not speech, it is money. But the expenditure of money enables speech; and that expenditure is often necessary to communicate a message, particularly in a political context. A law that forbids the expenditure of money to convey a message could effectively suppress that communication.

Nor does it resolve the matter simply to point out that campaign contribution limits inhibit the political "speech opportunities" of those who wish to contribute more. Indeed, that is so. But the question is whether, in context, such a limitation abridges "the freedom of speech." And to announce that this kind of harm could never prove justified in a political context is simply to state an ultimate constitutional conclusion; it is not to explain the underlying reasons.

To refer to the Constitution's general participatory self-government objective, its protection of "active liberty" is far more helpful. That is because that constitutional goal indicates that the First Amendment's constitutional role is not simply one of protecting the individual's "negative" freedom from governmental restraint. The Amendment in context also forms a necessary part of a constitutional system designed to sustain that democratic self-government. The Amendment helps to sustain the democratic process both by encouraging the exchange of ideas needed to make sound electoral decisions and by encouraging an exchange of views among ordinary citizens necessary to encourage their informed participation in the electoral process. It thereby helps to maintain a form of government open to participation (in Constant's words "by all citizens without exception").

The relevance of this conceptual view lies in the fact that the campaign finance laws also seek to further the latter objective. They hope to democratize the influence that money can bring to bear upon the electoral process, thereby building public confidence in that process, broadening the base of a candidate's meaningful financial support, and encouraging greater public participation. They consequently seek to maintain the integrity of the political process—a process that itself translates political speech into governmental action. Seen in this way, campaign finance laws, despite the limits they impose, help to further the kind of open public political discussion that the First Amendment also seeks to encourage, not simply as an end, but also as a means to achieve a workable democracy.

For this reason, I have argued that a court should approach most campaign finance questions with the understanding that important First Amendment-related interests lie on both sides of the constitutional equation and that a First Amendment presumption hostile to government regulation, such as "strict scrutiny" is consequently out of place. Rather, the Court considering the matter without benefit of presumptions, must look realistically at the legislation's impact, both its negative impact on the ability of some to engage in as much communication as they wish and the positive impact upon the public's confidence, and consequent ability to communicate through (and participate in) the electoral process.

The basic question the Court should ask is one of proportionality. Do the statutes strike a reasonable balance between their electoral speech-restricting and speech-enhancing consequences? Or do you instead impose restrictions on that speech that are disproportionate when measured against their corresponding electoral and speech-related benefits, taking into account the kind, the importance, and the extent of those benefits, as well as the need for the restrictions in order to secure them?

The judicial modesty discussed earlier suggests that, in answering these questions, courts should defer to the legislatures' own answers insofar as those answers reflect empirical matters about which the legislature is comparatively expert, for example, the extent of the campaign finance problem, a matter that directly concerns the realities of political life. But courts cannot defer when evaluating the risk that reform legislation will defeat the very objective of participatory self-government itself, for example, where laws would set limits so low that, by elevating the reputation-related or media-related advantages of incumbency to the point where they would insulate incumbents from effective challenge.

I am not saying that focus upon active liberty will automatically answer the constitutional question in particular campaign finance cases. I argue only that such focus will help courts find a proper route for arriving at an answer. The positive constitutional goal implies a systemic role for the First Amendment; and that role, in turn, suggests a legal framework, i.e., a more particular set of questions for the Court to ask. Modesty suggests where, and how, courts should defer to legislatures in doing so. The suggested inquiry is complex. But courts both here and abroad have engaged in similarly complex inquiries where the constitutionality of electoral laws is at issue. That complexity is demanded by a Constitution that provides for judicial review of the constitutionality of electoral rules while granting Congress the effective power to secure a fair electoral system.

I next turn to a different kind of example. It focuses upon current threats to the protection of privacy, defined as "the power to control what others can come to know about you." It seeks to illustrate what active liberty is like in modern America, when we seek to arrive democratically at solutions to important technologically based problems. And it suggests a need for judicial caution and humility when certain privacy matters, such as the balance between free speech and privacy, are at issue.

First, I must describe the "privacy" problem. That problem is unusually complex. It has clearly become even more so since the terrorist attacks. For one thing, those who agree that privacy is important disagree about why. Some emphasize the need to be left alone, not bothered by others, or that privacy is important because it prevents people from being judged out of context. Some emphasize the way in which relationships of love and friendship depend upon trust, which implies a sharing of information not available to all. Others find connections between privacy and individualism, in that privacy encourages non-conformity. Still others find connections between privacy and equality, in that limitations upon the availability of individualized information lead private businesses to treat all customers alike. For some, or all, of these reasons, legal rules protecting privacy help to assure an individual's dignity.

For another thing, the law protects privacy only because of the way in which technology interacts with different laws. Some laws, such as trespass, wiretapping, eavesdropping, and search-and-seizure laws, protect particular places or sites, such as homes or telephones, from searches and monitoring. Other laws protect not places, but kinds of information, for example laws that forbid the publication of certain personal information even by a person who obtained that information legally. Taken together these laws protect privacy to different degrees depending upon place, individual status, kind of intrusion, and type of information.

Further, technological advances have changed the extent to which present laws can protect privacy. Video cameras now can monitor shopping malls, schools, parks, office buildings, city streets, and other places that present law left unprotected. Scanners and interceptors can overhear virtually any electronic conversation. Thermal imaging devices can detect activities taking place within the home. Computers can record and collate information obtained in any of these ways, or others. This technology means an ability to observe, collate and permanently record a vast amount of information about individuals that the law previously may have made available for collection but which, in practice, could not easily have been recorded and collected. The nature of the current or future privacy threat depends upon how this technological/legal fact will affect differently situated individuals.

These circumstances mean that efforts to revise privacy law to take account of the new technology will involve, in different areas of human activity, the balancing of values in light of prediction about the technological future. If, for example, businesses obtain detailed consumer purchasing information, they may create individualized customer profiles. Those profiles may invade the customer's privacy. But they may also help firms provide publicly desired products at lower cost. If, for example, medical records are placed online, patient privacy may be compromised. But the ready availability of those records may lower insurance costs or help a patient carried unconscious into an operating room. If, for example, all information about an individual's genetic make-up is completely confidential, that individual's privacy is protected, but suppose a close relative, a nephew or cousin, needs the information to assess his own cancer risk?

Nor does a "consent" requirement automatically answer the dilemmas suggested, for consent forms may be signed without understanding and, in any event, a decision by one individual to release or to deny information can affect others as well.

Legal solutions to these problems will be shaped by what is technologically possible. Should video cameras be programmed to turn off? Recorded images to self-destruct? Computers instructed to delete certain kinds of information? Should cell phones be encrypted? Should web technology, making use of an individual's privacy preferences, automatically negotiate privacy rules with distant web sites as a condition of access?

The complex nature of these problems calls for resolution through a form of participatory democracy. Ideally, that participatory process does not involve legislators, administrators, or judges imposing law from above. Rather, it involves law revision that bubbles up from below. Serious complex changes in law are often made in the context of a national conversation involving, among others, scientists, engineers, businessmen and -women, the media, along with legislators, judges, and many ordinary citizens whose lives the new technology will affect. That conversation takes place through many meetings, symposia, and discussions, through journal articles and media reports, through legislative hearings and court cases. Lawyers participate fully in this discussion, translating specialized knowledge into ordinary English, defining issues, creating consensus. Typically, administrators and legislators then make decisions, with courts later resolving any constitutional issues that those decisions raise. This "conversation" is the participatory democratic process itself.

The presence of this kind of problem and this kind of democratic process helps to explain, because it suggests a need for, judicial caution or modesty. That is why, for example, the Court's decisions so far have hesitated to preempt that process. In one recent case the Court considered a cell phone conversation that an unknown private individual had intercepted with a scanner and delivered to a radio station. A statute forbid the broadcast of that conversation, even though the radio station itself had not planned or participated in the intercept. The Court had to determine the scope of the station's First Amendment right to broadcast given the privacy interests that the statute sought to protect. The Court held that the First Amendment trumped the statute, permitting the radio station to broadcast the information. But the holding was narrow. It focused upon the particular circumstances present, explicitly leaving open broadcaster liability in other, less innocent, circumstances.

The narrowness of the holding itself serves a constitutional purpose. The privacy "conversation" is ongoing. Congress could well rewrite the statute, tailoring it more finely to current technological facts, such as the widespread availability of scanners and the possibility of protecting conversations through encryption. A broader constitutional rule might itself limit legislative options in ways now unforeseeable. And doing so is particularly dangerous where statutory protection of an important personal liberty is at issue.

By way of contrast, the Court held unconstitutional police efforts to use, without a warrant, a thermal imaging device placed on a public sidewalk. The device permitted police to identify activities taking place within a private house. The case required the Court simply to ask whether the residents had a reasonable expectation that their activities within the house would not be disclosed to the public in this way—a well established Fourth Amendment principle. Hence the case asked the Court to pour new technological wine into old bottles; it did not suggest that doing so would significantly interfere with an ongoing democratic policy conversation.

The privacy example suggests more by way of caution. It warns against adopting an overly rigid method of interpreting the constitution—placing weight upon eighteenth-century details to the point where it becomes difficult for a twenty-first-century court to apply the document's underlying values. At a minimum it suggests that courts, in determining the breadth of a constitutional holding, should look to the effect of a holding on the ongoing policy process, distinguishing, as I have suggested, between the "eavesdropping" and the "thermal heat" types of cases. And it makes clear that judicial caution in such matters does not reflect the fact that judges are mitigating their legal concerns with practical considerations. Rather, the Constitution itself is a practical document—a document that authorizes the Court to proceed practically when it examines new laws in light of the Constitution's enduring, underlying values.

My fourth example concerns equal protection and voting rights, an area that has led to considerable constitutional controversy. Some believe that the Constitution prohibits virtually any legislative effort to use race as a basis for drawing electoral district boundaries—unless, for example, the effort seeks to undo earlier invidious race-based discrimination. Others believe that the Constitution does not so severely limit the instances in which a legislature can use race to create majority-minority districts. Without describing in detail the basic argument between the two positions, I wish to point out the relevance to that argument of the Constitution's democratic objective.

That objective suggests a simple, but potentially important, constitutional difference in the electoral area between invidious discrimination, penalizing members of a racial minority, and positive discrimination, assisting members of racial minorities. The Constitution's Fifteenth Amendment prohibits the former, not simply because it violates a basic Fourteenth Amendment principle, namely that the government must treat all citizens with equal respect, but also because it denies minority citizens the opportunity to participate in the self-governing democracy that the Constitution creates. By way of contrast, affirmative discrimination ordinarily seeks to enlarge minority participation in that self-governing democracy. To that extent it is consistent with, indeed furthers, the Constitution's basic democratic objective. That consistency, along with its more benign purposes, helps to mitigate whatever lack of equal respect any such discrimination might show to any disadvantaged member of a majority group.

I am not saying that the mitigation will automatically render any particular discriminatory scheme constitutional. But the presence of this mitigating difference supports the view that courts should not apply the strong presumptions of unconstitutionality that are appropriate where invidious discrimination is at issue. My basic purpose, again, is to suggest that reference to the Constitution's "democratic" objective can help us apply a different basic objective, here that of equal protection. And in the electoral context, the reference suggests increased legislative authority to deal with multiracial issues.

The instances I have discussed encompass different areas of law—speech, federalism, privacy, equal protection, and statutory interpretation. In each instance, the discussion has focused upon a contemporary social problem—campaign finance, workplace regulation, environmental regulation, information-based technological change, race-based electoral districting, and legislative politics. In each instance, the discussion illustrates how increased focus upon the Constitution's basic democratic objective might make a difference—in refining doctrinal rules, in evaluating consequences, in applying practical cautionary principles, in interacting with other constitutional objectives, and in explicating statutory silences. In each instance, the discussion suggests how that increased focus might mean better law. And "better" in this context means both (a) better able to satisfy the Constitution's purposes and (b) better able to cope with contemporary problems. The discussion, while not proving its point purely through logic or empirical demonstration, uses example to create a pattern. The pattern suggests a need for increased judicial emphasis upon the Constitution's democratic objective.

My discussion emphasizes values underlying specific constitutional phrases, sees the Constitution itself as a single document with certain basic related objectives, and assumes that the latter can inform a judge's understanding of the former. Might that discussion persuade those who prefer to believe that the keys to constitutional interpretation instead lie in specific language, history, tradition, and precedent and who fear that a contrary approach would permit judges too often to act too subjectively?

Perhaps so, for several reasons. First, the area of interpretive disagreement is more limited than many believe. Judges can, and should, decide most cases, including constitutional cases, through the use of language, history, tradition, and precedent. Judges will often agree as to how these factors determine a provision's basic purpose and the result in a particular case. And where they differ, their differences are often differences of modest degree. Only a handful of constitutional issues—though an important handful—are as open in respect to language, history, and basic purpose as those that I have described. And even in respect to those issues, judges must find answers within the limits set by the Constitution's language. Moreover, history, tradition, and precedent remain helpful, even if not determinative.

Second, those more literalist judges who emphasize language, history, tradition, and precedent cannot justify their practices by claiming that is what the framers wanted, for the framers did not say specifically what factors judges should emphasize when seeking to interpret the Constitution's open language. Nor is it plausible to believe that those who argued about the Bill of Rights, and made clear that it did not contain an exclusive detailed list, had agreed about what school of interpretive thought should prove dominant in the centuries to come. Indeed, the Constitution itself says that the "enumeration" in the Constitution of some rights "shall not be construed to deny or disparage others retained by the people." Professor Bailyn concludes that the Framers added this language to make clear that "rights, like law itself, should never be fixed, frozen, that new dangers and needs will emerge, and that to respond to these dangers and needs, rights must be newly specified to protect the individual's integrity and inherent dignity." Instead, justification for the literalist's practice itself tends to rest upon consequences. Literalist arguments often seek to show that such an approach will have favorable results, for example, controlling judicial subjectivity.

Third, judges who reject a literalist approach deny that their decisions are subjective and point to important safeguards of objectivity. A decision that emphasizes values, no less than any other, is open to criticism based upon (1) the decision's relation to the other legal principles (precedents, rules, standards, practices, institutional understandings) that it modifies and (2) the decision's consequences, i.e., the way in which the entire bloc of decision-affected legal principles subsequently affects the world. The relevant values, by limiting interpretive possibilities and guiding interpretation, themselves constrain subjectivity, indeed the democratic values that I have emphasized themselves suggest the importance of judicial restraint. An individual constitutional judge's need for consistency over time also constrains subjectivity. That is why Justice O'Connor has explained that need in terms of a constitutional judge's initial decisions creating "footprints" that later decisions almost inevitably will follow.

Fourth, the literalist does not escape subjectivity, for his tools, language, history, and tradition, can provide little objective guidance in the comparatively small set of cases about which I have spoken. In such cases, the Constitution's language is almost always nonspecific. History and tradition are open to competing claims and rival interpretations. Nor does an emphasis upon rules embodied in precedent necessarily produce clarity, particularly in borderline areas or where rules are stated abstractly. Indeed, an emphasis upon language, history, tradition, or prior rules in such cases may simply channel subjectivity into a choice about: Which history? Which tradition? Which rules? It will then produce a decision that is no less subjective but which is far less transparent than a decision that directly addresses consequences in constitutional terms.

Finally, my examples point to offsetting consequences—at least if "literalism" tends to produce the legal doctrines (related to the First Amendment, to federalism, to statutory interpretation, to equal protection) that I have criticized. Those doctrines lead to consequences at least as harmful, from a constitutional perspective, as any increased risk of subjectivity. In the ways that I have set out, they undermine the Constitution's efforts to create a framework for democratic government—a government that, while protecting basic individual liberties, permits individual citizens to govern themselves.

To reemphasize the constitutional importance of democratic self-government may carry with it a practical bonus. We are all aware of figures that show that the public knows ever less about, and is ever less interested in, the processes of government. Foundation reports criticize the lack of high school civics education. Comedians claim that more students know the names of the Three Stooges than the three branches of government. Even law school graduates are ever less inclined to work for government—with the percentage of those entering government (or nongovernment public interest) work declining at one major law school from 12% to 3% over a generation. Indeed, polls show that, over that same period of time, the percentage of the public trusting the government declined at a similar rate.

This trend, however, is not irreversible. Indeed, trust in government has shown a remarkable rebound in response to last month's terrible tragedy [September 11]. Courts cannot maintain this upward momentum by themselves. But courts, as highly trusted government institutions, can help some, in part by explaining in terms the public can understand just what the Constitution is about. It is important that the public, trying to cope with the problems of nation, state, and local community, understand that the Constitution does not resolve, and was not intended to resolve, society's problems. Rather, the Constitution provides a framework for the creation of democratically determined solutions, which protect each individual's basic liberties and assures that individual equal respect by government, while securing a democratic form of government. We judges cannot insist that Americans participate in that government, but we can make clear that our Constitution depends upon it. Indeed, participation reinforces that "positive passion for the public good," that John Adams, like so many others, felt a necessary condition for "Republican Government" and any "real Liberty."

That is the democratic ideal. It is as relevant today as it was 200 or 2,000 years ago. Today it is embodied in our Constitution. Two thousand years ago, Thucydides, quoting Pericles, set forth a related ideal—relevant in his own time and, with some modifications, still appropriate to recall today. "We Athenians," said Pericles, "do not say that the man who fails to participate in politics is a man who minds his own business. We say that he is a man who has no business here."

DISCUSSION QUESTIONS

1. Critics of the originalist perspective often point to ambiguities in the language of the Constitution. Justice Breyer outlines several of these in his speech. What are some other examples of ambiguous language in the Constitution? (Look at the Bill of Rights as a start.) What alternative interpretations can you develop?

2. Critics of the Living Constitution, such as Justice Scalia, often argue that judges substitute their own reading of what they think the law should be for what the law is. Do you think it is possible for justices to avoid having their own views shape their decisions? How could they protect against this happening?

3. Should judges take public opinion or changing societal standards into account when ruling on the constitutionality of a statute or practice? If so, what evidence of public opinion or societal standards should matter? Surveys? Laws enacted in states? If not, what are the risks in doing so?

4. Consider Scalia's examples of when the Court has employed a Living Constitution approach. How would Breyer's approach of active liberty decide these decisions? Which approach do you think leads to the better outcomes?

9

Public Opinion and the Media: The Future of Political Journalism

From the 1960s through the 1980s, when people thought of media and news, they thought of newspapers and the broadcast television networks (ABC, CBS, NBC). Cable news soon emerged to provide an alternative (CNN, Fox, MSNBC), but one that for the most part followed the same style in their major nightly newscasts as the big networks. Late in the 1980s, talk radio, which had been around for some time, boomed in popularity and hosts such as Rush Limbaugh became household names. Hosts gleefully tweaked the mainstream media and embraced a much more aggressive, hard-hitting style that was explicitly ideological and partisan. There was, in this new forum, no pretense to being objective but, talk-radio fans would argue, the mainstream media were also not objective—they just pretended to be. News-oriented talk shows on CNN, Fox, and MSNBC followed the same pattern.

The rise of the Internet in the 1990s was the most recent dramatic change in communications technology. Today, Twitter receives much of the attention for breaking stories, blogs are prominent in presenting wide-ranging opinion and analysis, and YouTube makes it possible for every misstep by a politician to be easily viewed by millions of viewers.

Major changes in communications technology have produced major changes in the practice of politics and the way people learn about government. Earlier technologies do not necessarily fade away, but their role changes and their dominance diminishes. Pamphlets, then newspapers, then radio, and then television all had their eras of ascendancy. All continued to play important roles when other technologies emerged. Political talk radio in the 1980s and 1990s, for example, gave new life to radio in the age of television, creating another kind of information exchange with which politicians had to become conversant. Inevitably, these technological shifts raise concerns that the new form of information dissemination will drive out some of the positive features of the previous technology.

Does the rise of new media inevitably mean that the old media must fade away? And if so, at what cost to democracy, if any? The struggles facing newspapers have received extensive attention, and for good reason. Even when Americans relied more on television than newspapers to get their news, newspaper coverage often influenced what was reported on TV. Fans of the new media argue that those media have the potential to provide a powerful check on politicians and to allow for a more participatory democracy. By combining the knowledge, memory, and energy of multitudes of contributors, blogs and new media such as Twitter can reveal faulty or absent reporting by the mainstream media. Critics, however, worry that blogs and other new media may gain increasing sway over politicians and the public while not being held to high journalistic standards, and that they are as likely to generate misleading interpretations as they are to uncover truth.

To Paul Starr, the decline of newspapers is a crisis for democracy. In his view, newspapers were uniquely able to hold government accountable and expose corruption. In large part, this was because the financial model that supported newspapers allowed extensive news staffs to be subsidized by advertisers, classified ads, and sections catering to sports and lifestyles. In the new media world, these components have become largely unbundled. News now has to be financially self-sustaining, which has proven to be a difficult task. Starr explores whether the idea that newspapers must make money has to be abandoned in favor of a model in which philanthropy subsidizes the news.

James Fallows discusses ways in which the new media and the old are mutually interdependent. In particular, Fallows focuses on concerns at Google. Because it thrives as a search engine when users find quality content, Google is concerned about the problems facing the news media, particularly newspapers. Fallows reports on Google's concerns and the ways in which the company is attempting to assist news organizations. According to company executives, there is no single big thing that will save newspapers, but lots of little things might.

Paul Starr

Goodbye to the Age of Newspapers (Hello to a New Era of Corruption)

I.

We take newspapers for granted. They have been so integral a part of daily life in America, so central to politics and culture and business, and so powerful and profitable in their own right, that it is easy to forget what a remarkable historical invention they are. Public goods are notoriously under-produced in the marketplace, and news is a public good—and yet, since the mid-nineteenth century, newspapers have produced news in abundance at a cheap price to readers and without need of direct subsidy. More than any other medium, newspapers have been our eyes on the state, our check on private abuses, our civic alarm systems. It is true that they have often failed to perform those functions as well as they should have done. But whether they can continue to perform them at all is now in doubt.

* * *

II.

These developments raise practical questions for anyone concerned about the future of American democracy. * * * To answer those practical questions, it is necessary first to ponder a more theoretical one. Along with other new technology, the Internet was supposed to bring us a cornucopia of information, and in many respects it has done so. But if one of its effects is to shrink the production of professionally reported news, perhaps we need to understand the emerging framework of post-industrial society and politics somewhat differently.

* * *

III.

Of course, a medium that 40 percent of the public still claim to read should not be pronounced dead yet. The situation is also a bit more complicated, and more hopeful, than these trends suggest. Total readership of news that originates from newspapers has probably at least stabilized. Online, many people read news items on blogs and other sites that take items from the press, and the news junkies among us are reading more news from more papers than they did before the Internet made the sampling of multiple publications so easy. And some newspapers are clearly gaining wider reach online.

* * *

Some critics of the companies wonder why they cannot adjust to lower profits and make do. The trouble is that the declines in print circulation and advertising are virtually certain to continue, and if newspapers try to maintain the size and the scope of their operations, they may not be able [to] make any profit even when the recession is over. Nor is it clear that they can cut deep enough fast enough while retaining enough readers to be profitable.

* * *

Among many journalists as well as investors, the hope has vanished that newspapers as we have known them can make the transition to a world of hybrid print-online publication. Like network TV news and weekly newsmagazines, newspapers have been living off aging audiences that acquired their media habits in earlier decades. A few years ago, it seemed that they could rely on that aging print readership to tide them over until revenue began gushing from the Web. But online ads still account for only 8 percent of ad sales, and their growth has stalled just as earnings from print have tumbled. The result is that newspapers are shrinking not just physically or in labor power, but in the most important dimension of all—their editorial mission.

* * *

Besides cutting back foreign, national, and state coverage, newspapers are also reducing space devoted to science and the arts, and laying off science and medical reporters, music critics, and book reviewers. But there is one type of coverage that newspapers have tried to protect, at least in the early phases of cutbacks. According to the 2008 Pew survey of news executives, they have devoted more resources to local news. The case for "hyperlocalism," as it is known, is that newspapers enjoy comparative advantage as sources of information about their immediate communities. But this strategy may not work commercially if it means moving downmarket. The less coverage of the wider world and cultural life that newspapers provide, the more they stand to lose readership among the relatively affluent who have those interests, and the less attractive newspapers will be to many advertisers. Hyperlocalism may be just a short step from hollowing out the newsroom to the point where most newspapers come to resemble the free tabloids distributed at supermarkets rather than the newspapers of the past.

* * *

* * * Many of the functions that were bundled together in the newspaper are being unbundled online. But if the emerging media environment favors niche journalism, how will public-service journalism be able to reach and influence the broad public that newspapers have had? There is no going back to the way things used to be. If independent news media capable of holding government accountable are going to flourish, they are going to have to do so in the new world of the news, not the one that used to exist.

IV.

After the dot-com bust, the effusive talk about the miracles of the information revolution thankfully went out of style. But the social transformation under way—and there ought to be no doubt that one is indeed underway—is breaking up old monopolies of communication and power and creating new possibilities for free expression and democratic politics. As in any upheaval, some effects are unanticipated, and not all of them are positive, and what is perhaps most confusing, the good and bad are often intertwined.

By vastly increasing the options for diversion as well as information, the Internet has extended a process that had already begun when cable began increasing the number of TV channels. And if the political scientist Markus Prior is right, that expansion of choice is partly responsible for one of the most worrisome trends in American life: diminished attention to the news and reduced engagement in civic life among a significant part of the public.

* * *

The decline of newspapers and the growth of the Internet as a source of news may have a similar impact. On the one hand, there is likely to be less incidental learning among those with low political interest. Like the entertainment-oriented TV viewers who learned about the world because they had no alternative except to sit through the national network news, many people who have bought a paper for the sports, the recipes, the comics, or the crossword puzzle have nonetheless learned something about the wider world because they have been likely at least to scan the front page. Online, by contrast, they do not necessarily see what would be front-page news in their city, and so they are likely to become less informed about news and politics as the reading of newspapers drops. * * *

But there is another side to the story. As Yochai Benkler argues in his brilliant book *The Wealth of Networks: How Social Production Transforms Markets and Freedom*, the new "networked information economy" has some critical advantages for realizing democratic values. The old "industrial model" mass media have required large investments of capital and provided a platform to speak to the public for a relatively small number of people, but now the falling costs of computers and communication have "placed the material means of information and cultural production in the hands of a significant fraction of the world's population—on the order of a billion people around the globe." Instead of being confined to a passive role, ordinary people can talk back to the media or circumvent them entirely and enter the public conversation.

The new public sphere, in Benkler's view, is also developing mechanisms for filtering information for reliability and relevance, organizing it into easily navigated paths, and raising it to higher levels of public debate, contrary to critics who have worried that the Internet would be a chaotic Babel or a polarized system of "echo chambers" (as Cass Sunstein argued in his book *Republic.com*). And, unlike the old mass media, the new digital environment facilitates decentralized individual and cooperative action, often organized on an open and voluntary basis. Benkler invests a great deal of hope in this type of non-market collaborative production—the kind that has generated new social media such as Wikipedia, which, amazingly, despite being an encyclopedia, has also become an important news medium because it is so rapidly updated.

Of course, some of these innovations are mixed blessings: people can now share their misinformation as well as their knowledge. Viral email, Twitter, and social network sites can be used to spread rumors and malice through channels hidden from the wider public and insulated from criticism. Benkler is right about the many important gains from new technology, but he does not adequately balance the gains against the losses that the emerging networked economy is also bringing about—among them the problems that Prior identifies, such as the diminished share of the public following the news, and perhaps most important, the toll on the institutions of professional journalism.

* * *

The non-market collaborative networks on the Web celebrated by Benkler represent an alternative way of producing information as a public good. Before Wikipedia was created, hardly anyone supposed it would work as well as it has. But it has severe limitations as a source of knowledge. Its entries, including news items, are rewritten from other sources, and it does not purport to offer original research or original reporting. The blogosphere and the news aggregators are also largely parasitic: they feed off the conventional news media. Citizen journalists contribute reports from the scene of far-flung events, but the reports may just be the propaganda of self-interested parties.

Voluntary networks cannot easily duplicate certain critical advantages that large-scale and professionally run media have had—the financial wherewithal to invest in trained reporters and editors and to assign them to beats and long projects, and a well-established system of professional norms that has been a source of conscientious motivation and restraint in the reporting of news. The new social media add value when they are a supplement to professional journalism. To the extent that they supplant it, however, the wildfires of rumor and malice will be harder to check.

* * *

V.

And this returns us to the central problem. If newspapers are no longer able to cross-subsidize public-service journalism and if the de-centralized, non-market forms of collaboration cannot provide an adequate substitute, how is that work going to be paid for? The answer, insofar as there is one, is that we are going to need much more philanthropic support for journalism than we have ever had in the United States.

When a society requires public goods, the solution is often to use government to subsidize them or to produce them directly. But if we want a press that is independent of political control, we cannot have government sponsoring or bailing out specific papers. In the late eighteenth and nineteenth centuries, besides using printing contracts to subsidize favored party organs, the federal government supported the press in what First Amendment lawyers today would call a "viewpoint-neutral" way—through cheap postal rates that were available to all newspapers. And since the 1960s, both the federal and state governments have aided public broadcasting, which has enabled public TV and radio stations to become important sources of news.

Public radio has been a particularly notable success. In a period when commercial radio stations have abandoned all but headline news, National Public Radio has become the last refuge of original reporting on the dial. But as Charles Lewis, a long-time leader in investigative reporting, has pointed out in the *Columbia Journalism Review*, public radio stations, for all their excellent work, have not done a lot of investigative stories. The dependence of many local stations on state government funding makes them vulnerable to political pressure and unlikely to fill the void left by the decline in newspaper coverage of the states. Virtually any proposal for government subsidies of the press today would likely fail on just these grounds: funding by the federal government or the states has too much potential for political manipulation. Elsewhere governments are subsidizing the press. In an effort to aid newspapers in France, President Nicolas Sarkozy recently announced a program to give eighteen-year-olds a free year-long subscription to a daily paper of their choice. In America this would be a joke, though depending on how many teenagers chose one of our racier tabloids, it could give added meaning to the concept of a "stimulus package."

The other standard means of supporting the production of public goods is through private non-profit organization. In fact, non-profit support of journalism has recently been increasing. But much of the discussion about non-profit journalism has failed to recognize that it can mean at least three different things. The first, though not necessarily the most relevant, is the conversion of newspapers from commercial to non-profit status as a way of preserving their public-service role. Florida's *St. Petersburg Times*, which is owned by a journalism school, the Poynter Institute for Media Studies, is often mistakenly cited as a model for this approach. In fact, the *Times* itself has been run at a profit, which has been used to build up the Poynter Institute into a major center for training in journalism. Today, however, the question is not whether to use a money-making newspaper to support philanthropy, but whether non-profit organizations can sustain newspapers that may be losing money. Britain's Guardian Media Group, owned by the Scott Trust, comes closer to present demands. The trust uses profits from its money-making media subsidiaries to ensure the survival of the daily *Guardian*, which has lost money in recent years. But the *Guardian* model depends on having profitable subsidiaries to offset losses in a daily paper.

Before stopping the presses for the last time, the owners of some declining newspapers may try to convert them into non-profits in the hope of raising contributions to keep them in operation. I would not be surprised if some papers do have a devoted core of readers who would be willing to give more in tax-deductible contributions than they currently pay in subscriptions. But no paper has yet tested whether this option could raise enough money to stay in business.

Besides full non-profit operation of a newspaper, a second approach is philanthropic support of specific kinds of journalism, available through multiple outlets, whether they are commercial or non-profit. The best-known example of this solution is ProPublica, which describes itself as "an independent, non-profit newsroom that produces investigative journalism in the public interest." Publishing online as of last June, ProPublica also works in partnership on some stories with newspapers such as the *New York Times*. The partnerships enable newspapers to keep down the costs of investigative stories, and they give ProPublica access to mass distribution as well as a check on quality. Similarly, the Kaiser Family Foundation, which focuses on health policy, announced last fall that it would begin directly employing reporters to create a health policy news service. According to Drew Altman, Kaiser's president, besides making some stories freely available to newspapers and online, the news service will establish partnerships with newspapers for specific stories, which the papers will then have the right to release first. Some other foundations that focus on specific areas of policy may follow this approach as a way to promote public awareness of their concerns.

Both the non-profit operation of newspapers and the philanthropic subsidy of particular types of reporting are aimed at fostering forms of public-service journalism that would otherwise be in jeopardy. But there is yet a third use of non-profits—and it is for underwriting new models of journalism in the online environment. A good example of this approach is the Center for Independent Media, which, according to its director David Bennahum, receives about $4 million annually from seventy funders to support online political news sites in five states as well as one for national news, The Washington Independent. Bennahum says that "the narrative voice of newspapers is not what [online] readers want" and that the sites his center finances are instead doing a kind of journalism that brings readers into dialogue.

The notion that the digital medium requires a more inclusive relationship with the "people formerly called the audience" is a common theme among online journalists. Joshua Micah Marshall, the founder of Talking-PointsMemo.com, which runs on a commercial basis, says that many of the stories on his site grow out of ideas and tips supplied by readers in thousands of emails daily. Any news operation has information flowing in and out; an online publication can productively open up this process to anyone who is able and prepared to help. Stories develop online incrementally, often through participation in a collaborative network, rather than being written behind the scenes and released only when checked and finished. This is entirely different from "citizen journalism," and has the potential to be just as rigorous as traditional journalistic practices.

In cities around the country, journalists are experimenting with a variety of strategies for building up Web-only news sites to make up for the shrinking newsrooms of local papers. MinnPost.com in Minneapolis-St. Paul, the most substantial of these ventures, hopes to attract a wide range of readers and sponsors with news coverage of relatively broad scope, according to its CEO and editor Joel Kramer. But its annual budget of $1.3 million cannot support an operation on the scale of a metropolitan daily; with only seven full-time staff, MinnPost.com relies primarily on freelancers, many of them journalists who have left St. Paul's *Pioneer Press* or Minneapolis's *Star-Tribune* (which in January filed for bankruptcy protection despite having cut its editorial staff by 25 percent). Another non-profit online metropolitan news site, the VoiceofSanDiego.org, developed as a response to scandals in the city and has specialized in investigative stories. Like public radio, these ventures raise money through individual membership contributions and grants from local foundations, though not from government.

Doubtful that they can ever achieve the scale of the big metros, Rosenstiel compares the Web-based city news sites to aggressive city magazines. If one major concern is keeping government accountable, that kind of aggressive reporting is certainly a valuable function and well worth supporting. But owing to their more limited economic basis, the non-profit news sites are unlikely to be able to offer the coverage, or to exert the influence, of a daily newspaper read by half the people in a city. The great metros did not emerge just because cities needed newspapers to inform citizens—after all, cities need lots of things that they are never able to develop. Newspapers flourished at the metropolitan level because their role as local market intermediaries enabled them to generate substantial advertising as well as circulation income and thereby to become strong and independent. Non-profit news sites that lack a strong advertising base depend on donors for their survival and are at risk of being destroyed by a single lawsuit, and so they are unlikely to be able to match the traditional power of the press.

Many people have been expecting the successors of newspapers to emerge on the Web. But there may be no successor, at least none like the papers we have known. The metropolitan daily may be a peculiar historical invention whose time is passing. We may be approaching not the end of newspapers, but the end of the age of newspapers—the long phase in history when newspapers published in major cities throughout the United States have been central to both the production of news and the life of their metropolitan regions.

Metropolitan newspapers have dominated news gathering, set the public agenda, served as the focal point of controversy, and credibly represented themselves as symbolizing and speaking for the cities whose names they have carried. They have tried to be everyone's source of news, appealing across the ideological spectrum, and to be comprehensive, providing their readers with whatever was of daily interest to them. Some newspapers, a smaller number than exist today, will survive the transition to the Web, but they probably will not possess the centrality, the scope, or the authoritative voice—much less the monopolies on metropolitan advertising—that newspapers have had.

* * *

For those with the skills and interest to take advantage of this new world of news, there should be much to be pleased with. Instead of being limited to a local paper, such readers already enjoy access to a broader range of publications and discussions than ever before. But without a local newspaper or even with a shrunken one, many other people will learn less about what is going on in the world. As of now, moreover, no source in any medium seems willing and able to pay for the general-interest reporting that newspapers are abandoning. Philanthropy can help to offset some of these cutbacks, but it is unlikely to make up fully for what we are losing.

News coverage is not all that newspapers have given us. They have lent the public a powerful means of leverage over the state, and this leverage is now at risk. If we take seriously the notion of newspapers as a fourth estate or a fourth branch of government, the end of the age of newspapers implies a change in our political system itself. Newspapers have helped to control corrupt tendencies in both government and business. If we are to avoid a new era of corruption, we are going to have to summon that power in other ways. Our new technologies do not retire our old responsibilities.

James Fallows

How to Save the News

Everyone knows that Google is killing the news business. Few people know how hard Google is trying to bring it back to life, or why the company now considers journalism's survival crucial to its own prospects.

Of course this overstates Google's power to destroy, or create. The company's chief economist, Hal Varian, likes to point out that perhaps the most important measure of the newspaper industry's viability—the number of subscriptions per household—has headed straight down, not just since Google's founding in the late 1990s but ever since World War II. In 1947, each 100 U.S. households bought an average of about 140 newspapers daily. Now they buy fewer than 50, and the number has fallen nonstop through those years. If Google had never been invented, changes in commuting patterns, the coming of 24-hour TV news and online information sites that make a newspaper's information stale before it appears, the general busyness of life, and many other factors would have created major problems for newspapers. Moreover, "Google" is shorthand for an array of other Internet-based pressures on the news business, notably the draining of classified ads to the likes of Craigslist and eBay. On the other side of the balance, Google's efforts to shore up news organizations are extensive and have recently become intense but are not guaranteed to succeed.

* * *

Let's start with the diagnosis: If you are looking at the troubled ecology of news from Google's point of view, how do you define the problem to be solved? You would accept from the outset that something "historic," "epochal," "devastating," "unprecedented," "irresistible," and so on was happening to the news business—all terms I heard used in interviews to describe the challenges facing newspapers in particular and the journalism business more broadly.

"There really is no single cause," I was told by Josh Cohen, a former Web-news manager for Reuters who now directs Google's dealings with publishers and broadcasters, at his office in New York. "Rather, you could pick any single cause, and that on its own would be enough to explain the problems—except it's not on its own." The most obvious cause is that classified advertising, traditionally 30 to 40 percent of a newspaper's total revenue, is disappearing in a rush to online sites. "There are a lot of people in the business who think that in the not-too-distant future, the classified share of a paper's revenue will go to zero," Cohen said. "Stop right there. In any business, if you lose a third of your revenue, you're going to be in serious trouble."

You can't stop right there, Cohen said, and he went through the list of the other, related trends weighing on newspapers in particular, each pointing downward and each making the others worse. First, the relentless decline of circulation—"fewer people using your product," as he put it. Then, the consequent defection of advertisers from the lucrative "display" category—the big ads for cars, banks, airlines—as well as from classifieds. The typical newspaper costs much more to print and deliver than a subscriber pays. Its business rationale is as an advertising-delivery vehicle, with 80 percent of the typical paper's total revenue coming from ads. That's what's going away. In hopes of preserving that advertising model, newspapers have decided to defend their hold on the public's attention by giving away, online, the very information they were trying to sell in print. However that decision looks in the long run, for now it has created a rising generation of "customers" who are out of the habit of reading on paper and are conditioned to think that information should be free.

"It's the triple whammy," [Google CEO] Eric Schmidt said when I interviewed him. "Loss of classifieds, loss of circulation, loss of the value of display ads in print, on a per-ad basis. Online advertising is growing but has not caught up."

So far, this may sound familiar. To me, the interesting aspects of the Google diagnosis, which of course sets the stage for the proposed cure, were these:

First, it was strikingly not moralistic or mocking. This was a change, not simply from what I'd grown used to hearing at tech conferences over the past decade—the phrase "dead-tree edition" captures the tone—but also from the way Americans usually talk about distressed industries. Think of the connotations of "Big Auto" or "Rust Belt." * * *

Next in the Google assessment is the emphasis on "unbundling" as an insurmountable business problem for journalism. "Bundling" was the idea that all parts of the paper came literally in one wrapper—news, sports, comics, grocery-store coupons—and that people who bought the paper for one part implicitly subsidized all the rest. This was important not just because it boosted overall revenue but because it kept publishers from having to figure out whether enough people were reading stories from the statehouse or Mexico City to pay the costs of reporters there.

* * * The Internet has been one giant system for stripping away such cross-subsidies. Why look to the newspaper real-estate listings when you can get more

up-to-date, searchable info on Zillow—or better travel deals on Orbitz, or a broader range of movie showtimes on Yahoo? Google has been the most powerful unbundling agent of all. It lets users find the one article they are looking for, rather than making them buy the entire paper that paid the reporter. It lets advertisers reach the one customer who is searching for their product, rather than making them advertise to an entire class of readers.

Next, and significantly for the company's vision of the future, nearly everyone at Google emphasized that prospects look bleak for the printed versions of newspapers—but could be bright for the news industry as a whole, including newspaper publishers. This could seem an artificial distinction, but it is fundamental to the company's view of how news organizations will support themselves.

* * *

Publishers would be overjoyed to stop buying newsprint—if the new readers they are gaining for their online editions were worth as much to advertisers as the previous ones they are losing in print. Here is a crucial part of the Google analysis: they certainly will be. The news business, in this view, is passing through an agonizing transition—bad enough, but different from dying. The difference lies in the assumption that soon readers will again pay for subscriptions, and online display ads will become valuable.

"Nothing that I see suggests the 'death of newspapers,'" Eric Schmidt told me. The problem was the high cost and plummeting popularity of their print versions. "Today you have a subscription to a print newspaper," he said. "In the future model, you'll have subscriptions to information sources that will have advertisements embedded in them, like a newspaper. You'll just leave out the print part. I am quite sure that this will happen." We'll get to the details in a moment, but the analytical point behind his conviction bears emphasis. "I observe that as print circulation falls, the growth of the online audience is dramatic," Schmidt said. "Newspapers don't have a demand problem; they have a business-model problem." Many of his company's efforts are attempts to solve this, so that newspaper companies can survive, as printed circulation withers away.

Finally, and to me most surprisingly, the Google analysis reveals something about journalism that people inside the business can't easily see about themselves. This involves a kind of inefficiency that a hard-pressed journalistic establishment may no longer be able to afford.

* * *

Except for an 18-month period when [Krishna] Bharat founded and ran Google's R&D center in Bangalore, his original hometown, he has been guiding Google News ever since. In this role, he sees more of the world's news coverage daily than practically anyone else on Earth. I asked him what he had learned about the news business.

He hesitated for a minute, as if wanting to be very careful about making a potentially offensive point. Then he said that what astonished him was the predictable and pack-like response of most of the world's news outlets to most stories. Or, more positively, how much opportunity he saw for anyone who was willing to try a different approach.

The Google News front page is a kind of air-traffic-control center for the movement of stories across the world's media, in real time. "Usually, you see essentially the same approach taken by a thousand publications at the same time," he told me. "Once something has been observed, nearly everyone says approximately the same thing." He didn't mean that the publications were linking to one another or syndicating their stories. Rather, their conventions and instincts made them all emphasize the same things. This could be reassuring, in indicating some consensus on what the "important" stories were. But Bharat said it also indicated a faddishness of coverage—when Michael Jackson dies, other things cease to matter—and a redundancy that journalism could no longer afford. "It makes you wonder, is there a better way?" he asked. "Why is it that a thousand people come up with approximately the same reading of matters? Why couldn't there be five readings? And meanwhile use that energy to observe something else, equally important, that is currently being neglected." He said this was not a purely theoretical question. "I believe the news industry is finding that it will not be able to sustain producing highly similar articles."

With the debut of Krishna Bharat's Google News in 2002, Google began its first serious interactions with news organizations. Two years later, it introduced Google Alerts, which sent e-mail or instant-message notifications to users whenever Google's relentless real-time indexing of the world's news sites found a match for a topic the user had flagged. Two years after that, in the fall of 2006, Google began scanning the paper or microfilmed archives of many leading publications so that articles from their pre-digital era could be indexed, searched for, and read online.

* * *

"About two years ago, we started hearing more and more talk about the decline of the press," Schmidt told me. "A set of people [inside the company] began looking at what might be the ways we could help newspapers."

Why should the company bother? Until recently, I would have thought that the answer was a combination of PR concerns and Schmidt's personal interest. * * *

Before this year, when I asked Google employees about the health of the news business, their answers often seemed dutiful. During my interviews this year, people sounded as if they meant it. Google is valuable, by the logic I repeatedly heard, because the information people find through it is valuable. If the information is uninteresting, inaccurate, or untimely, people will not want to search for it. How valuable would Google Maps be, if the directions or street listings were wrong?

Nearly everyone I spoke with made this point in some way. Nikesh Arora's version was that Google had a "deeply symbiotic relationship" with serious news organizations. "We help people find content," he told me. "We don't generate content ourselves. As long as there is great content, people will come looking for it. When there's no great content, it's very hard for people to be interested in finding it. That's what we do for a living." * * *

"For the last eight years, we mainly focused on getting the algo- rithms better," Krishna Bharat said, referring to the automated systems for finding and ranking items in Google News. "But lately, a lot of my time has gone into thinking about the basis on which the product"—news—"is built. A lot of our thinking now is focused on making the news sustainable."

So how can news be made sustainable? The conceptual leap in Google's vision is simply to ignore print. It's not that everyone at the company assumes "dead tree" newspapers and magazines will disappear. * * * No one I spoke with at Google went quite that far. But all of their plans for reinventing a business model for journalism involve attracting money to the Web-based news sites now available on computers, and to the portable information streams that will flow to whatever devices evolve from today's smart phones, iPods and iPads, Nooks and Kindles, and mobile devices of any other sort. This is a natural approach for Google, which is, except for its Nexus One phone, a strictly online company.

The three pillars of the new online business model, as I heard them invariably described, are distribution, engagement, and monetization. That is: getting news to more people, and more people to news-oriented sites; making the presentation of news more interesting, varied, and involving; and converting these larger and more strongly committed audiences into revenue, through both subscription fees and ads. Conveniently, each calls on areas of Google's expertise. "Not knowing as much about the news business as the newspapers do, it is unlikely that we can solve the problems better than they can," Nikesh Arora told me. "But we are willing to support any formal and informal effort that newspapers or journalists more generally want to make" to come up with new sources of money.

In practice this involves projects like the ones I'm about to describe, which share two other traits beyond the "distribution, engagement, monetization" strategy that officially unites them. One is the Google concept of "permanent beta" and continuous experimentation—learning what does work by seeing all the things that don't. "We believe that teams must be nimble and able to fail quickly," Josh Cohen told me. (I resisted making the obvious joke about the contrast with the journalism world, which believes in slow and statesmanlike failure.) "The three most important things any newspaper can do now are experiment, experiment, and experiment," Hal Varian said.

* * *

The other implicitly connecting theme is that an accumulation of small steps can together make a surprisingly large difference. The forces weighing down the news industry are titanic. In contrast, some of the proposed solutions may seem disappointingly small-bore. But many people at Google repeated a maxim from Clay Shirley, of New York University, in an essay last year about the future of the news: "Nothing will work, but everything might."

In all, Google teams are working with hundreds of news organizations, which range in scale from the Associated Press, the Public Broadcasting System, and *The New York Times* to local TV stations and papers. The last two efforts I'll mention are obviously different in scale and potential from all the others, but these examples give a sense of what "trying everything" means.

Living Stories

News reporting is usually incremental. Something happens in Kabul today. It's related to what happened there yesterday, plus 20 years ago, and further back. It has a bearing on what will happen a year from now. High-end news organizations reflect this continuous reality in hiring reporters and editors who (ideally) know the background of today's news and in the way they present it, usually with modest additions to the sum of established knowledge day by day.

The modest daily updating of the news—another vote in Congress, another debate among political candidates—matches the cycle of papers and broadcasts very well, but matches the Internet very poorly, in terms of both speed and popularity rankings. *The Financial Times* might have given readers better sustained coverage of European economic troubles than any other paper. But precisely because it has done so many incremental stories, no one of them might rise to the top of a Google Web search, compared with an occasional overview story somewhere else. By the standards that currently generate online revenue, better journalism gets a worse result.

This past winter, the Google News team worked with *The New York Times* and *The Washington Post* to run the Living Stories experiment, essentially a way to rig Google's search results to favor serious, sustained reporting. All articles about a big topic—the war in Afghanistan, health-care reform—were grouped on one page that included links to all aspects of the paper's coverage (history, videos, reader comments, related articles). "It is a repository of information, rather than ephemeral information," Krishna Bharat said, explaining that it was a repository designed to prosper in what he called "today's link economy." In February, Google called off the *Times-Post* experiment—and declared it a success, by making the source code available free online, for any organization that would like to create a Living Stories feature for its site.

* * *

Fast Flip

The Internet is a great way to get news but often a poor way to read it. Usually the longer the item, the worse the experience; a screenful is fine, clicking through thousands of words is an ordeal. * * *

The Fast Flip project, which began last summer and has now graduated to "official" status, is an attempt to approximate the inviting aspects of leafing through a magazine. It works by loading magazine pages not as collections of text but as highly detailed photos of pages as a whole, cached in Google's system so they load almost as quickly as a (human) reader can leaf through them. "It was an experiment in giving you a preview of an article that was more than just a link to the title," Krishna Bharat said. "It gives you a sense of the graphics, the emphasis, the quality, the feel. Whether you would like to spend time with it." Spending time with an article, whether in print or online, is of course the definition of "engagement" and the behavior advertisers seek. * * *

"We're not saying we have worked out exactly the right model," Krishna Bharat said when I asked about Fast Flip details. "We just want news to be available, fast, all over the place on the Internet."

YouTube Direct

Projects like Living Stories and Fast Flip are tactical in their potential. Google's hope is that broader use of YouTube videos could substantially boost a news organization's long-term ability to engage an audience. Amateur-produced video is perhaps the most powerful new tool of the Internet era in journalism, making the whole world a potential witness to dramas, tragedies, achievements almost anywhere. The idea behind the various YouTube projects is that the same newspapers that once commanded an audience with printed reports of local news, sports, crime, and weather could re-create their central role by becoming a clearinghouse for video reports.

* * * For instance, Google offers, for free, the source code for YouTube Direct, which any publication can put on its own Web site. Readers can then easily send in their video clips, for the publication to review, censor, combine, or shorten before putting them up on its site. After a blizzard, people could send in clips of what they had seen outside. Same for a local football game, or a train wreck, or a city-council meeting, or any other event when many people would be interested in what their neighbors had seen. The advertising potential might be small, for YouTube and the local paper alike. The point would be engagement. Al Jazeera used YouTube Direct during the elections in Iraq this spring to show footage from around the country.

* * *

Another tool extends the lessons of the YouTube Debates during the 2008 presidential campaign, in which [Google] invited YouTube users from around the country to send in clips of brief questions for the candidates. Anderson Cooper of CNN then introduced YouTube clips of the questions CNN had chosen to use. They ranged from serious to silly and included one asking Barack Obama whether he was "black enough." YouTube has added a feature that lets users vote for the questions they want asked and has used the method effectively many times since then. . . .

Whatever comes of these experiments, two other broad initiatives are of unquestionable importance, because they address the two biggest business emergencies today's news companies face: they can no longer make enough money on display ads, and they can no longer get readers to pay. According to the Google view, these are serious situations, but temporary.

Display Ads

The idea for improving display-ad prospects begins with insignificant-sounding adjustments that have great potential payoff. For instance: Neal Mohan of Google pointed out that news organizations now typically sell their online ad space in two very different ways. Premium space—on the home page, facing certain featured articles or authors—is handled by "direct sales," through the publication's own sales staff. "Remnant" space, anything left over, is generally franchised out to a national sales network or "exchange" that digs up whatever advertisers it can. Publications decide on the division of space ahead of time, and hope the real-world results more or less fit.

One of Google's new systems does for online ad space what the airlines' dreaded "yield management" systems do for seats on a plane. Airlines constantly adjust the fares on a route, and the size of the planes that will fly it, toward the goal of making each plane as full as it can be before it takes off. The Google system does the same thing, allowing publishers to adjust the allocation of high- and low-priced space, second by second. "Your top salesperson might just have had dinner with the biggest client, who decides to run a big campaign," Mohan told me. The dynamic allocation system ensures that the publisher doesn't lose a penny of potential ad revenue to avoidable supply/demand glitches. If an advertiser wants to spend more on "premium" ads, the necessary space will be automatically redeployed from lower-value sections. * * * Yield management has allowed airlines to survive; according to Mohan, the advertising equivalent in Google's new system "has generated a lift for publishers of 130 percent, versus what they did when dividing the space themselves."

Mohan suggested a variety of other small but significant operational improvements, which together led to a proposal so revolutionary that it challenges all despairing conclusions about the economic future of the press. * * * Online display ads may not be so valuable now, he said, but that is because we're still in the drawn-out "transition" period. Sooner or later—maybe in two years, certainly in 10—display ads will, per eyeball, be worth more online than they were in print.

How could this be? In part, he said, today's discouraging ad results simply reflect a lag time. The audience has shifted dramatically from print to online. So has the accumulation of minutes people choose to spend each day reading the news. Wherever people choose to spend their time, Mohan said, they can eventually be "monetized"—the principle on which every newspaper and magazine (and television network) has survived until today.

* * *

* * * "The online world will be a lot more attuned to who you are and what you care about, and it will be interactive in a way it never has been before." Advertising has been around forever, Mohan said, "but until now it has always been a one-way conversation. Now your users can communicate back to you." His full argument is complex, but his conclusion is: eventually news operations will wonder why they worried so much about print display ads, since online display will be so much more attractive.

* * *

Designing the Paywall

The other hugely consequential effort Google is exploring involves reviving the idea of "subscriptions"—the quaint old custom of an audience paying for what it receives. Most Google people I spoke with had zero interest in the paywall question as an abstraction, because it seemed so obvious that different publications in different circumstances with different business models will make different decisions about how customers should pay.

* * *

"We don't want to encourage anyone to start charging for content, or not to charge for content," Chris Gaither said. "That is entirely up to them." But Google teams based in Mountain View and New York have been working with newspapers and magazines on the surprisingly complex details of making any kind of payment system work. Paywalls themselves come in a wide variety: absolute barriers to anyone who is not a subscriber, metered approaches that allow nonsubscribers a certain number of free views per day or month, "first click free" schemes to let anyone see the start of an article but reserve the full text for subscribers, and many more. Each involves twists in how the publication's results show up in Google searches and on Google News. For instance: if you are a paid subscriber to the *Financial Times*, any Web search you run should include FT results—and indeed rank them all the higher, since your status as a subscriber means you place extra value on the paper's reports. If you don't subscribe, those FT links should come lower in the search results, since you won't be able to read them—but the results should still appear, in case you decide you want them enough to subscribe. But when you run the search, how can Google tell whether or not you subscribe? How can it know that you are you, whether you're using your computer, or a friend's, or one at an Internet cafe, or an iPhone? And how can its Web crawlers index the FTs stories in the first place, if they're behind the paywall? All these questions have answers, but they're not always obvious.

"We often hear from publishers saying, 'We're thinking of this approach, and we want to understand it fully,'" Josh Cohen told me. "'We want to be sure this works the way we intend it to work. Can you give it a look?' We will tell them how their ideas would turn out with our system." Then, without giving the newspaper's name or the proprietary details of its specific plan, the Google team will also post its findings and advice on its public Web site. And for publications thinking of the "E-ZPass" approach—some automatic way to collect small per-article charges without slowing the user down or involving cumbersome forms—another Google team is working on the practicalities.

As for the very idea of paid subscriptions: How can they have a future in the Google-driven world of atomized spot information? "It is probable that unbundling has a limit," Eric Schmidt said. Something basic in human nature craves surprise and new sources of stimulation. Few people are "so monomaniacal," as he put it, that they will be interested only in a strict, predefined list of subjects. Therefore people will still want to buy subscriptions to sources of information and entertainment—"bundles," the head of the world's most powerful unbundler said—and advertisers will still want to reach them. His example:

"It's obvious that in five or 10 years, most news will be consumed on an electronic device of some sort. Something that is mobile and personal, with a nice color screen. Imagine an iPod or Kindle smart enough to show you stories that are incremental to a story it showed you yesterday, rather than just repetitive. And it knows who your friends are and what they're reading and think is hot. And it has display advertising with lots of nice color, and more personal and targeted, within the limits of creepiness. And it has a GPS and a radio network and knows what is going on around you. If you think about that, you get to an interesting answer very quickly, involving both subscriptions and ads."

This vision, which Schmidt presented as Utopian, helps illustrate the solution Google believes it will find; the problem it knows it can't solve; and another problem that goes well beyond its ambitions.

The solution is simply the idea that there can be a solution. The organization that dominates the online-advertising world says that much more online-ad money can be flowing to news organizations. The company whose standard price to consumers is zero says that subscribers can and will pay for news. The name that has symbolized disruption of established media says it sees direct self-interest in helping the struggling journalism business. In today's devastated news business, these are major and encouraging developments, all the more so for their contrast with what other tech firms are attempting.

The problem Google is aware of involves the disruption still ahead. Ten years from now, a robust and better-funded news business will be thriving. What next year means is harder to say. * * * But this is consistent with the way the news has always worked, rather than a threatening change. Fifteen years ago, Fox News did not exist. A decade ago, Jon Stewart was not known for political commentary. The news business has continually been reinvented by people in their 20s and early 30s. . . .

The challenge Google knows it has not fully coped with is a vast one, which involves the public function of the news in the broadest sense. The company views the survival of "premium content" as important to its own welfare. But Schmidt and his colleagues realize that a modernized news business might conceivably produce "enough" good content for Google's purposes even if no one has fully figured out how to pay for the bureau in Baghdad, or even at the state-house. This is the next challenge, and a profound one, for a reinvented journalistic culture. The fluid history of the news business, along with today's technological pattern of Google-style continuous experimentation, suggests that there will be no one big solution but a range of partial remedies. Google's efforts may have bought time for a panicked, transitional news business to see a future for itself and begin discovering those new remedies and roles.

DISCUSSION QUESTIONS

1. Which part or parts of the news media—newspapers, television, websites, blogs, radio, social networks, Twitter—do you rely on most? Which would you say you trust the most? Should all news-oriented media, whether new or old, use the same journalistic standards in determining what to broadcast or publish?

2. Imagine you are a blogger and you have come across some damaging information about a presidential candidate. Do you blog it? On one hand, it might not be true. On the other, if it is true, it is critical information that voters should know. Do you put the information into the blogosphere and trust it will be filtered and proven true or false by other media? Or do you approach it as mainstream media journalists traditionally would, requiring more corroboration for the story—which can take time to obtain—before presenting it to the public? Would your answer depend on how late in the campaign it is? Now imagine the same scenario, except that the office in question is an elected position in your hometown, where people know you. Would you handle this situation differently?

3. Both articles express concerns about the fate of newspapers. What are the key concerns? Do you share them? Why or why not?

4. What do you see as the strengths and weaknesses of the solutions described by Starr and Fallows for the problems facing newspapers?

10

Elections and Voting: Voter Identification

Recent national elections have raised many concerns about the voting system and the standards for administering elections in the United States. Charges of impropriety in voting procedures and vote counting, as well as complaints that certain voting technologies were systematically likely to produce more voter error or not accurately record voter choices, were legion. Massive voter mobilization campaigns on both the political left and right registered millions of new voters. Huge sums were poured into campaign advertising, further stoking the interest of these newly registered voters and the public in general. In such a charged political environment, concerns about the integrity of the process took on a particular urgency. One issue on which battle lines are frequently drawn is voter identification, especially requiring voters to show a photo ID. In 2012, thirty states required some form of identification, with eleven of those states requiring photo ID. Several other states had photo ID laws that were on hold pending legal challenges and U.S. Department of Justice investigations.

One argument, presented here by Chandler Davidson, contends that these complaints about fraud are part of a strategy to discourage or scare away potential voters. Voter ID laws are most likely to restrict turnout among minorities and the elderly, and the threat of fraud is minimal. To Davidson, voter ID laws are intended to promote the fortunes of the Republican Party and are little different from other attempts to suppress voter turnout, such as the poll tax.

The opposing argument, presented here by Hans von Spakovsky, is that voter fraud is a reality. He points to voters registered in multiple locations, voting more than once, illegally registered, paid an inducement to vote, and to felons voting as symptomatic of the lack of control over the voting process. Spakovsky supports voter-ID laws and rejects the idea that they will systematically discriminate against minorities or other groups.

Edward Foley argues that conservatives and liberals both have valid points. Even if voting fraud is minimal, he writes, it is real and should be a concern, as conservatives argue. Similarly, liberals are right to be concerned that the cost of obtaining a photo ID might discourage some citizens from voting. Foley suggests the solution is to delink the photo ID from voting. Instead, potential voters would be able to get free digital photos from government offices if they do not have one. They would have to show this photo when they register to vote. When a voter arrives at the polls to vote, poll workers could pull up an electronic file of the photo and match it to the person standing in front of them. This solution, Foley argues, ensures that anyone who wants to register can, while also guaranteeing that the person voting at the polling place is the same person who is registered under that name.

Chandler Davidson
The Historical Context of Voter Photo-ID Laws

The issue before the U.S. Supreme Court in the *Crawford* case (*Crawford v. Marion County Election Bd.* 2008) was whether a law (Indiana Senate Enrolled Act No. 483) passed by the Indiana legislature requiring most voters to show a photo ID in order to cast a ballot violates the First and Fourteenth Amendments. Plaintiffs argued that it works an unfair hardship on many people who do not have the government-issued documents that count as a legitimate ID. They argued that the law, in effect, constitutes a poll tax, inasmuch as there are costs to obtain the right kind of photo ID, costs that unduly burden many eligible citizens wanting to exercise their right to vote.

Given the long history of legally sanctioned disfranchisement of large and disparate groups of citizens, from the founding of the Republic to the recent past, the case raised important questions to scholars of voting rights. Indeed, Indiana's new law brought to mind events during the half-century following the Civil War, when the language of "progressive reform" cloaked the disfranchisement of blacks and poor whites in the South—those most likely to vote for Republican or Populist candidates. Actually adopted for partisan and racially discriminatory purposes, these laws were often presented as high-minded attacks on fraud—efforts to "purify" the electorate that would only inconvenience "vote sellers" or the ignorant and "shiftless."

To be sure, unlike today, when proponents of voter identification must strain mightily to find the rarest examples of fraud, particularly in-person voter fraud at the polls, in the nineteenth century there was widespread and readily admitted fraud. However, this was often committed against African Americans and the Republican Party to which they then overwhelmingly adhered. Louisiana senator and former governor Samuel D. McEnery stated in 1898 that his state's 1882 election law "was intended to make it the duty of the governor to treat the law as a formality and count in the Democrats." A leader of the 1890 Mississippi constitutional convention admitted that "it is no secret that there has not been a full vote and a fair count in Mississippi since 1875," which was the last year until 1967 in which blacks voted at all freely in the state. Nonetheless, these same Democrats invoked the language of reform in calling for a wide range of restrictions on the suffrage: registration acts, poll taxes, literacy and property tests, "understanding" qualifications, and white primaries, among others.

Between 1889 and 1913, for example, nine states outside the South made the ability to read English a prerequisite for voting. Literacy tests were said to reduce the influence of immigrants or African Americans who supported "bosses" and "demagogues." Moreover, between 1890 and 1908, seven of the 11 ex-Confederate states adopted state constitutional amendments allowing only literate voters or those with a certain amount of property to vote. There were sometimes loopholes like "understanding" qualifications or "grandfather" clauses that allowed some whites to vote who could not meet literacy or property tests. Shortly after passage of these amendments, less than 10% of African Americans managed to register to vote in most states, and no more than 15% in any.

The poll tax was one of the most notorious disfranchising mechanisms of its day. The current debate over the Indiana photo-ID requirement—as well as similar laws in other states—has led to claims that they are a "modern-day poll tax." This implies that the new Indiana law, too, falls within the ignominious American tradition of disfranchising laws passed under the guise of "good government" reform.

Frederick Ogden, perhaps the foremost scholar of the poll tax, wrote in the 1950s: "While critics of legalized restrictions on Negro voting may find it hard to discover any high moral tone in such activities, these restrictions reflected a movement for purifying the electoral process in southern states." Ogden quotes the editor of the *San Antonio Express* writing in 1902: "By requiring a poll tax receipt, secured six months previous to an election, fraudulent elections can be prevented almost entirely."

Other essays in this symposium address the nature and extent of burdens imposed on various subsets of Indiana citizens by the photo-ID law, and I shall forgo discussing them. Suffice it to say that the most accessible photo-ID in Indiana consists either of the state's driver's license or a state-issued ID card. Obtaining one or the other has been shown to be a good deal more difficult for some people than it might seem at first glance. At least 43,000 persons of voting age in Indiana are estimated to have neither.

The demographic characteristics of persons lacking the requisite ID are suggested by a November 2006 telephone survey of 987 randomly selected voting-age American citizens by the independent Opinion Research Corporation conducted for the Brennan Center for Justice at NYU School of Law: 11% did not have valid government-issued photo ID, while 18% of citizens 65 years of age or older lacked it, as did 25% of African Americans. The latter two demographic groups, the elderly and African Americans, are more likely to self-identify as Democrats—African-Americans disproportionately so. Elderly African Americans, who are even more unlikely than members of their ethnic group in general to have a photo ID, would be strongly predisposed to vote Democratic. In close elections, the additional burdens placed on both the elderly and African Americans by the photo-ID law could help elect Republican candidates. There is no reason to believe this national pattern is much different from that in Indiana.

Nonetheless, it is often asserted that such barriers should not prevent a truly motivated citizen from voting. In a classic article by Kelley, Ayres, and Bowen attempting to measure determinants of voter turnout, the authors make the following observation:

> A frequent objection to such efforts [to get out the vote] is that voters not interested enough to vote are not apt to vote wisely and so should be left alone. This view recalls the statement of a New York voter regarding the adequacy of the facilities for registering in New York City in 1964: "I sure do want to vote against that man . . . but I don't think I hate him enough to

stand on that line all day long." How much interest should a voter have to qualify him for voting? Enough to stand in line all day? For half a day? For two days? We cannot say, but those who think voting should be limited to the "interested" ought to be prepared to do so.

Their question, posed in terms of the burden of time alone, can also be posed with regard to money: particularly concerning the least well off, how large a monetary imposition should be placed on the right to vote before it becomes the functional equivalent of a poll tax? Regarding these twin burdens, two questions may be posed to help determine whether the Indiana photo-ID law should be interpreted according to the good-government language of its proponents: First, how will the application of the law help shape the Indiana electorate "to a size and composition deemed desirable by those in power," as Kelley, Ayres, and Bowen put it? In other words, to what extent is the law motivated by partisan efforts to disfranchise voters who are undesirable to Republicans and thus increase their chances of winning elections? Second, did supporters of the law demonstrate a significant degree of fraud of the kind the law was fashioned to prevent? Let us consider each question in turn.

While it is impossible to know the motives of those lawmakers who favored the photo-ID bill under consideration by the Indiana legislature in April 2005, we can ascertain whether it was passed by a partisan vote. Significantly, Indiana's photo-ID bill was one of at least 10 bills introduced by Republicans in state legislatures between 2005 and 2007 requiring voters to show a photo ID at the polls. Two of these states' bills were initially enjoined, and a second bill was introduced in one state. (Besides Indiana, the other states included Georgia, Florida, Missouri, Kansas, New Hampshire, Pennsylvania, Texas, and Wisconsin.) If the House and Senate votes for all 10 proposals are combined, 95.3% of the 1,222 Republicans voting and 2.1% of the 796 Democrats voting supported the bills. Moreover, in the five cases in which both houses passed a bill and a Republican was governor, he signed it. In the three cases in which both houses passed a bill and a Democrat was governor, he vetoed it. (In two cases, only one house passed a bill.) The Indiana vote was part of this pattern, although even more extreme. In the vote on Senate Bill 483, 85 Republicans voted for it and none against; 62 Democrats voted against it and none in favor. The Republican governor signed the bill into law.

Did supporters of the law demonstrate that there is a significant degree of fraud of the kind the law was fashioned to prevent? The debate over the extent and kind of vote fraud that exists in the United States today has been wide-spread and acerbic at least since the 2000 presidential election, and it shows no signs of abating. There are numerous kinds of vote fraud, and distinctions among them—which are necessary to determine the most effective means of their prevention—are often lost in popular debate. As critics of the Indiana law have asserted, the photo-ID requirement was implemented to prevent one type of fraud: voter impersonation at the polls on Election Day. Among the many kinds it does not prevent is that involving mail-in ballots, which some believe to be more common than impersonation at the polls. What makes the statute particularly suspect in the case of Indiana is the fact that there has not been a single prosecution for in-person vote fraud in the history of the state—a fact that Richard Posner, judge on the U.S. Court of Appeals for the Seventh Circuit and author of that court's split decision favoring Indiana, attributed to lax law enforcement.

Recent events in Texas are relevant in this regard. In both 2005 and 2007 Republicans in the legislature introduced photo-ID bills less restrictive than that in Indiana. In 2007, according to a newspaper reporter: "Republicans like the voter ID bill because they believe it will weaken Democrats, but can argue that it is a reasonable requirement" because it would prevent vote fraud. Not all Republicans, however, shared the belief that it would curtail fraud. Royal Masset, former political director of the Texas Republican Party, was one. He told the reporter he agreed that among his fellow Republicans it was "an article of religious faith that voter fraud is causing us to lose elections." He was not convinced. He did believe, however, that requiring photo IDs could cause enough of a drop-off in legitimate Democratic voting to add 3% to the Republican vote.

In January 2006, after his party's first failure to pass a photo-ID bill, Greg Abbott, the Republican attorney general of Texas, announced a "training initiative to identify, prosecute [and] prevent voter fraud." This was the most ambitious and costly effort in recent Texas history—perhaps ever—by the state's government to attack the alleged problem. "Vote fraud has been an epidemic in Texas for years, but it hasn't been treated like one," Abbott said. "It's time for that to change." He promised that his newly created Special Investigations Unit (SIU) would "help police departments, sheriff's offices, and district and county attorneys successfully identify, investigate and prosecute various types of voter fraud offences." Established with a $1.5 million grant from the governor's office, the SIU would have as one of its prime responsibilities investigating voter-fraud allegations, he said. Abbott targeted 44 counties containing 78% of registered voters in the state. According to the *Austin American-Statesman,* "Complaints originate from voting officials, district attorneys or citizens and are sent to the secretary of state or the attorney general. Each complaint is evaluated by a professional employee to determine whether the complaint is legitimate and warrants further investigation."

Such an initiative would seem to constitute a model of the aggressive, responsible, multi-level law-enforcement effort that Judge Posner seemed to believe had been lacking in Indiana. Moreover, given Republicans' desire to provide evidence of widespread voter fraud in order to justify new statutes criticized by Democrats and some media sources, one would expect Abbott to have conducted the effort with enthusiasm. What has been the result?

Texas is a large state, with thousands of elections occurring in a four-year period in its numerous governmental units. In 2006, there were 16.6 million persons of voting age, and of those, 13.1 million were registered to vote. An anti-immigration organization estimated that 1.7 million Texas inhabitants resided there illegally in 2007. Given these facts, one would expect an aggressive, centralized vote-fraud initiative by the state's highest law-enforcement officer to yield a sizable number of indictments during the more than 21 months of its existence if, in fact, vote fraud had reached "epidemic" proportions.

The data presented by Attorney General Abbot on his Web site told a different story. In the almost two years between the day the initiative was announced in late January 2006 and October 2007, 13 persons had either been indicted, found guilty, or sentenced for vote fraud, six on misdemeanor counts typically involving helping others with mail-in ballots. Of the 13, five were accused of having committed fraud before 2006, the year the initiative was announced, and the remaining eight in 2006. A total of 4.4 million Texans voted in the general elections for governor or U.S. senator that year, in addition to those who voted in primaries and local nonpartisan elections. At that point, six of the 13 persons mentioned above had not yet been found guilty. This, then, is the extent of vote fraud in Texas that has been uncovered after the announcement and implementation of the $1.5 million vote-fraud initiative. Moreover, of the seven found guilty and the six remaining under indictment, *none of the types of fraud they had been charged with would have been prevented by the photo-ID requirement advocated by Republicans in the 2007 legislative session.* That is to say, none involved voter impersonation at the polls. Most either involved political officials who were charged with engaging in illegal efforts to affect the election outcome, or persons who helped elderly or disabled friends with their mail-in ballots, apparently unaware of a law passed in 2003 requiring them to sign the envelope containing the friend's ballot before mailing it.

These data do not appear to be anomalous. A survey of the director or deputy director of all 88 Ohio boards of election in June 2005 found that a total of only four votes cast in the state's general elections in 2002 and 2004 (in which over nine million votes were cast) were judged ineligible and thus likely constituted actual voter fraud. Interviews by *New York Times* reporters with election-law-enforcement officials and academic experts suggest that the pattern in Ohio is not anomalous. Professor Richard L. Hasen, an election law expert at Loyola Law School, summed up knowledgeable opinion about vote fraud to the reporters as follows: "what we see is isolated, small-scale activities that often have not shown any kind of criminal intent."

While it is possible, as Judge Posner implied in his Seventh Circuit decision, that aggressive vote-fraud enforcement in Indiana might uncover its existence in the state, the Texas investigation suggests otherwise, and the burden of proof rests on those who allege that vote fraud there is widespread and of the kind that is deterred by a photo-ID requirement. Until that burden is responsibly shouldered by state authorities, the question of whether the Indiana voter-ID law has accomplished its ostensible purpose must be answered in the negative. When this conclusion is placed alongside our earlier findings that the legislative vote for the law was strictly along partisan lines and that the people most likely to be disfranchised by it are Democratic voters—particularly African Americans—Indiana's law appears to fit comfortably within the long and unsavory history of those in positions of power disfranchising blacks and less-well-off whites for partisan gain. Moreover, Indiana's attempt to justify its new law with claims of voter fraud is as dubious as those that justified the now unconstitutional poll tax.

A great deal of progress has been made over the past 50 years in combating racial discrimination in politics, thanks in part to such epochal events as passage of the Twenty-Fourth Amendment and the Voting Rights Act. However, race, class, and partisanship continue to be inextricably intertwined in the United States, just as they were from the end of Reconstruction to the Civil Rights Era. The 2005 Indiana voter-ID law, if the above analysis is correct, is an excellent example of this fact.

Hans von Spakovsky

Requiring Identification by Voters

Testimony Before the Texas Senate
Delivered March 10, 2009

I appreciate the invitation to be here today to discuss the importance of states such as Texas requiring individuals to authenticate their identity at the polls through photo and other forms of identification.

By way of background, I have extensive experience in voting matters, including both the administration of elections and the enforcement of federal voting rights laws. Prior to becoming a Legal Scholar at the Heritage Foundation, I was a member for two years of the Federal Election Commission. I spent four years at the Department of Justice as a career lawyer, including as Counsel to the Assistant Attorney General for Civil Rights. I also spent five years in Atlanta, Georgia, on the Fulton County Board of Registration and Elections, which is responsible for administering elections in the largest county in Georgia, a county that is almost half African American. I have published extensively on election and voting issues, including on the subject of voter ID.

Guaranteeing the integrity of elections requires having security throughout the entire election process, from voter registration to the casting of votes to the counting of ballots at the end of the day when the polls have closed. For example, jurisdictions that use paper ballots seal their ballot boxes when all of the ballots have been deposited, and election officials have step-by-step procedures for securing election ballots and other materials throughout the election process.

I doubt any of you think that it would be a good idea for a county to allow world wide Internet access to the computer it uses in its election headquarters to tabulate ballots and count votes—we are today a computer-literate generation and you understand that allowing that kind of outside access to the software used for counting votes would imperil the integrity of the election.

Requiring voters to authenticate their identity at the polling place is part and parcel of the same kind of security necessary to protect the integrity of elections. Every illegal vote steals the vote of a legitimate voter. Voter ID can prevent:

- impersonation fraud at the polls;
- voting under fictitious voter registrations;

- double voting by individuals registered in more than one state or locality; and
- voting by illegal aliens.

As the Commission on Federal Election Reform headed by President Jimmy Carter and Secretary of State James Baker said in 2005:

> The electoral system cannot inspire public confidence if no safeguards exist to deter or detect fraud or to confirm the identity of voters. Photo identification cards currently are needed to board a plane, enter federal buildings, and cash a check. Voting is equally important.

Voter fraud does exist, and criminal penalties imposed after the fact are an insufficient deterrent to protect against it. In the Supreme Court's voter ID case decided last year, the Court said that despite such criminal penalties:

> It remains true, however, that flagrant examples of such fraud in other parts of the country have been documented throughout this Nation's history by respected historians and journalists, that occasional examples have surfaced in recent years, and that [they] demonstrate that not only is the risk of voter fraud real but that it could affect the outcome of a close election.

The relative rarity of voter fraud prosecutions for impersonation fraud at the polls, as the Seventh Circuit Court of Appeals pointed out in the Indiana case, can be explained in part because the fraud cannot be detected without the tools—a voter ID—available to detect it. However, as I pointed out in a paper published by the Heritage Foundation last year, a grand jury in New York released a report in the mid-1980s detailing a widespread voter fraud conspiracy involving impersonation fraud at the polls that operated successfully for 14 years in Brooklyn without detection. That fraud resulted in thousands of fraudulent votes being cast in state and congressional elections and involved not only impersonation of legitimate voters at the polls, but voting under fictitious names that had been successfully registered without detection by local election officials. This fraud could have been easily stopped and detected if New York had required voters to authenticate their identity at the polls. According to the grand jury, the advent of mail-in registration was also a key factor in perpetrating the fraud. In recent elections, thousands of fraudulent voter registration forms have been detected by election officials. But given the minimal to nonexistent screening efforts engaged in by most election jurisdictions, there is no way to know how many others slipped through. In states without identification requirements, election officials have no way to prevent bogus votes from being cast by unscrupulous individuals based on fictitious voter registrations.

The problem of possible double voting by someone who is registered in two states is illustrated by one of the Indiana voters who was highlighted by the League of Women Voters in their amicus brief before the Supreme Court in the Indiana case. After an Indiana newspaper interviewed her, it turned out that the problems she encountered voting in Indiana stemmed from her trying to use a Florida driver's license to vote in Indiana. Not only did she have a Florida driver's license, but she was also registered to vote in Florida where she owned a second home. In fact, she had claimed residency in Florida by claiming a homestead exemption on her property taxes, which as you know is normally only available to residents. So the Indiana law worked perfectly as intended to prevent someone who could have illegally voted twice without detection.

I don't want to single out Texas, but just like Indiana, New York, and Illinois, Texas has a long and unfortunate history of voter fraud. In the late 1800s, for example, Harrison County was so infamous for its massive election fraud that the phrase "Harrison County Methods" became synonymous with election fraud. From Ballot Box 13 in Lyndon Johnson's 1948 Senate race, to recent reports of voting by illegal aliens in Bexar County, Texas does have individuals who are willing to risk criminal prosecution in order to win elections. I do not claim that there is massive voter fraud in Texas or anywhere else. In fact, as a former election official, I think we do a good job overall in administering our elections. But the potential for abuse exists, and there are many close elections that could turn on a very small number of votes. There are enough incidents of voter fraud to make it very clear that we must take the steps necessary to make it hard to commit. Requiring voter ID is just one such common sense step.

Not only does voter ID help prevent fraudulent voting, but where it has been implemented, it has not reduced turnout. There is no evidence that voter ID decreases the turnout of voters or has a disparate impact on minority voters, the poor, or the elderly—the overwhelming majority of Americans have photo ID or can easily obtain one.

Numerous studies have borne this out. A study by a University of Missouri professor of turnout in Indiana showed that turnout actually increased by about two percentage points overall in Indiana after the voter ID law went into effect. There was no evidence that counties with higher percentages of minority, poor, elderly or less-educated populations suffered any reduction in voter turnout. In fact, "the only consistent and statistically significant impact of photo ID in Indiana is to increase voter turnout in counties with a greater percentage of Democrats relative to other counties."

The Heritage Foundation released a study in September of 2007 that analyzed 2004 election turnout data for all states. It found that voter ID laws do not reduce the turnout of voters, including African Americans and Hispanics—such voters were just as likely to vote in states with ID as in states where just their name was asked at the polling place.

A study by professors at the Universities of Delaware and Nebraska–Lincoln examined data from the 2000, 2002, 2004, and 2006 elections. At both the aggregate and individual levels, the study found that voter ID laws do not affect turnout including across racial/ethnic/socioeconomic lines. The study concluded that "concerns about voter identification laws affecting turnout are much ado about nothing."

In 2007 as part of the MIT/CalTech Voter Project, an MIT professor did an extensive national survey of 36,500 individuals about Election Day practices. The survey found:

- overwhelming support for photo ID requirements across ethnic and racial lines with "over 70% of Whites, Hispanics and Blacks support[ing] the requirement"; and
- Only twenty-three people out of the entire 36,500 person sample said that they were not allowed to vote because of voter ID, although the survey did not indicate whether they were even eligible to vote or used provisional ballots.

A similar study by John Lott in 2006 also found no effect on voter turnout, and in fact, found an indication that efforts to reduce voter fraud such as voter ID may have a positive impact on voter turnout. That is certainly true in a case study of voter fraud in Greene County, Alabama that I wrote about recently for the Heritage Foundation. In that county, voter turnout went up after several successful voter fraud prosecutions instilled new confidence in local voters in the integrity of the election process.

Recent election results in Georgia and Indiana also confirm that the suppositions that voter ID will hurt minority turnout are incorrect. Turnout in both states went up dramatically in 2008 in both the presidential preference primary and the general election.

In Georgia, there was record turnout in the 2008 presidential primary election—over 2 million voters, more than twice as much as in 2004 when the voter photo ID law was not in effect. The number of African-Americans voting in the 2008 primary also doubled from 2004. In fact, there were 100,000 more votes in the Democratic Primary than in the Republican Primary. And the number of individuals who had to vote with a provisional ballot because they had not gotten the free photo ID available from the state was less that 0.01%.

In the general election, Georgia, with one of the strictest voter ID laws in the nation, had the largest turnout in its history—more than 4 million voters. Democratic turnout was up an astonishing 6.1 percentage points from the 2004 election. Overall turnout in Georgia went up 6.7 percentage points, the second highest increase of any state in the country. The black share of the statewide vote increased from 25% in 2004 to 30% in 2008. By contrast, the Democratic turnout in the nearby state of Mississippi, also a state with a high percentage of black voters but without a voter ID requirement, increased by only 2.35 percentage points.

I should point out that the Georgia voter ID law was upheld in final orders issued by every state and federal court in Georgia that reviewed the law, including most recently by the Eleventh Circuit Court of Appeals. Just as in Texas, various organizations in Georgia made the specious claims that there were hundreds of thousands of Georgians without photo ID. Yet when the federal district court dismissed all of their claims, the court pointed out that after two years of litigation, none of the plaintiff organizations like the NAACP had been able to produce a single individual or member who did not have a photo ID or could not easily obtain one. The district court judge concluded that this "failure to identify those individuals is particularly acute in light of the Plaintiffs' contention that a large number of Georgia voters lack acceptable Photo ID . . . the fact that Plaintiffs, in spite of their efforts, have failed to uncover anyone who can attest to the fact that he/she will be prevented from voting provides significant support for a conclusion that the photo ID requirement does not unduly burden the right to vote."

In Indiana, which the Supreme Court said has the strictest voter ID law in the country, turnout in the Democratic presidential preference primary in 2008 quadrupled from the 2004 election when the photo ID law was not in effect— in fact, there were 862,000 more votes cast in the Democratic primary than the Republican primary. In the general election in November, the turnout of Democratic voters increased by 8.32 percentage points from 2004, the largest increase in Democratic turnout of any state in the nation. The neighboring state of Illinois, with no photo ID requirement and President Obama's home state, had an increase in Democratic turnout of only 4.4 percentage points—nearly half of Indiana's increase.

Just as in the federal case in Georgia, the federal court in Indiana noted the complete inability of the plaintiffs in that case to produce anyone who would not be able to vote because of the photo ID law:

> Despite apocalyptic assertions of wholesale vote disenfranchisement, Plaintiffs have produced not a single piece of evidence of any identifiable registered voter who would be prevented from voting pursuant to [the photo ID law] because of his or her inability to obtain the necessary photo identification.

One final point on the claims that requiring an ID, even when it is free, is a "poll tax" because of the incidental costs like possible travel to a registrar's office or obtaining a birth certificate that may be involved. That claim was also raised in Georgia. The federal court dismissed this claim, pointing out that such an "argument represents a dramatic overstatement of what fairly constitutes a 'poll tax'. Thus, the imposition of tangential burdens does not transform a regulation into a poll tax. Moreover, the cost of time and transportation cannot plausibly qualify as a prohibited poll tax because those same 'costs' also result from voter registration and in-person voting requirements, which one would not reasonably construe as a poll tax."

We are [the only] one of about one hundred democracies that do not uniformly require voters to present photo ID when they vote. All of those countries administer that law without any problems and without any reports that their citizens are in any way unable to vote because of that requirement. In fact, our southern neighbor Mexico, which has a much larger population in poverty than Texas or the United States, requires both a photo ID and a thumbprint to vote—and turnout has increased in their elections since this requirement went into effect in the 1990s.

Requiring voters to authenticate their identity is a perfectly reasonable and easily met requirement. It is supported by the vast majority of voters of all races and ethnic backgrounds. As the Supreme Court said, voter ID protects the integrity and reliability of the electoral process. Texas has a valid and legitimate state interest not only in deterring and detecting voter fraud, but in maintaining the confidence of its citizens in the security of its elections.

Edward B. Foley

Is There a Middle Ground in the Voter ID Debate?

The left and the right are increasingly trading accusations in the debate over new voter ID laws, and the rhetoric is heating up. Georgia's new law has been called the new "Jim Crow," although similar measures have recently been enacted in non-Southern states like Arizona and Indiana. Defenders of such measures say opponents are willfully blind to the possibility of fraud unless a photo ID requirement is imposed.

Given that heels are digging in, it might seem naïve to search for a compromise. Yet it is imperative to do so. Election laws cannot serve their intended function unless they are accepted by both the left and the right as fair means for conducting the competition between these two political camps to win approval from the citizenry. If the right insists that a voter ID law is necessary to make the electoral process legitimate, while the left simultaneously says that the same ID law makes the electoral process illegitimate, then it becomes impossible for our society to settle upon rules of procedure for a fair contest between opposing political forces.

With that observation in mind, it is worth searching for a middle position on the voter ID issue, even if at the outset a successful conclusion to this endeavor is far from assured.

In principle, some form of identification requirement should not be objectionable to liberals. Voting is an activity that only the eligible are entitled to engage in, and so it is not unreasonable to ask citizens for some information to demonstrate their eligibility. For example, liberals do not generally object to the traditional requirements that voters provide their names, addresses, and signatures before casting their ballots.

Conservatives, however, say that these traditional requirements no longer suffice because an imposter easily could forge a signature and, in contemporary society, poll workers are unlikely to distinguish eligible from ineligible voters simply by looking at their visages. Therefore, according to these conservatives, a photo ID is necessary to show the voter's eligibility. The picture will show that the person standing before the poll worker is the same one who, according to the poll book, is registered to vote under that particular name and address.

Liberals object, however, to a photo ID requirement on the ground that it is burdensome to citizens who do not have a driver's license, passport, or comparable document. Part of the burden is cost, which can be addressed by making a valid photo ID free of charge. Another part of the burden is the difficulty of accessing locations where no-charge IDs may be obtained. That problem could be remedied by making them available at any post office, public library, or public school, as well as other social service agencies (hospitals, police stations, and so forth).

But a remaining concern of liberals is that, even if photo IDs are easily obtained, many voters will fail to bring them to the polls on Election Day. Public reminders may be issued, including public service announcements on TV. Still, some voters are forgetful, perhaps senior citizens more so than younger adults, and thus the obligation to carry an ID to the polls might serve as a barrier for these eligible citizens.

A potential solution to this problem is to break the connection with the photo requirement and the obligation to produce identification at the polls. Eligible citizens could be required to provide a photograph at the time they *register* to vote, and poll workers would match this photograph with the image of the person standing in front of them. Given the availability of digital photography, the photos of registered voters could be stored in electronic poll books and easily "pulled up" with a click of a computer mouse when voters sign in to vote.

These electronic photos should satisfy the anti-fraud concerns of conservatives as much as printed photos that citizens would be required to bring to the polls. After all, the purpose of a *photo* ID requirement— beyond the traditional requirement of providing one's name, address, and signature—is to compare the likeness of the person seeking to vote with the photograph that is linked to the name and address of the registered voter (whom the flesh-and-blood person purports to be). This function can just as easily occur by comparing the likeness of the person with the computerized photo in the electronic poll book, which was linked to the name and address of the registered voter at time of registration.

Of course, to satisfy the concerns of liberals, a requirement to provide a digital photograph at time of registration would have to address the cost and accessibility issues identified earlier. But, again, a system in which citizens could go to a wide variety of public offices (including post offices, libraries, and schools), where clerical officials would be authorized to take a digital photo of the citizen and then email it to the applicable board of election, without any cost to the citizen, would satisfactorily address these concerns. In addition, for those citizens seeking to register by mail, they could be permitted to email their own digital photos of themselves, if they conform to "passport style" specifications. In this way, nursing homes and other senior citizens centers could take "at home" digital photos of their elderly residents and email them to the board of election, without requiring these elderly citizens to travel to a post office, library, or other public building. (Another comparable approach would be to permit individuals to become a kind of "deputized notary public," trained to take the right sort of digital photo, so that other citizens could meet with any of these designated individuals whenever and wherever it would be convenient.) Moreover, as an alternative, those citizens who do not submit a digital photo at time of registration could provide the more conventional form of photo ID (like a driver's license) at time of voting, making either approach an equally available option, depending solely on which the particular citizen prefers.

Liberals might still complain that any form of photo ID requirement is unnecessary to reduce the risk of fraud and, in any event, will be ineffective if inapplicable to absentee voting. The point about absentee voting is surely a valid one. (For this reason, one wonders whether it is wise to expand the availability of at-home voting, as many states are doing.) If individuals sitting at home can vote without providing any form of photo ID, the opportunity for fraud exists even if voters who go to the polls are subject to a photograph requirement. One way around this discrepancy would be to require absentee voters to submit a photocopy of their photo ID when they mail in their absentee ballot. Or, if the digital photo proposal is adopted, absentee voters could mail with their ballot a printed copy of the digital photo they submitted as part of their registration. In the future, absentee voters might simply email a second copy of their digital photo when emailing their absentee ballots.

A liberal objection to any form of photo ID requirement is more difficult to sustain, particularly if the goal is a compromise acceptable to both sides. To be sure, the frequency of fraud at polling places that would be preventable by a photo ID requirement may be fairly low—there is clearly a debate between conservatives and liberals on this factual point—but it is not non-existent. Liberals acknowledge the possibility of fraudulent absentee voting, saying that its risk is greater than polling place voting. But if an imposter can obtain and submit an absentee ballot, he or she can show up at a polling place purporting to be someone else. Even if the latter is more difficult, the lack of a photo ID requirement makes this deceit easier than it otherwise would be.

Thus, an acceptable compromise must take the form of a photo ID requirement that is not unduly onerous. The proposal here, to permit voters to submit an easily obtainable and no-charge digital photo at the time they register, as an alternative to having to produce a driver's license or comparable photo ID when they go to the polls on Election Day, satisfies this objective. Pursuing this proposal would enable both sides to move beyond the vituperative rhetoric that increasingly, and unfortunately, is clouding the policy debate on this topic.

DISCUSSION QUESTIONS

1. Would you approve of a proposal that all voters had to show photo identification at polling places? Do you think it would decrease turnout? If so, is that a reasonable cost to pay to ensure that people cannot vote using another person's name? Or should turnout be prioritized and the risk that some people will vote inappropriately be accepted as a reasonable risk?

2. Would you have any concerns with having voting conducted over the Internet or by mail (as is done in Washington and Oregon)? Are there benefits that outweigh these concerns?

3. What might be some possible objections raised against Foley's proposal by the two sides in the voter-ID debate?

4. As a general matter, do you believe there is a trade-off between maximizing turnout and minimizing fraud? Or are these goals compatible? Why?

11

Political Parties: Red America versus Blue America—Are We Polarized?

In 1992, presidential nominee contender Patrick Buchanan famously stated at the Republican National Convention that the United States was in the midst of a culture war that posited traditional, conservative social values against liberal, secular values. Bill Clinton's defeat of President George H. W. Bush seemed to defuse that idea: Clinton was a southern Democrat who had pushed his party toward the ideological center and, although garnering only 43 percent of the vote, he won states in all regions of the country. His 1996 victory was broader, adding some states he had lost in 1992. In the 2000 presidential election, however, a striking regional pattern emerged in the results. Al Gore, the Democratic candidate, did well on the coasts and in the upper Midwest, while George W. Bush, the Republican candidate, picked up the remaining states. Many analysts were struck by this "red state/blue state" pattern—named after the coloring of the states on post-election maps—and suggested that it told us something more fundamental about American politics. Indeed, these analysts argued, Patrick Buchanan was in large measure right: the American public was deeply divided and polarized and in many respects living in two different worlds culturally. This polarization showed up not only in voting, but in presidential approval ratings, with the partisan gap in evaluations of Bill Clinton and George W. Bush being larger than for any previous presidents. The 2004 presidential election looked very much like 2000: with a few exceptions, the red states stayed red and the blue states stayed blue. Eighty-five percent of conservatives voted for Bush; the same percentage of liberals voted for Kerry; and moderates split 54–45 percent for Kerry.

In 2008, Barack Obama campaigned on the idea of practicing a new kind of politics that set aside red-America/blue-America distinctions. His victory scattered the red/blue map, as he picked up nine states Bush had won in 2004. Shortly into his presidency, however, Obama's policy plans became engulfed in deep partisan and ideological strife. Like those of Clinton and Bush before him, President Obama's approval ratings were sharply different among Democrats and Republicans. And like those two presidents, Obama invigorated his opponents. Where the Bush presidency played a major role in galvanizing the liberal blogosphere, Obama's contributed to the rise of the Tea Party, a political movement deeply skeptical about the effectiveness and growing size of American government. Victorious in the 2010 election, the Tea Party suffered a set back in 2012 when President Obama was reelected.

Is America deeply polarized along partisan lines? Is there a culture war? Is the red-America/blue-America split real? Is there division on certain highly charged issues but not on most others? Are the divisions just artifacts of the way that survey questions are worded? In this debate, the political scientists James Q. Wilson and Morris Fiorina agree that the political elite—elected leaders, the news media, and interest groups—are polarized, but they disagree on the answers to the rest of the questions. Wilson argues that the cultural split is deep and is reflected in party competition and the public opinion of partisans within and across the red and blue states. Fiorina counters that the idea of a culture war is vastly exaggerated—there might be a skirmish, but there is no war.

John Judis aligns more with Wilson. Although not a fan of the Tea Party, Judis nonetheless argues that it is a real movement with the potential for lasting influence. Its issues, anxieties, and ideological orientation, he states, draw on a deep populist tradition in American politics. As with other populist movements, supporters see the Tea Party as engaged in a struggle to define America, a struggle between "the people" and "the elites."

Morris P. Fiorina

What Culture Wars? Debunking the Myth of a Polarized America

> "There is a religious war going on in this country, a cultural war as critical to the kind of nation we shall be as the Cold War itself, for this war is for the soul of America."

With those ringing words insurgent candidate Pat Buchanan fired up his supporters at the 1992 Republican National Convention. To be sure, not all delegates cheered Buchanan's call to arms, which was at odds with the "kinder, gentler" image that George H. W. Bush had attempted to project. Election analysts later included Buchanan's fiery words among the factors contributing to the defeat of President Bush, albeit one of lesser importance than the slow economy and the repudiation of his "Read my lips, no new taxes" pledge.

In the years since Buchanan's declaration of cultural war, the idea of a clash of cultures has become a common theme in discussions of American politics. The culture war metaphor refers to a displacement of the classic economic conflicts that animated twentieth-century politics in the advanced democracies by newly emergent moral and cultural ones. The literature generally attributes Buchanan's inspiration to a 1991 book, *Culture Wars*, by sociologist James Davison Hunter, who divided Americans into the culturally "orthodox" and the culturally "progressive" and argued that increasing conflict was inevitable.

No one has embraced the concept of the culture war more enthusiastically than journalists, ever alert for subjects that have "news value." Conflict is high in news value. Disagreement, division, polarization, battles, and war make good copy. Agreement, consensus, moderation, compromise, and peace do not. Thus, the notion of a culture war fits well with the news sense of journalists who cover politics. Their reports tell us that contemporary voters are sharply divided on moral issues. As David Broder wrote in the *Washington Post* in November 2000, "The divide went deeper than politics. It reached into the nation's psyche. . . . It was the moral dimension that kept Bush in the race."

Additionally, it is said that close elections do not reflect indifferent or ambivalent voters; rather, such elections reflect evenly matched blocs of deeply committed partisans. According to a February 2002 report in *USA Today*, "When George W. Bush took office, half the country cheered and the other half seethed"; some months later the *Economist* wrote that "such political divisions cannot easily be shifted by any president, let alone in two years, because they reflect deep demographic divisions. . . . The 50-50 nation appears to be made up of two big, separate voting blocks, with only a small number of swing voters in the middle."

The 2000 election brought us the familiar pictorial representation of the culture war in the form of the "red" and "blue" map of the United States. Vast areas of the heartland appeared as Republican red, while coastal and Great Lakes states took on a Democratic blue hue. Pundits reified the colors on the map, treating them as prima facie evidence of deep cultural divisions: Thus "Bush knew that the landslide he had wished for in 2000 . . . had vanished into the values chasm separating the blue states from the red ones" (John Kenneth White, in *The Values Divide*). In the same vein, the *Boston Herald* reported Clinton adviser Paul Begala as saying, on November 18, 2000, that "tens of millions of good people in Middle America voted Republican. But if you look closely at that map you see a more complex picture. You see the state where James Byrd was lynched—dragged behind a pickup truck until his body came apart—it's red. You see the state where Matthew Shepard was crucified on a split-rail fence for the crime of being gay—it's red. You see the state where right-wing extremists blew up a federal office building and murdered scores of federal employees—it's red."

Claims of bitter national division were standard fare after the 2000 elections, and few commentators publicly challenged them. On the contrary, the belief in a fractured nation was expressed even by high-level political operatives. Republican pollster Bill McInturff commented to the *Economist* in January 2001 that "we have two massive colliding forces. One is rural, Christian, religiously conservative. [The other] is socially tolerant, pro-choice, secular, living in New England and the Pacific Coast." And Matthew Dowd, a Bush re-election strategist, explained to the *Los Angeles Times* why Bush has not tried to expand his electoral base: "You've got 80 to 90 percent of the country that look at each other like they are on separate planets."

The journalistic drumbeat continues unabated. A November 2003 report from the Pew Research Center led E. J. Dionne Jr. of the *Washington Post* to comment: "The red states get redder, the blue states get bluer, and the political map of the United States takes on the coloration of the Civil War."

And as the 2004 election approaches, commentators see a continuation, if not an intensification, of the culture war. *Newsweek*'s Howard Fineman wrote in October 2003, "The culture war between the Red and Blue Nations has erupted again—big time—and will last until Election Day next year. Front lines are all over, from the Senate to the Pentagon to Florida to the Virginia suburbs where, at the Bush-Cheney 2004 headquarters, they are blunt about the shape of the battle: 'The country's split 50–50 again,' a top aide told me, 'just as it was in 2000.' "

In sum, observers of contemporary American politics have apparently reached a new consensus around the proposition that old disagreements about economics now pale in comparison to new divisions based on sexuality, morality, and religion, divisions so deep and bitter as to justify talk of war in describing them.

Yet research indicates otherwise. Publicly available databases show that the culture war script embraced by journalists and politicos lies somewhere between simple exaggeration and sheer nonsense. There is no culture war in the United States; no battle for the soul of America rages, at least none that most Americans are aware of.

Certainly, one can find a few warriors who engage in noisy skirmishes. Many of the activists in the political parties and the various cause groups do hate each other and regard themselves as combatants in a war. But their hatreds and battles are not shared by the great mass of Americans—certainly nowhere near "80–90 percent of the country"—who are for the most part moderate in their views and tolerant in their manner. A case in point: To their embarrassment, some GOP senators recently learned that ordinary Americans view gay marriage in somewhat less apocalyptic terms than do the activists in the Republican base.

If swing voters have disappeared, how did the six blue states in which George Bush ran most poorly in 2000 all elect Republican governors in 2002 (and how did Arnold Schwarzenegger run away with the 2003 recall in blue California)? If almost all voters have already made up their minds about their 2004 votes, then why did John Kerry surge to a 14-point trial-heat lead when polls offered voters the prospect of a Kerry-McCain ticket? If voter partisanship has hardened into concrete, why do virtually identical majorities in both red and blue states favor divided control of the presidency and Congress, rather than unified control by their party? Finally, and ironically, if voter positions have become so uncompromising, why did a recent CBS story titled "Polarization in America" report that 76 percent of Republicans, 87 percent of Democrats, and 86 percent of Independents would like to see elected officials compromise more rather than stick to their principles?

Still, how does one account for reports that have almost 90 percent of Republicans planning to vote for Bush and similarly high numbers of Democrats planning to vote for Kerry? The answer is that while voter *positions* have not polarized, their *choices* have. There is no contradiction here; positions and choices are not the same thing. Voter choices are functions of their positions and the positions and actions of the candidates they choose between.

Republican and Democratic elites unquestionably have polarized. But it is a mistake to assume that such elite polarization is equally present in the broader public. It is not. However much they may claim that they are responding to the public, political elites do not take extreme positions because *voters* make them. Rather, by presenting them with polarizing alternatives, elites make voters appear polarized, but the reality shows through clearly when voters have a choice of more moderate alternatives—as with the aforementioned Republican governors.

Republican strategists have bet the Bush presidency on a high-risk gamble. Reports and observation indicate that they are attempting to win in 2004 by getting out the votes of a few million Republican-leaning evangelicals who did not vote in 2000, rather than by attracting some modest proportion of 95 million other non-voting Americans, most of them moderates, not to mention moderate Democratic voters who could have been persuaded to back a genuinely compassionate conservative. Such a strategy leaves no cushion against a negative turn of events and renders the administration vulnerable to a credible Democratic move toward the center. Whether the Democrats can capitalize on their opportunity remains to be seen.

James Q. Wilson

How Divided Are We?

The 2004 election left our country deeply divided over whether our country is deeply divided. For some, America is indeed a polarized nation, perhaps more so today than at any time in living memory. In this view, yesterday's split over Bill Clinton has given way to today's even more acrimonious split between Americans who detest George Bush and Americans who detest John Kerry, and similar divisions will persist as long as angry liberals and angry conservatives continue to confront each other across the political abyss. Others, however, believe that most Americans are moderate centrists, who, although disagreeing over partisan issues in 2004, harbor no deep ideological hostility. I take the former view.

By polarization I do not have in mind partisan disagreements alone. These have always been with us. Since popular voting began in the 19th century, scarcely any winning candidate has received more than 60 percent of the vote, and very few losers have received less than 40 percent. Inevitably, Americans will differ over who should be in the White House. But this does not necessarily mean they are polarized.

By polarization I mean something else: an intense commitment to a candidate, a culture, or an ideology that sets people in one group definitively apart from people in another, rival group. Such a condition is revealed when a candidate for public office is regarded by a competitor and his supporters not simply as wrong but as corrupt or wicked; when one way of thinking about the world is assumed to be morally superior to any other way; when one set of political beliefs is considered to be entirely correct and a rival set wholly wrong. In extreme form, as defined by Richard Hofstadter in *The Paranoid Style in American Politics* (1965), polarization can entail the belief that the other side is in thrall to a secret conspiracy that is using devious means to obtain control over society. Today's versions might go like this: "Liberals employ their dominance of the media, the universities, and Hollywood to enforce a radically secular agenda"; or, "conservatives, working through the religious Right and the big corporations, conspired with their hired neocon advisers to invade Iraq for the sake of oil."

Polarization is not new to this country. It is hard to imagine a society more divided than ours was in 1800, when pro-British, pro-commerce New Englanders supported John Adams for the presidency while pro-French, pro-agriculture Southerners backed Thomas Jefferson. One sign of this hostility was the passage of the Alien and Sedition Acts in 1798; another was that in 1800, just as in 2000, an extremely close election was settled by a struggle in one state (New York in 1800, Florida in 2000).

The fierce contest between Abraham Lincoln and George McClellan in 1864 signaled another national division, this one over the conduct of the Civil War. But thereafter, until recently, the nation ceased to be polarized in that sense. Even in the half-century from 1948 to (roughly) 1996, marked as it was by sometimes strong expressions of feeling over whether the presidency should go to Harry Truman or Thomas Dewey, to Dwight Eisenhower or Adlai Stevenson, to John F. Kennedy or Richard Nixon, to Nixon or Hubert Humphrey, and so forth, opinion surveys do not indicate widespread detestation of one candidate or the other, or of the people who supported him.

Now they do. Today, many Americans and much of the press regularly speak of the president as a dimwit, a charlatan, or a knave. A former Democratic presidential candidate has asserted that Bush "betrayed" America by launching a war designed to benefit his friends and cor-porate backers. A senior Democratic Senator has characterized administration policy as a series of "lies, lies, and more lies" and has accused Bush of plotting a "mindless, needless, senseless, and reckless" war. From the other direction, similar expressions of popular disdain have been directed at Senator John Kerry (and before him at President Bill Clinton); if you have not heard them, that may be because (unlike many of my relatives) you do not live in Arkansas or Texas or other locales where the *New York Times* is not read. In these places, Kerry is widely spoken of as a scoundrel.

In the 2004 presidential election, over two-thirds of Kerry voters said they were motivated explicitly by the desire to defeat Bush. By early 2005, President Bush's approval rating, which stood at 94 percent among Republicans, was only 18 percent among Democrats—the largest such gap in the history of the Gallup poll. These data, moreover, were said to reflect a mutual revulsion between whole geographical sections of the country, the so-called Red (Republican) states versus the so-called Blue (Democratic) states. As summed up by the distinguished social scientist who writes humor columns under the name of Dave Barry, residents of Red states are "ignorant racist fascist knuckle-dragging NASCAR-obsessed cousin-marrying roadkill-eating tobacco-juice-dribbling gun-fondling religious fanatic rednecks," while Blue-state residents are "godless unpatriotic pierced-nose Volvo-driving France-loving leftwing Communist latte-sucking tofu-chomping holistic-wacko neurotic vegan weenie perverts."

To be sure, other scholars differ with Dr. Barry. To them, polarization, although a real enough phenomenon, is almost entirely confined to a small number of political elites and members of Congress. In *Culture War?*, which bears the subtitle "The Myth of a Polarized America," Morris Fiorina of Stanford argues that policy differences between voters in Red and Blue states are really quite small, and that most are in general agreement even on issues like abortion and homosexuality.

But the extent of polarization cannot properly be measured by the voting results in Red and Blue states. Many of these states are in fact deeply divided internally between liberal and conservative areas, and gave the nod to one candidate or the other by only a narrow margin. Inferring the views of individual citizens from the gross results of presidential balloting is a questionable procedure.

Nor does Fiorina's analysis capture the very real and very deep division over an issue like abortion. Between 1973, when *Roe v. Wade* was decided, and now, he writes, there has been no change in the degree to which people will or will not accept any one of six reasons to justify an abortion: (1) the woman's health is endangered; (2) she became pregnant because of a rape; (3) there is a strong chance of a fetal defect; (4) the family has a low income; (5) the woman is not married; and (6) the woman simply wants no more children. Fiorina may be right about that. Nevertheless, only about 40 percent of all Americans will support abortion for any of the last three reasons in his series, while over 80 percent will support it for one or another of the first three.

In other words, almost all Americans are for abortion in the case of maternal emergency, but fewer than half if it is simply a matter of the mother's preference. That split—a profoundly important one—has remained in place for over three decades, and it affects how people vote. In 2000 and again in 2004, 70 percent of those who thought abortion should always be legal voted for Al Gore or John Kerry, while over 70 percent of those who thought it should always be illegal voted for George Bush.

Division is just as great over other high-profile issues. Polarization over the war in Iraq, for example, is more pronounced than any war-related controversy in at least a half-century. In the fall of 2005, according to Gallup, 81 percent of Democrats but only 20 percent of Republicans thought the war in Iraq was a mistake. During the Vietnam war, by contrast, itself a famously contentious cause, there was more unanimity across party lines, whether for or against: in late 1968 and early 1969, about equal numbers of Democrats and Republicans thought the intervention there was a mistake. Pretty much the same was true of Korea: in early 1951, 44 percent of Democrats and 61 percent of Republicans thought the war was a mistake—a partisan split, but nowhere near as large as the one over our present campaign in Iraq.

Polarization, then, is real. But what explains its growth? And has it spread beyond the political elites to influence the opinions and attitudes of ordinary Americans?

The answer to the first question, I suspect, can be found in the changing politics of Congress, the new competitiveness of the mass media, and the rise of new interest groups.

That Congress is polarized seems beyond question. When, in 1998, the House deliberated whether to impeach President Clinton, all but four Republican members voted for at least one of the impeachment articles, while only five Democrats voted for even one. In the Senate, 91 percent of Republicans voted to convict on at least one article; every single Democrat voted for acquittal.

The impeachment issue was not an isolated case. In 1993, President Clinton's budget passed both the House and the Senate without a single Republican vote in favor. The same deep partisan split occurred over taxes and supplemental appropriations. Nor was this a blip: since 1950, there has been a steady increase in the percentage of votes in Congress pitting most Democrats against most Republicans.

In the midst of the struggle to pacify Iraq, Howard Dean, the chairman of the Democratic National Committee, said the war could not be won and Nancy Pelosi, the leader of the House Democrats, endorsed the view that American forces should be brought home as soon as possible. By contrast, although there was congressional grumbling (mostly by Republicans) about Korea and complaints (mostly by Democrats) about Vietnam, and although Senator George Aiken of Vermont famously proposed that we declare victory and withdraw, I cannot remember party leaders calling for unconditional surrender.

The reasons for the widening fissures in Congress are not far to seek. Each of the political parties was once a coalition of dissimilar forces: liberal Northern Democrats and conservative Southern Democrats, liberal coastal Republicans and conservative Midwestern Republicans. No longer; the realignments of the South (now overwhelmingly Republican) and of New England (now strongly Democratic) have all but eliminated legislators who deviate from the party's leadership. Conservative Democrats and liberal Republicans are endangered species now approaching extinction. At the same time, the ideological gap between the parties is growing: if there was once a large overlap between Democrats and Republicans— remember "Tweedledum and Tweedledee"?—today that congruence has almost disappeared. By the late 1990s, virtually every Democrat was more liberal than virtually every Republican.

The result has been not only intense partisanship but a sharp rise in congressional incivility. In 1995, a Republican-controlled Senate passed a budget that President Clinton proceeded to veto; in the loggerhead that followed, many federal agencies shut down (in a move that backfired on the Republicans). Congressional debates have seen an increase not only in heated exchanges but in the number of times a representative's words are either ruled out of order or "taken down" (that is, written by the clerk and then read aloud, with the offending member being asked if he or she wishes to withdraw them).

It has been suggested that congressional polarization is exacerbated by new districting arrangements that make each House seat safe for either a Democratic or a Republican incumbent. If only these seats were truly competitive, it is said, more centrist legislators would be elected. That seems plausible, but David C. King of Harvard has shown that it is wrong: in the House, the more competitive the district, the more extreme the views of the winner. This odd finding is apparently the consequence of a nomination process dominated by party activists. In primary races, where turnout is low (and seems to be getting lower), the ideologically motivated tend to exercise a preponderance of influence.

All this suggests a situation very unlike the half-century before the 1990s, if perhaps closer to certain periods in the eighteenth and nineteenth centuries. Then, too, incivility was common in Congress, with members not only passing the most scandalous remarks about each other but on occasion striking their rivals with canes or fists. Such partisan feeling ran highest when Congress was deeply divided over slavery before the Civil War and over Reconstruction after it. Today the issues are different, but the emotions are not dissimilar.

Next, the mass media: Not only are they themselves increasingly polarized, but consumers are well aware of it and act on that awareness. Fewer people now subscribe to newspapers or watch the network evening news. Although some of this decline may be explained by a preference for entertainment over news, some undoubtedly reflects the growing conviction that the mainstream press generally does not tell the truth, or at least not the whole truth.

In part, media bias feeds into, and off, an increase in business competition. In the 1950s, television news amounted to a brief 30-minute interlude in the day's programming, and not a very profitable one at that; for the rest of the time, the three networks supplied us with westerns and situation comedies. Today, television news is a vast, growing, and very profitable venture by the many broadcast and cable outlets that supply news twenty-four hours a day, seven days a week.

The news we get is not only more omnipresent, it is also more competitive and hence often more adversarial. When there were only three television networks, and radio stations were forbidden by the fairness doctrine from broadcasting controversial views, the media gravitated toward the middle of the ideological spectrum, where the large markets could be found. But now that technology has created cable news and the Internet, and now that the fairness doctrine has by and large been repealed, many media outlets find their markets at the ideological extremes.

Here is where the sharper antagonism among political leaders and their advisers and associates comes in. As one journalist has remarked about the change in his profession, "We don't deal in facts [any longer], but in attributed opinions." Or, these days, in unattributed opinions. And those opinions are more intensely rivalrous than was once the case.

The result is that, through commercial as well as ideological self-interest, the media contribute heavily to polarization. Broadcasters are eager for stories to fill their round-the-clock schedules, and at the same time reluctant to trust the government as a source for those stories. Many media outlets are clearly liberal in their orientation; with the arrival of Fox News and the growth of talk radio, many are now just as clearly conservative.

The evidence of liberal bias in the mainstream media is very strong. The Center for Media and Public Affairs (CMPA) has been systematically studying television broadcasts for a quarter-century. In the 2004 presidential campaign, John Kerry received more favorable mentions than any presidential candidate in CMPA's history, especially during the month before election day. This is not new: since 1980 (and setting aside the recent advent of Fox News), the Democratic candidate has received more favorable mentions than the Republican candidate in every race except the 1988 contest between Michael Dukakis and George H. W. Bush. A similarly clear orientation characterizes weekly newsmagazines like *Time* and *Newsweek*.

For its part, talk radio is listened to by about one-sixth of the adult public, and that one-sixth is made up mostly of conservatives. National Public Radio has an audience of about the same size; it is disproportionately liberal. The same breakdown affects cable-television news, where the rivalry is between CNN (and MSNBC) and Fox News. Those who watch CNN are more likely to be Democrats than Republicans; the reverse is emphatically true of Fox. As for news and opinion on the Internet, which has become an important source for college graduates in particular, it, too, is largely polarized along political and ideological lines, emphasized even more by the culture that has grown up around news blogs.

At one time, our culture was only weakly affected by the media because news organizations had only a few points of access to us and were largely moderate and audience-maximizing enterprises. Today the media have many lines of access, and reflect both the maximization of controversy and the cultivation of niche markets. Once the media talked to us; now they shout at us.

And then there are the interest groups. In the past, the major ones—the National Association of Manufacturers, the Chamber of Commerce, and labor organizations like the AFL-CIO—were concerned with their own material interests. They are still active, but the loudest messages today come from very different sources and have a very different cast to them. They are issued by groups concerned with social and cultural matters like civil rights, managing the environment, alternatives to the public schools, the role of women, access to firearms, and so forth, and they directly influence the way people view politics.

Interest groups preoccupied with material concerns can readily find ways to arrive at compromise solutions to their differences; interest groups divided by issues of rights or morality find compromise very difficult. The positions taken by many of these groups and their supporters, often operating within the two political parties, profoundly affect the selection of candidates for office. In brief, it is hard to imagine someone opposed to abortion receiving the Democratic nomination for President, or someone in favor of it receiving the Republican nomination.

Outside the realm of party politics, interest groups also file briefs in important court cases and can benefit from decisions that in turn help shape the political debate. Abortion became a hot controversy in the 1970s not because the American people were already polarized on the matter but because their (mainly centrist) views were not consulted; instead, national policy was determined by the Supreme Court in a decision, *Roe v. Wade*, that itself reflected a definition of "rights" vigorously promoted by certain well-defined interest groups.

Polarization not only is real and has increased, but it has also spread to rank-and-file voters through elite influence.

In *The Nature and Origins of Mass Opinion* . . . , John R. Zaller of UCLA listed a number of contemporary issues—homosexuality, a nuclear freeze, the war in Vietnam, busing for school integration, the 1990–91 war to expel Iraq from Kuwait—and measured the views held about them by politically aware citizens. (By "politically aware," Zaller meant people who did well answering neutral factual questions about politics.) His findings were illuminating.

Take the Persian Gulf war. Iraq had invaded Kuwait in August 1990. From that point through the congressional elections in November 1990, scarcely any elite voices were raised to warn against anything the United States might contemplate doing in response. Two days after the mid-term elections, however, President George H. W. Bush announced that he was sending many more troops to the Persian Gulf. This provoked strong criticism from some members of Congress, especially Democrats.

As it happens, a major public-opinion survey was under way just as these events were unfolding. Before criticism began to be voiced in Congress, both registered Democrats and registered Republicans had supported Bush's vaguely announced intention of coming to the aid of Kuwait; the more politically aware they were, the greater their support. After the onset of elite criticism, the support of Republican voters went up, but Democratic support flattened out. As Bush became more vigorous in indicating his aims, politically aware voters began to differ sharply, with Democratic support declining and Republican support increasing further.

Much the same pattern can be seen in popular attitudes toward the other issues studied by Zaller. As political awareness increases, attitudes split apart, with, for example, highly aware liberals favoring busing and job guarantees and opposing the war in Vietnam, and highly aware conservatives opposing busing and job guarantees and supporting the war in Vietnam.

But why should this be surprising? To imagine that extremist politics has been confined to the chattering classes is to believe that Congress, the media, and American interest groups operate in an ideological vacuum. I find that assumption implausible.

As for the extent to which these extremist views have spread, that is probably best assessed by looking not at specific issues but at enduring political values and party preferences. In 2004, only 12 percent of Democrats approved of George Bush; at earlier periods, by contrast, three to four times as many Democrats approved of Ronald Reagan, Gerald Ford, Richard Nixon, and Dwight D. Eisenhower. Over the course of about two decades, in other words, party affiliation had come to exercise a critical influence over what people thought about a sitting President.

The same change can be seen in the public's view of military power. Since the late 1980s, Republicans have been more willing than Democrats to say that "the best way to ensure peace is through military strength." By the late 1990s and on into 2003, well over two-thirds of all Republicans agreed with this view, but far fewer than half of all Democrats did. In 2005, three-fourths of all Democrats but fewer than a third of all Republicans told pollsters that good diplomacy was the best way to ensure peace. In the same survey, two-thirds of all Republicans but only one fourth of all Democrats said they would fight for this country "whether it is right or wrong."

Unlike in earlier years, the parties are no longer seen as Tweedledum and Tweedledee. To the contrary, as they sharpen their ideological differences, attentive voters have sharpened their ideological differences. They now like either the Democrats or the Republicans more than they once did, and are less apt to feel neutral toward either one.

How deep does this polarization reach? As measured by opinion polls, the gap between Democrats and Republicans was twice as great in 2004 as in 1972. In fact, rank-and-file Americans disagree more strongly today than did politically active Americans in 1972.

To be sure, this mass polarization involves only a minority of all voters, but the minority is sizable, and a significant part of it is made up of the college-educated. As Marc Hetherington of Vanderbilt puts it: "people with the greatest ability to assimilate new information, those with more formal education, are most affected by elite polarization." And that cohort has undeniably grown.

In 1900, only 10 percent of all young Americans went to high school. My father, in common with many men his age in the early twentieth century, dropped out of school after the eighth grade. Even when I graduated from college, the first in my family to do so, fewer than one-tenth of all Americans over the age of twenty-five had gone that far. Today [2006], 84 percent of adult Americans have graduated from high school and nearly 27 percent have graduated from college. This extraordinary growth in schooling has produced an ever larger audience for political agitation.

Ideologically, an even greater dividing line than undergraduate education is postgraduate education. People who have proceeded beyond college seem to be very different from those who stop with a high-school or college diploma. Thus, about a sixth of all voters describe themselves as liberals, but the figure for those with a postgraduate degree is well over a quarter. In mid-2004, about half of all voters trusted George Bush; less than a third of those with a postgraduate education did. In November of the same year, when over half of all college graduates voted for Bush, well over half of the smaller cohort who had done postgraduate work voted for Kerry. According to the Pew Center for Research on the People and the Press, more than half of all Democrats with a postgraduate education supported the antiwar candidacy of Howard Dean.

The effect of postgraduate education is reinforced by being in a profession. Between 1900 and 1960, write John B. Judis and Ruy Teixeira in *The Emerging Democratic Majority* . . . , professionals voted pretty much the same way as business managers; by 1988, the former began supporting Democrats while the latter supported Republicans. On the other hand, the effect of postgraduate education seems to outweigh the effect of affluence. For most voters, including college graduates, having higher incomes means becoming more conservative; not so for those with a postgraduate education, whose liberal predilections are immune to the wealth effect.

The results of this linkage between ideology, on the one hand, and congressional polarization, media influence, interest-group demands, and education on the other are easily read in the commentary surrounding the 2004 election. In their zeal to denigrate the President, liberals, pronounced one conservative pundit, had "gone quite around the twist." According to liberal spokesmen, conservatives with their "religious intolerance" and their determination to rewrite the Constitution had so befuddled their fellow Americans that a "great nation was felled by a poisonous nut."

If such wholesale slurs are not signs of polarization, then the word has no meaning. To a degree that we cannot precisely measure, and over issues that we cannot exactly list, polarization has seeped down into the public, where it has assumed the form of a culture war. The sociologist James Davison Hunter, who has written about this phenomenon in a mainly religious context, defines culture war as "political and social hostility rooted in different systems of moral understanding." Such conflicts, he writes, which can involve "fundamental ideas about who we are as Americans," are waged both across the religious/secular divide and within religions themselves, where those with an "orthodox" view of moral authority square off against those with a "progressive" view.

To some degree, this terminology is appropriate to today's political situation as well. We are indeed in a culture war in Hunter's sense, though I believe this war is itself but another component, or another symptom, of the larger ideological polarization that has us in its grip. Conservative thinking on political issues has religious roots, but it also has roots that are fully as secular as anything on the Left. By the same token, the liberal attack on conservatives derives in part from an explicitly "progressive" religious orientation—liberal Protestantism or Catholicism, or Reform Judaism—but in part from the same secular sources shared by many conservatives.

But what, one might ask, is wrong with having well-defined parties arguing vigorously about the issues that matter? Is it possible that polarized politics is a good thing, encouraging sharp debate and clear positions? Perhaps that is true on those issues where reasonable compromises can be devised. But there are two limits to such an arrangement.

First, many Americans believe that unbridgeable political differences have prevented leaders from addressing the problems they were elected to address. As a result, distrust of government mounts, leading to an alienation from politics altogether. The steep decline in popular approval of our national officials has many causes, but surely one of them is that ordinary voters agree among themselves more than political elites agree with each other—and the elites are far more numerous than they once were.

In the 1950s, a committee of the American Political Science Association (APSA) argued the case for a "responsible" two-party system. The model the APSA had in mind was the more ideological and therefore more "coherent" party system of Great Britain. At the time, scarcely anyone thought our parties could be transformed in such a supposedly salutary direction. Instead, as Governor George Wallace of Alabama put it in his failed third-party bid for the presidency, there was not a "dime's worth of difference" between Democrats and Republicans.

What Wallace forgot was that, however alike the parties were, the public liked them that way. A half-century ago, Tweedledum and Tweedledee enjoyed the support of the American people; the more different they have become, the greater has been the drop in popular confidence in both them and the federal government.

A final drawback of polarization is more profound. Sharpened debate is arguably helpful with respect to domestic issues, but not for the management of important foreign and military matters. The United States, an unrivaled superpower with unparalleled responsibilities for protecting the peace and defeating terrorists, is now forced to discharge those duties with its own political house in disarray.

We fought World War II as a united nation, even against two enemies (Germany and Italy) that had not attacked us. We began the wars in Korea and Vietnam with some degree of unity, too, although it was eventually whittled away. By the early 1990s, when we expelled Iraq from Kuwait, we had to do so over the objections of congressional critics; the first President Bush avoided putting the issue to Congress altogether. In 2003 we toppled Saddam Hussein in the face of catcalls from many domestic leaders and opinion-makers. Now, in stabilizing Iraq and helping that country create a new free government, we have proceeded despite intense and mounting criticism, much of it voiced by politicians who before the war agreed that Saddam Hussein was an evil menace in possession of weapons of mass destruction and that we had to remove him.

Denmark or Luxembourg can afford to exhibit domestic anguish and uncertainty over military policy; the United States cannot. A divided America encourages our enemies, disheartens our allies, and saps our resolve—potentially to fatal effect. What General Giap of North Vietnam once said of us is even truer today. America cannot be defeated on the battlefield, but it can be defeated at home. Polarization is a force that can defeat us.

Polarized America?

February 21, 2006

To the editor:
James Q. Wilson (February) takes issue with my demonstration in *Culture War? The Myth of a Polarized America* (with Samuel Abrams and Jeremy Pope) that the polarization evident among the members of the American political class has only a faint reflection in the American public. As a long-time admirer of Wilson's work I am naturally concerned when his take on some aspect of American politics differs from mine. But I believe that his criticisms are a result of misunderstanding. I would like to address two of them.

First, Wilson discounts our red state-blue state comparisons with the comment that "Inferring the views of individual citizens from the gross results of presidential balloting is a questionable procedure." Indeed it is, which is why we did not do that. As we wrote in the book, inferring polarization from close elections is precisely what pundits have done and why their conclusions have been wrong. In contrast, we report detailed analyses of the policy views expressed by voters in 2000 and 2004 and contrary to the claims of Garry Wills, Maureen Dowd, and other op-ed columnists, we find surprisingly small differences between the denizens of the blue states and the red states. As we show in the book and emphasize repeatedly, people's *choices* (as expressed, say, in presidential balloting) can be polarized while their *positions* are not, and the evidence strongly indicates that this is the case.

Moreover, we report that not only are red and blue state citizens surprisingly similar in their views, but other studies find little evidence of growing polarization no matter how one slices and dices the population—affluent v. poor, white v. black v. brown, old v. young, well educated v. the less educated, men v. women, and so on. Like many before him, Wilson confuses partisan *sorting* with polarization—the Democrats have largely shed their conservative southern wing while Republicans have largely shed their liberal Rockefeller wing, resulting in more distinct parties, even while the aggregate distribution of ideology and issue stances among the citizenry remains much the same as in the past.

Second, Wilson criticizes our analysis of Americans' views on the specific issue of abortion, contending that the small numerical differences expressed by people on a General Social Survey scale constitute a significantly larger substantive difference. Although we disagree, even if one accepted Wilson's contention, it would not apply to our supporting analysis of a differently-worded Gallup survey item that yields the same conclusions, or to numerous other survey items that clearly show that most Americans are "pro-choice, buts."

For example, Wilson notes that "70 percent of those who thought abortion should always be legal voted for Al Gore or John Kerry, while over 70 percent of those who thought it should always be illegal voted for George Bush." True enough, but he does not mention that Gallup repeatedly finds that a majority of the American people place themselves between those polar categories—they think abortion should be "legal only under certain circumstances." Even limiting the analysis to avowed partisans, in 2005 only 30 percent of Democrats thought abortion should always be legal, and fewer than 30 percent of Republicans thought it should always be illegal. One can raise questions about every survey item that has ever been asked, but the cumulative weight of the evidence on Americans' abortion views is overwhelming. Contrary to the wishes of the activists on both sides, the American people prefer a middle ground on abortion, period.

Wilson approvingly cites James Davison Hunter, whose book, *Culture War*, inspired Patrick Buchanan's 1992 speech at the Republican National Convention. In a forthcoming Brookings Institution volume, Hunter now limits his thesis to "somewhere between 10 and 15 percent who occupy these opposing moral and ideological universes." That leaves more than 80 percent of the American public not engaged in the moral and ideological battles reveled in by the political class. Note that Wilson's examples of incivil discourse reference "the press," "a former Democratic presidential candidate," "a senior Democratic Senator," "liberal spokesmen," and "one conservative pundit." Absent from this list are well-intentioned, ordinary working Americans not given to the kind of incendiary remarks that get quoted by journalists.

I share Wilson's concern with the potentially harmful consequences of polarization. But the first step in addressing those concerns is to get the facts correct. I remain convinced that we have done that. If Americans are offered competent, pragmatic candidates with a problem-solving orientation, the shallow popular roots of political polarization will be exposed for all to see.

Morris P. Fiorina
Stanford, California

John B. Judis
Tea Minus Zero

Liberals have responded to the Tea Party movement by reaching a comforting conclusion: that there is no way these guys can possibly be for real. The movement has variously been described as a "front group for the Republican party" and a "media creation"; Paul Krugman has called Tea Party rallies "AstroTurf (fake grass roots) events, manufactured by the usual suspects."

I can understand why liberals would want to dismiss the Tea Party movement as an inauthentic phenomenon; it would certainly be welcome news if it were. The sentiments on display at Tea Party rallies go beyond run-of-the-mill anti-tax, anti-spending conservatism and into territory that rightly strikes liberals as truly disturbing. Among the signs I saw at an April 15 protest in Washington: "IF IT SOUNDS LIKE MARX AND ACTS LIKE STALIN IT MUST BE OBAMA," "STOP OBAMA'S BROWNSHIRT INFILTRAITORS," and "OBAMA BIN LYIN," which was accompanied by an illustration of the president looking like a monkey.

But the Tea Party movement is not inauthentic, and—contrary to the impression its rallies give off—it isn't a fringe faction either. It is a genuine popular movement, one that has managed to unite a number of ideological strains from U.S. history—some recent, some older. These strains can be described as many things, but they cannot be dismissed as passing phenomena. Much as liberals would like to believe otherwise, there is good reason to think the Tea Party movement could exercise considerable influence over our politics in the coming years.

The movement essentially began on February 19, 2009, when CNBC commentator Rick Santelli, speaking from the floor of the Chicago Mercantile Exchange, let loose against the Obama administration's plan to help homeowners who could no longer pay their mortgages. "This is America!" Santelli exclaimed. "How many of you people want to pay for your neighbors' mortgage that has an extra bathroom and can't pay their bills?" Santelli called for a "Chicago Tea Party" to protest the administration's plan.

Santelli's appeal was answered by a small group of bloggers, policy wonks, and Washington politicos who were primarily drawn from the libertarian wing of the conservative movement. They included John O'Hara from the Illinois Policy Institute (who has written a history of the movement, titled *A New American Tea Party*); Brendan Steinhauser of FreedomWorks, a Washington lobbying group run by former Representative Dick Armey; and blogger Michael Patrick Leahy, a founder of Top Conservatives on Twitter. The initial round of Tea Party protests took place at the end of February in over 30 cities. There were more protests in April, and, by the time of the massive September 12 protest last year, the Tea Party movement had officially arrived as a political force.

Like many American movements, the Tea Parties are not tightly organized from above. They are a network of local groups and national ones (Tea Party Patriots, Tea Party Express, Tea Party Nation), Washington lobbies and quasi-think tanks (FreedomWorks, Americans for Prosperity), bloggers, and talk-show hosts. There are no national membership lists, but extensive polls done by Quinnipiac, the Winston Group, and Economist/YouGov suggest that the movement commands the active allegiance of between 13 percent and 15 percent of the electorate. That is a formidable number, and, judging from other polls that ask whether someone has a "favorable" view of the Tea Parties, the movement gets a sympathetic hearing from as much as 40 percent of the electorate.

Tea Partiers' favorite politician is undoubtedly Sarah Palin—according to the Economist/YouGov poll, 71 percent of Tea Partiers think Palin "is more qualified to be president than Barack Obama" (and another 15 percent are "not sure")—but, more than anyone else, the movement takes its cues from Glenn Beck. Unlike fellow talkers Rush Limbaugh and Sean Hannity, Beck has never been a conventional Republican; he calls himself a conservative rather than a member of the GOP. While Limbaugh has attempted to soft-pedal his personal failings, the baby-faced Beck makes his into a story of redemption. He is, in his own words, an "average, everyday person." You need to have followed Beck's conspiratorial meanderings to understand what preoccupies many members of the Tea Party movement. At the Washington demonstration in April, for instance, there were people holding signs attacking Frances Fox Piven and Richard Cloward, two 1960s-era Columbia University sociologists who, Beck claims, were the brains behind both the community group ACORN and Obama's attempt to destroy capitalism by bankrupting the government through national health care reform.

In the last year, the movement's focus has shifted from demonstrations to elections. Currently, Tea Party groups are backing Republican Senate candidates in Kentucky, Utah, and Florida, while trying to knock off Democratic Senators Harry Reid in Nevada and Arlen Specter in Pennsylvania. In some places, Tea Party organizations have begun to displace the state GOP. Last month, Action is Brewing, the northern Nevada Tea Party affiliate, hosted a televised debate for the Republican gubernatorial and senatorial candidates. In addition, numerous candidates are running for Congress as Tea Party supporters.

The Tea Parties are the descendants of a number of conservative insurgencies from the past two generations: the anti-tax rebellion of the late '70s, the Moral Majority and Christian Coalition of the '80s and '90s, and Pat Buchanan's presidential runs. Like the Tea Partiers I saw in Washington—and the picture of the Tea Partiers put forward by the Winston and Quinnipiac polls—these movements have been almost entirely white, disproportionately middle-aged or older, and more male than female (though parts of the Christian right are an exception on this count). A majority of their adherents generally are not college-educated, with incomes in the middle range—attributes that also closely match the Tea Party movement's demographic profile. (A misleading picture of Tea Partiers as college-educated and affluent came from a *New York Times*/CBS poll of people who merely "support," but don't necessarily have anything to do with, the Tea Party movement. The other polls surveyed people who say they are "part of" the movement.)

Sociologists who have studied these earlier movements describe their followers as coming from the "marginal segments of the middle class." That's a sociological, but also a political, fact. These men and women look uneasily upward at corporate CEOs and investment bankers, and downward at low-wage service workers and laborers, many of whom are minorities. And their political outlook is defined by whether they primarily blame those below or above for the social and economic anxieties they feel. In the late nineteenth and early twentieth century, the marginal middle class was the breeding ground for left-wing attacks against Wall Street. For the last half-century, it has nourished right-wing complaints about blacks, illegal immigrants, and the poor.

It isn't just demography that the Tea Parties have in common with recent conservative movements; it's also politics. To be sure, some of the original Tea Party organizers were young libertarians, many of whom, like Brendan Steinhauser, voted for Ron Paul in 2008 and have rediscovered Ayn Rand's ethic of rational selfishness. They remain part of the movement—one sign I saw at the Washington rally read, "WE ARE JOHN GALT," referring to the hero of *Atlas Shrugged*—but, as the movement has grown, its adherents have become more conventionally conservative. As Grover Norquist likes to point out, what distinguishes one conservative group from another is not their members' overall views, but what "moves" them to demonstrate or to vote. The Christian right, for instance, went to the barricades over abortion and gay marriage, yet most members also hold conservative economic views. Likewise, the Tea Partiers have been moved to action by economic issues, but they share the outlook of social conservatives. According to the Economist/YouGov poll, 74 percent of Tea Party members think abortion is "murder," and 81 percent are against gay marriage. Sixty-three percent are in favor of public school students learning that "the Book of Genesis in the Bible explains how God created the world"; 62 percent think that "the only way to Heaven is through Jesus Christ." These beliefs are on display at rallies: In Washington, one demonstrator in clerical garb held a sign saying, "GOD HATES TAXES." Moreover, aside from the followers of Ron Paul, Tea Party members also share the post-September 11 national security views of the GOP. When Tea Partiers were asked to name the "most important issue" to them, terrorism came in third out of ten, behind only the economy and the budget deficit.

If you look at the people who are running as pro–Tea Party candidates, you discover that some of them have simply graduated from one stage of the conservative movement to another. Jason Meade, who is running for Congress in Ohio, was just out of school, working in his father's business and playing music, when he "returned to the church and left the music world behind." Now 38, he sees his participation in Tea Party politics as a continuation of his twelve subsequent years in ministry school. "I decided to try and minister in a new way; by trying to be involved in the protection of the freedoms and liberty that God has given us and that have been woven into the fabric of our country," he wrote on his Web site. Jason Sager, 36, who is running in a Republican congressional primary northeast of Tampa, got into conservative politics in the wake of September 11. A Navy veteran, he joined a group called Protest Warrior that staged counter-demonstrations at antiwar rallies, and he was a volun-teer in George W. Bush's 2004 campaign. After Obama's election, he got involved with Glenn Beck's 912 Project and, then, with the local Tea Parties.

But the Tea Parties' roots in U.S. history go back much further than the conservative movements of recent decades. The Tea Parties are defined by three general ideas that have played a key role in U.S. politics since the country's early days. The first is an obsession with decline. This idea, which traces back to the outlook of New England Puritans during the seventeenth century, consists of a belief that a golden age occurred some time ago; that we are now in a period of severe social, economic, or moral decay; that evil forces and individuals are the cause of this situation; that the goal of politics is to restore the earlier period; and that the key to doing so is heeding a special text that can serve as a guidebook for the journey backward. (The main difference between the far right and far left is that the left locates the golden age in the future.) The Puritans were trying to reproduce the circumstances of early Christianity in New England, using the Bible as their guiding text. Their enemies were Catholics and the Church of England, who they believed had corrupted the religion. For the Tea Partiers, the golden age is the time of the Founders, and adherence to the Constitution is the means to restore this period in the face of challenges from secular humanism, radical Islam, and especially socialism.

Beck has been instrumental in sacralizing the Constitution. He has touted the works of the late W. Cleon Skousen, a John Birch Society defender who projected his ultraconservative views back onto the Founding Fathers. In *The 5000 Year Leap*, which has been reissued with a foreword by Beck, Skousen claimed that the Founders "warned against the 'welfare state' " and against "the drift toward the collectivist left."

In Arizona, Tea Party members hand out copies of the Constitution at political meetings the way a missionary group might hand out Bibles. The San Antonio Tea Party group has demanded that politicians sign a "contract with the Constitution." In speeches, Tea Partiers cite articles and amendments from the Constitution the same way that clerics cite Biblical verses. Speaking at the Lakeland Tea Party rally on tax day, Jason Sager said, "You are now able to see the most pressing issue that faces our nation and our society. Do you know what that issue is? We are now witnessing the fundamental breakdown of the republican form of government that we are guaranteed in Article Four, Section Four of our Constitution." In typical fashion, Sager did not go on to explain what Article Four, Section Four was. (You can look it up. I had to.)

Just as the Puritans believed Catholics and the Church of England were undermining Christianity, the Tea Partiers have fixated on nefarious individuals and groups—Saul Alinsky, ACORN, and, of course, Obama himself—who they believe are destroying the country. (According to the Economist/YouGov poll, 52 percent of Tea Party members think ACORN stole the 2008 election from John McCain; another 24 percent are still not sure.) "America has let thieves into her home," writes Beck, "and that nagging in your gut is a final warning that our country is about to be stolen." Their determination to locate the threat outside the United States accounts for their emphasis on Obama being a socialist, Marxist, communist, or even fascist—all of which are foreign faiths—rather than what he is: a conventional American liberal. It also helps explain the repeated references to Obama's African father. And it explains why some Tea Partiers continue to believe, in the face of incontrovertible evidence, that Obama was born outside the United States. The Economist/YouGov poll found that 34 percent of Tea Party members think he was not born in the United States, and another 34 percent are not sure.

But how could a movement that cultivates such crazy, conspiratorial views be regarded favorably by as much as 40 percent of the electorate? That is where the Tea Party movement's second link to early U.S. history comes in. The Tea Partiers may share the Puritans' fear of decline, but it is what they share with Thomas Jefferson that has far broader appeal: a staunch anti-statism. What began as a sentiment of the left—a rejection of state monopolies—became, after the industrial revolution and the rise of the labor movement, a weapon against progressive reforms. The basic idea—that government is a "necessary evil"—has retained its power, and, when the economy has faltered, Americans have been quick to blame Washington, perhaps even before they looked at Wall Street or big corporations. It happened in the late '70s under Jimmy Carter and in the early '90s under George H. W. Bush; and it has happened again during Obama's first 18 months in office. According to a Pew poll, the percentage of Americans "angry" with government has risen from 10 percent in February 2000 to 21 percent today, while another 56 percent are "frustrated" with government.

Of course, during Franklin Roosevelt's first term, most voters didn't blame the incumbent administration for the Great Depression. Roosevelt was able to deflect blame for the depression back onto the Hoover administration and the "economic royalists" of Wall Street and corporate America. But Roosevelt took office at the nadir of the Great Depression, and his policies achieved dramatic improvements in unemployment and economic growth during his first term. Obama took office barely four months after the financial crisis visibly hit, and he has had to preside over growing unemployment.

Simmering economic frustration also accounts for the final historical strain that defines the Tea Parties: They are part of a tradition of producerism that dates to Andrew Jackson. Jacksonian Democrats believed that workers should enjoy the fruits of what they produce and not have to share them with the merchants and bankers who didn't actually create anything. The Populists of the late nineteenth century invoked this ethic in denouncing the Eastern bankers who held their farms hostage. Producerism also underlay Roosevelt's broadsides against economic royalists and Bill Clinton's promise to give priority to those who "work hard and play by the rules."

During the 1970s, conservatives began invoking producerism to justify their attacks on the welfare state, and it was at the core of the conservative tax revolt.

While the Jacksonians and Populists had largely directed their anger upward, conservatives directed their ire at the people below who were beneficiaries of state programs—from the "welfare queens" of the ghetto to the "illegal aliens" of the barrio. Like the attack against "big government," this conservative producerism has most deeply resonated during economic downturns. And the Tea Parties have clearly built their movement around it.

Producerism was at the heart of Santelli's rant against government forcing the responsible middle class to subsidize those who bought homes they couldn't afford. In his history of the Tea Party movement, O'Hara described an America divided between "moochers, big and small, corporate and individual, trampling over themselves with their hands out demanding endless bailouts" and "disgusted, hardworking citizens getting sick of being played for chumps and punished for practicing personal responsibility." The same theme recurs in the Tea Partiers' rejection of liberal legislation. Beck dismissed Obama's health care reform plan as "good old socialism . . . raping the pocketbooks of the rich to give to the poor." Speaking to cheers at the April 15 rally in Washington, Armey denounced the progressive income tax in the same terms. "I can't steal your money and give it to this guy," he declared. "Therefore, I shouldn't use the power of the state to steal your money and give it to this guy."

The Tea Parties are not managed by the Republican National Committee, and they are not really a wing of the GOP. It is telling that Beck devoted his February speech at the Conservative Political Action Conference to bashing Republicans—and that, in a survey of 50 Tea Party leaders, the Sam Adams Alliance found that 28 percent identify themselves as Independents and 11 percent as Tea Party members rather than Republicans. Still, the Tea Partiers' political objective is clearly to push the GOP to the right. They agitated last summer for a Republican party-line vote against health care reform and are now arguing that states have a constitutional right to refuse to comply with it. They have been calling the offices of Republican senators to demand that they oppose a bipartisan compromise on financial regulatory reform. In South Carolina, they have attacked Senator Lindsey Graham, who is also a favorite Beck target, for backing a cap-and-trade [environmental] bill. The Arizona Tea Party pressured Governor Jan Brewer to sign the now-infamous bill targeting illegal immigrants. And Tea Party Nation has issued a "Red Alert" to prevent Congress from adopting "amnesty" legislation.

If the GOP wins back at least one house of Congress in November, the Tea Parties will be able to claim victory and demand a say in Republican congressional policies. That could lead to a replay of the Newt Gingrich Congress of 1995–1996, from which the country was lucky to escape relatively unscathed. But, beyond this, it's hard to say what will become of the movement. If the economy improves in a significant way next year, it is likely to fade. That is what happened to the tax revolt, which peaked from 1978 to 1982 and then subsided. But, if the economy limps along—say, in the manner of Japan over the last 15 years—then the Tea Parties will likely remain strong, and may even become a bigger force in U.S. politics than they are now.

For all of its similarities to previous insurgencies, the Tea Party movement differs in one key respect from the most prominent conservative movement of recent years, the Christian right: The Tea Parties do not have the same built-in impediments to growth. The Christian right looked like it was going to expand in the early '90s, but it ran up against the limit of its politics, which were grounded ultimately in an esoteric theology and a network of churches. If it strayed too far from the implications of that theology, it risked splitting its membership. But, if it articulated it—as Pat Robertson and others did at various inopportune moments—then it risked alienating the bulk of Americans. The Tea Parties do not have the same problem. They have their own crazy conspiracy theories, but even the wackiest Tea Partiers wouldn't demand that a candidate seeking their endorsement agree that ACORN fixed the election or that Obama is foreign-born. And their core appeal on government and spending will continue to resonate as long as the economy sputters. None of this is what liberals want to hear, but we might as well face reality: The Tea Party movement—firmly grounded in a number of durable U.S. political traditions and well-positioned for a time of economic uncertainty—could be around for a while.

DISCUSSION QUESTIONS

1. According to Wilson and Judis, what are the chief factors contributing to polarization and cultural division in the United States? Are these factors likely to change any time soon? What part, if any, of Wilson's and Judis's arguments would Fiorina agree with?

2. Based on the articles and other information you might have, do you think Fiorina is right that the American public is not deeply split on a range of issues and that

they tend to favor more moderate solutions to problems? Can you think of issues for which this would be true?

3. If you were an adviser for one of the two major parties, how would you advise them to address the issue of polarization or culture war? Should they emphasize issues where broader consensus might be possible? Or is it the job of political parties to emphasize precisely those issues that might be the most divisive in order to appeal to their strongest supporters? Which is better for voters—a focus on consensus or on contrasts?

4. Party strategists often talk about changing a party's public image. In your view, what would a party have to do to change its public image significantly? What would convince you that a party had changed?

12

Groups and Interests: Corporate and Labor Spending in Campaigns

The First Amendment of the U.S. Constitution says that "Congress shall make no law . . . abridging the freedom of speech." The Supreme Court must define the boundaries of what that broad prohibition means. Does it apply to pornography? To commercial speech? To speech that advocates the overthrow of the government or incites violence? Political advertising and campaign spending similarly generate a difficult set of questions. In its rulings, the Court has equated the use of money in campaigns with speech. In other words, money facilitates the making and spreading of messages. Supporting a candidate with a contribution is making a statement, and is thus speech, and the money itself helps the candidate speak through advertisements and other means. Spending independently to promote a candidate or message and not giving the money to a candidate is similarly a kind of speech—spending the money allows you to distribute the message. The Court has recognized a government interest in promoting fair elections that are free from corruption, so it has determined that some regulation of campaign finance is warranted. But the question is where to draw the line between activity that is permissible and that which is prohibited.

In its January 2010 decision in *Citizens United v. Federal Election Commission* (FEC), the Supreme Court decided that the First Amendment protects the right of non-profit and for-profit corporations and labor unions to spend directly to run ads calling for the election or defeat of a candidate in political campaigns, rather than having to set up political action committees (PACs). Political action committees must raise donations that they then either contribute directly to candidates and parties or spend independently to send a campaign message. The Court decision said that corporations and unions could bypass PACs and spend directly from their treasuries to speak on matters of interest to their organizations, including who they believe would be preferable candidates to elect. The amounts they could spend to support these messages, so long as they were not giving the money directly to a candidate or party, was not limited. The premise in the Court's decision was that the risk of the corrupting influence of money is most powerful when the money is going directly to a candidate or party's campaign coffers, not when an organization is spending money to transmit a message independently. *Citizens United* and subsequent lower court rulings and Federal Election Commission decisions also paved the way for so-called Super PACs, which could collect unlimited donations so long as they spent the money independently—for example, on TV ads—and did not contribute it to a candidate or party.

Ronald Dworkin, a law professor at New York University, says *Citizens United* "threatens democracy" because it will create "an avalanche of negative political commercials financed by huge corporate wealth." He also is concerned that the decision has "generated open hostilities among the three branches of our government," pointing to comments from President Barack Obama in his 2010 State of the Union message and the subsequent negative reaction from Supreme Court Justices Samuel Alito and John Roberts. Dworkin argues that this radical a decision cannot be grounded in any theory of the First Amendment, ignored relevant precedent despite the conservative majority's avowed belief in judicial restraint, and opened American electoral campaigns to influence from foreign corporations. Dworkin concludes with a plea for stronger disclosure laws and public financing for congressional elections.

Bradley Smith, a law professor and former chair of the Federal Election Commission, strongly disagrees. He calls the decision a "wonderful affirmation of the primacy of political speech in First Amendment jurisprudence." Furthermore, he says, the impact of the decision is almost certainly overstated: over half the states already allowed corporations to advertise in state elections at the time of the ruling, and most large corporations are unlikely to start spending huge amounts of money because they prefer lobbying to spending money in elections. Also, he notes the decision empowers not only corporations but also labor unions, which are more likely to want to spend in elections.

Matt Bai agrees with Smith that critics have overstated the impact of *Citizens United* and that much of what has happened in elections since the ruling was already happening before it. Bai argues that criticizing the Court's decision is a useful organizing device by liberal politicians because they know fellow liberals strongly disapprove of the ruling. But Bai doubts the ruling has had anywhere near the effects claimed by critics. Instead, he suggests that the surge of money in recent elections can be attributed to two factors. First, the Bipartisan Campaign Reform Act of 2002 made it more difficult to give money to political parties, which resulted in a rise in independent campaign spending. Second, the major issues under discussion in the Bush and Obama presidencies naturally led citizens with strong views on these issues, including but not exclusively, wealthy individuals, to attempt to have some influence on the direction of the country through campaign-related messages.

Ronald Dworkin

The Decision That Threatens Democracy

No Supreme Court decision in decades has generated such open hostilities among the three branches of our government as has the Court's 5–4 decision in *Citizens United v. FEC* in January 2010. The five conservative justices, on their own initiative, at the request of no party to the suit, declared that corporations and unions have a constitutional right to spend as much as they wish on television election commercials specifically supporting or targeting particular candidates. President Obama immediately denounced the decision as a catastrophe for American democracy and then, in a highly unusual act, repeated his denunciation in his State of the Union address with six of the justices sitting before him.

"With all due deference to separation of powers," he said, "last week the Supreme Court reversed a century of law that I believe will open the floodgates for special interests—including foreign corporations—to spend without limit in our elections." As he spoke one of the conservative justices, Samuel Alito, in an obvious breach of decorum, mouthed a denial, and a short time later Chief Justice John Roberts publicly chastised the President for expressing that opinion on that occasion. The White House press secretary, Robert Gibbs, then explained Obama's remarks: "The President has long been committed to reducing the undue influence of special interests and their lobbyists over government. That is why he spoke out to condemn the decision and is working with Congress on a legislative response." Democrats in Congress have indeed called for a constitutional amendment to repeal the decision and several of them, more realistically, have proposed statutes to mitigate its damage.

The history of the Court's decision is as extraordinary as its reception. At least since 1907, when Congress passed the Tillman Act at the request of President Theodore Roosevelt, it had been accepted by the nation and the Court that corporations, which are only fictitious persons created by law, do not have the same First Amendment rights to political activity as real people do. In 1990, in *Austin v. Michigan Chamber of Commerce*, the Court firmly upheld that principle. In 2002, Congress passed the Bipartisan Campaign Reform Act (BCRA) sponsored by Senators John McCain and Russell Feingold, which forbade corporations to engage in television electioneering for a period of thirty days before a primary for federal office and sixty days before an election. In 2003, in *McConnell v. Federal Election Commission (FEC)*, the Court upheld the constitutionality of that prohibition.

In the 2008 presidential primary season a small corporation, Citizens United, financed to a minor extent by corporate contributions, tried to broadcast a derogatory movie about Hillary Clinton. The FEC declared the broadcast illegal under the BCRA. Citizens United then asked the Supreme Court to declare it exempt from that statute on the ground, among others, that it proposed to broadcast its movie only on a pay-per-view channel. It did not challenge the constitutionality of the act. But the five conservative justices—Chief Justice Roberts and Justices Samuel Alito, Anthony Kennedy, Antonin Scalia, and Clarence Thomas—decided on their own initiative, after a rehearing they themselves called for, that they wanted to declare the act unconstitutional anyway.

They said that the BCRA violated the First Amendment, which declares that Congress shall make no law infringing the freedom of speech. They agreed that their decision was contrary to the *Austin* and *McConnell* precedents; they therefore overruled those decisions as well as repealing a century of American history and tradition. Their decision threatens an avalanche of negative political commercials financed by huge corporate wealth, beginning in this year's midterm elections. Overall these commercials can be expected to benefit Republican candidates and to injure candidates whose records dissatisfy powerful industries. The decision gives corporate lobbyists, already much too influential in our political system, an immensely powerful weapon. It is important to study in some detail a ruling so damaging to democracy.

The First Amendment, like many of the Constitution's most important provisions, is drafted in the abstract language of political morality: it guarantees a "right" of free speech but does not specify the dimensions of that right—whether it includes a right of cigarette manufacturers to advertise their product on television, for instance, or a right of a Ku Klux Klan chapter publicly to insult and defame blacks or Jews, or a right of foreign governments to broadcast political advice in American elections. Decisions on these and a hundred other issues require interpretation and if any justice's interpretation is not to be arbitrary or purely partisan, it must be guided by principle—by some theory of why speech deserves exemption from government regulation in principle. Otherwise the Constitution's language becomes only a meaningless mantra to be incanted whenever a judge wants for any reason to protect some form of communication. Precedent—how the First Amendment has been interpreted and applied by the Supreme Court in the past—must also be respected. But since the meaning of past decisions is also a matter of interpretation, that, too, must be guided by a principled account of the First Amendment's point.

A First Amendment theory is therefore indispensible to responsible adjudication of free speech issues. Many such theories have been offered by justices, lawyers, constitutional scholars, and philosophers, and most of them assign particular importance to the protection of political speech—speech about candidates for public office and about issues that are or might be topics of partisan political debate. But none of these theories—absolutely none of them—justifies the damage the five conservative justices have just inflicted on our politics.

The most popular of these theories appeals to the need for an informed electorate. Freedom of political speech is an essential condition of an effective democracy because it ensures that voters have access to as wide and diverse a range of information and political opinion as possible. Oliver Wendell Holmes Jr., Learned Hand, and other great judges and scholars argued that citizens are more likely to reach good decisions if no ideas, however radical, are censored. But even if that is not so, the basic justification of majoritarian democracy—that it gives power to the informed and settled opinions of the largest number of people—nevertheless requires what Holmes called a "free marketplace of ideas."

Kennedy, who wrote the Court's opinion in *Citizens United* on behalf of the five conservatives, appealed to the "informed electorate" theory. But he offered no reason for supposing that allowing rich corporations to swamp elections with money will in fact produce a better-informed public—and there are many reasons to think it will produce a worse-informed one. Corporations have no ideas of their own. Their ads will promote the opinions of their managers, who could publish or broadcast those opinions on their own or with others of like mind through political action committees (PACs) or other organizations financed through voluntary individual contributions. So though allowing them to use their stockholders' money rather than their own will increase the volume of advertising, it will not add to the diversity of ideas offered to voters.

Corporate advertising will mislead the public, moreover, because its volume will suggest more public support than there actually is for the opinions the ads express. Many of the shareholders who will actually pay for the ads, who in many cases are members of pension and union funds, will hate the opinions they pay to advertise. Obama raised a great deal of money on the Internet, mostly from small contributors, to finance his presidential campaign, and we can expect political parties, candidates, and PACs to tap that source much more effectively in the future. But these contributions are made voluntarily by supporters, not by managers using the money of people who may well be opposed to their opinions. Corporate advertising is misleading in another way as well. It purports to offer opinions about the public interest, but in fact managers are legally required to spend corporate funds only to promote their corporation's own financial interests, which may very well be different.

There is, however, a much more important flaw in the conservative justices' argument. If corporations exercise the power that the Court has now given them, and buy an extremely large share of the television time available for political ads, their electioneering will undermine rather than improve the public's political education. Kennedy declared that speech may not be restricted just to make candidates more equal in their financial resources. But he misunderstood why other nations limit campaign expenditures. This is not just to be fair to all candidates, like requiring a single starting line for runners in a race, but to create the best conditions for the public to make an informed decision when it votes—the main purpose of the First Amendment, according to the marketplace theory. The Supreme Court of Canada understands the difference between these different goals. Creating "a level playing field for those who wish to engage in the electoral discourse," it said, ". . . enables voters to be better informed; no one voice is overwhelmed by another."

Monopolies and near monopolies are just as destructive to the marketplace of ideas as they are to any other market. A public debate about climate change, for instance, would not do much to improve the understanding of its audience if speaking time were auctioned so that energy companies were able to buy vastly more time than academic scientists. The great mass of voters is already very much more aware of electoral advertising spots constantly repeated, like beer ads, in popular dramatic series or major sports telecasts than of opinions reported mainly on public broadcasting news programs. Unlimited corporate advertising will make that distortion much greater.

The difference between the two goals I distinguished—aiming at electoral equality for its own sake and reducing inequality in order to protect the integrity of political debate—is real and important. If a nation capped permissible electoral expenditure at a very low level, it would achieve the greatest possible financial equality. But it would damage the quality of political debate by not permitting enough discussion and by preventing advocates of novel or unfamiliar opinion from spending enough funds to attract any public attention. Delicate judgment is needed to determine how much inequality must be permitted in order to ensure robust debate and an informed population. But allowing corporations to spend their corporate treasure on television ads conspicuously fails that test. Judged from the perspective of this theory of the First Amendment's purpose—that it aims at a better-educated populace—the conservatives' decision is all loss and no gain.

A second popular theory focuses on the importance of free speech not to educate the public at large but to protect the status, dignity, and moral development of individual citizens as equal partners in the political process. Justice John Paul Stevens summarized this theory in the course of his very long but irresistibly powerful dissenting opinion in *Citizens United*. Speaking for himself and Justices Stephen Breyer, Ruth Ginsburg, and Sonia Sotomayor, he said that "one fundamental concern of the First Amendment is to 'protec[t] the individual's interest in self-expression.'" Kennedy tried to appeal to this understanding of the First Amendment to justify free speech for corporations. "By taking the right to speak from some and giving it to others," he stated, "the Government deprives the disadvantaged person or class of the right to use speech to strive to establish worth, standing, and respect for the speaker's voice." But this is bizarre. The interests the First Amendment protects, on this second theory, are only the moral interests of individuals who would suffer frustration and indignity if they were censored. Only real human beings can have those emotions or suffer those insults. Corporations, which are only artificial legal inventions, cannot. The right to vote is surely at least as important a badge of equal citizenship as the right to speak, but not even the conservative justices have suggested that every corporation should have a ballot.

A third widely accepted purpose of the First Amendment lies in its contribution to honesty and transparency in government. If government were free to censor its critics, or to curtail the right to a free press guaranteed in a separate phrase of the First Amendment, then it would be harder for the public to discover official corruption. The Court's *Citizens United* decision does nothing to serve that further purpose. Corporations do not need to run television ads in the run-up to an election urging votes against particular candidates in order to report discoveries they may make about official dishonesty, or in order to defend themselves against any accusation of dishonesty made against them. And of course they have everyone else's access to print and television reporters.

Though the Court's decision will do nothing to deter corruption in that way, it will do a great deal to encourage one particularly dangerous form of it. It will sharply increase the opportunity of corporations to tempt or intimidate congressmen facing reelection campaigns. Obama and Speaker Nancy Pelosi had great difficulty persuading some members of the House of Representatives to vote for the health care reform bill, which finally passed with a dangerously thin majority, because those members feared they were risking their seats in the coming midterm elections. They knew, after the Court's decision, that they might face not just another party and candidate but a tidal wave of negative ads financed by health insurance companies with enormous sums of their shareholders' money to spend.

Kennedy wrote that there is no substantial risk of such corrupting influence so long as corporations do not "coordinate" their electioneering with any candidate's formal campaign. That seems particularly naive. Few congressmen would be unaware of or indifferent to the likelihood of a heavily financed advertising campaign urging voters to vote for him, if he worked in a corporation's interests, or against him if he did not. No coordination—no role of any candidate or his agents in the design of the ads—would be necessary.

Kennedy's naiveté seems even stranger when we notice the very substantial record of undue corporate influence laid before Congress when it adopted the BCRA. Before that act, corporations and other organizations were free to broadcast "issue" ads that did not explicitly endorse or oppose any candidates. The district court judge who first heard the *Citizens United* case found that, according to testimony of lobbyists and political consultants, at least some "Members of Congress are particularly grateful when negative issue advertisements are run by these organizations . . . [that] . . . use issue advocacy as a means to influence various Members of Congress." That influence can be expected to be even greater now that the Court has permitted explicit political endorsements or opposition as well. Kennedy's optimism went further: he denied that heavy corporate spending would lead the public to suspect that form of corruption. But the district court judge had reported that

> eighty percent of Americans polled are of the view that corporations and other organizations that engage in electioneering communications, which benefit specific elected officials, receive special consideration from those officials when matters arise that affect these corporations and organizations.

So the radical decision of the five conservative justices is not only not supported by any plausible First Amendment theory but is condemned by them all. Was their decision nevertheless required by the best reading of past Supreme Court decisions? That seems initially unlikely because, as I said, the decision overruled the two most plainly pertinent such decisions: *Austin* and *McConnell*. Nothing had happened to the country, or through further legislation, that cast any doubt on those decisions. The change that made the difference was simply Justice Sandra Day O'Connor's resignation in 2006 and President George W. Bush's appointment of Alito to replace her.

Overruling these decisions is itself remarkable, particularly for Roberts and Alito, who promised to respect precedent in their Senate confirmation hearings. One of the reasons that Kennedy offered to justify his decision is alarming. He said that since the conservative justices who dissented in those past cases and who remain on the Court had continued to complain about them, the decisions were only weak precedents. "The simple fact that one of our decisions remains controversial," he announced, "is, of course, insufficient to justify overruling it. But it does undermine the precedent's ability to contribute to the stable and orderly development of the law." In other words, if the four more liberal justices who dissented in this case continue to express their dissatisfaction with it, they would be free to overrule it if the balance of the Court shifts again. That novel view would mean the effective end of the doctrine of precedent on the Supreme Court.

* * *

* * * [T]he central issue in *Citizens United* * * * is whether corporations are entitled to the First Amendment protection that individuals and groups of individuals have. We have already noticed a variety of arguments that they do not. Very few individuals have anything like the capital accumulation of any of the

Fortune 500 corporations, the smallest of which had revenues of $5 billion (the top of the list—Exxon Mobil—had $443 billion) in 2008. Individuals speak and spend for themselves, together or in association with other individuals, while corporations speak for their commercial interests and spend other people's money, not their own. Individuals have rights, on which their dignity and standing depend, to play a part in the nation's government; corporations do not. No one thinks corporations should vote, and their rights to speak as institutions have been limited for over a century. * * *

* * *

Two Democrats—Senator Charles Schumer of New York and Representative Chris Van Hollen of Maryland—have announced proposals for legislation to protect the country from the Court's ruling. The Court might reject some of their proposals—forbidding corporate advertising by TARP recipients who have not paid back the government's loan, for example—as unconstitutional attempts to ban speech according to the speaker's identity. Kennedy left open the possibility, however, that Congress might constitutionally accept another of their proposals: banning electioneering by corporations controlled by foreigners.

He also explicitly recognized the constitutionality of another of the Democrats' proposals: he said that Congress might require public disclosure of a corporation's expenses for electioneering. (Thomas dissented from that part of Kennedy's ruling.) Congress should require prompt disclosures on the Internet so that the information could be made quickly available to voters. It would be even more important for Congress to provide for ample disclosure within a television advertisement itself. The disclosure should name not only fronting organizations, like Citizens United, but also at least the major corporate contributors to that organization. Congress should also require that any corporation that wished to engage in electioneering obtain at least the annual consent of its stockholders to that activity and to a proposed budget for it, and that the required disclosure in an ad report the percentage of stockholders who have refused that blanket consent. Finally, Congress should require that the CEO of the major corporate contributor to any ad appear in that ad to state that he or she believes that broadcasting it is in the corporation's own financial interests.

The conservative justices might object that such disclosure requirements would unduly burden corporate speech and impermissibly target one type of speaker for special restriction. They might say, to use one of Kennedy's favorite terms, that these requirements would "chill" corporate speech. But we must distinguish measures designed to deter speech from those designed to guard against deception. The in-ad disclosures I describe need not take significantly more broadcast time than the "Stand By My Ad" rule that now requires a candidate to declare in his campaign's ad that he approves it. If several corporations finance an ad together, much of the required information—the amount of shareholder dissent, for instance—could be disclosed as an aggregate figure. If these requirements discourage a corporation's speech not because of the expense but for the different reason that managers are unwilling to report shareholder opposition or to acknowledge their fiduciary duty to act only in the financial interests of their own company, then their fear only shows the pertinence of Kennedy's own claim that "shareholder democracy" is the right remedy to protect shareholders who oppose a corporation's politics.

* * *

The Supreme Court's conservative phalanx has demonstrated once again its power and will to reverse America's drive to greater equality and more genuine democracy. It threatens a step-by-step return to a constitutional stone age of right-wing ideology. Once again it offers justifications that are untenable in both constitutional theory and legal precedent. Stevens's remarkable dissent in this case shows how much we will lose when he soon retires. We must hope that Obama nominates a progressive replacement who not only is young enough to endure the bad days ahead but has enough intellectual firepower to help construct a rival and more attractive vision of what our Constitution really means.

Bradley A. Smith

Citizens United We Stand

March 24, 2009, was a turning point in the long-running battle to restrict political speech, aka "campaign finance reform." On that day, the Supreme Court heard oral argument in *Citizens United v. Federal Election Commission*, in which the conservative activist group Citizens United challenged the provisions of the McCain-Feingold law that had prohibited it from airing a documentary film, *Hillary: The Movie*, through video on demand within 30 days of any 2008 Democratic presidential primary.

In the course of the argument, Deputy Solicitor General Malcolm Stewart, an experienced Supreme Court litigator, argued that a 1990 precedent, *Austin v. Michigan Chamber of Commerce*, gave the government the power to limit any political communication funded by a corporation, even a nonprofit such as Citizens United. Justice Samuel Alito asked Stewart if that power would extend to censoring political books published by corporations. Stewart responded—consistent with the government's position at all stages of the case—that yes, it would. There was an audible hush—if such a thing is possible—in the court. Then Justice Alito, appearing to speak for the room, merely said, "I find that pretty incredible."

Incredible or not, that was, and had been for many years, the position of the U.S. government. But until that moment, it seemed to have never quite sunken in with the justices. Americans are willing to accept far more abridgements of free speech than we sometimes like to believe, but the idea of banning books strikes an emotional chord that something described simply as "prohibitions and limits on campaign spending" does not. Americans may not always live up to the Bill of Rights, but Americans do not ban books. A stunned Court eventually asked the parties to reargue the case, to consider whether *Austin* should be overruled.

On reargument last September, Solicitor General Elena Kagan tried to control the damage, arguing that the government never actually had tried to censor books, even as she reaffirmed its claimed authority to do just that. She also stated that "pamphlets," unlike books, were clearly fair game for government censorship. (Former Federal Election Commissioner Hans von Spakovksy has noted that in fact the FEC has conducted lengthy investigations into whether certain books violated campaign finance laws, though it has not yet held that a book publisher violated the law through publication. And the FEC has attempted to penalize publishers of magazines and financial newsletters, only to be frustrated by the courts.) With the endgame of "campaign finance reform" finally laid out plainly, the Supreme Court's decision seemed a foregone conclusion. Sure enough, in January, the Court ruled that corporations, as associations of natural persons, have a right to spend funds from their general treasuries to support or oppose political candidates and causes—including through the publication or distribution of books and movies.

Though this ruling is obviously a correct interpretation of the First Amendment, reaction to the Court's decision in *Citizens United* has been loud, often disingenuous, and in some cases nearly hysterical. President Obama used his

State of the Union address to publicly scold the Court, in the process so mischaracterizing the Court's decision that he prompted Judge Alito's now famous, spontaneous rejoinder, "Not true."

Meanwhile, Democrats in Congress and the states have been working overtime to come up with "fixes," ranging from the absurd (a Vermont legislator proposed forcing corporate sponsors to be identified every five seconds during any broadcast ad), to the merely pernicious (such as proposals that seek to immobilize corporate speech by forcing corporations to hold a majority vote of shareholders before each and every expenditure). The fact that virtually all of these proposed "fixes" have been sponsored by Democrats, with the aim of silencing what they perceive to be the pro-Republican voices of the business community, merely illustrates once again the basic problem with campaign finance reform that *Citizens United* sought to alleviate: the desire to manipulate the law for partisan purposes.

Citizens United is at once both a potential game-changer and a decision whose "radicalism" has been widely overstated. Why overstated? Well, to start, one would never guess from the left's hysteria that even prior to *Citizens United*, 28 states, representing roughly 60 percent of the U.S. population, already allowed corporations and unions to make expenditures promoting or opposing candidates for office in state elections; in 26 states, such corporate and union expenditures were unlimited. Moreover, while the first bans on corporate spending were enacted more than a century ago, prior to the 1990 *Austin* decision, the Supreme Court had never upheld a ban, or even a limitation, on independent expenditures supporting or opposing a political candidate. It was the misleading contention that the decision overturned "100 years of law and precedent," that appears to have evoked Justice Alito's "not true" response to the president's State of the Union comments.

The president also stated, again misleadingly, that the decision would open the door for foreign corporations to spend unlimited sums in American elections. In fact, another provision of federal law, not at issue in the case, already prohibits any foreign national, including foreign corporations, from spending money in any federal campaign. FEC regulations, which have the force of the law, further prohibit any foreign national from playing any role in the political spending decisions of any U.S. corporation, political action committee, or association. And the Court specifically stated that *Citizens United* was not addressing these laws at all. So while some states may tweak their state rules in the wake of *Citizens United* to limit the ability of U.S. incorporated and headquartered subsidiaries of foreign corporations to spend money in campaigns, the "foreign corporation" bogeyman is little more than leftist demagoguery.

What is much more alarming than the prospect of U.S. corporations with some foreign ownership participating in campaigns is the fact that the four most liberal justices on the Supreme Court would have upheld the *Austin* precedent, and with it the authority of the federal government to censor books and movies published, produced, or distributed by U.S. corporations. But by affirming the rights of citizens to speak out on political issues, even when organized through the corporate form, the Supreme Court quite rightly put political speech back at the core of the First Amendment.

After four decades in which the Court had given greater First Amendment protection to such activities as topless dancing, simulated child pornography, Internet porn, flag burning, and the transfer of stolen information than to political speech, *Citizens United* is a wonderful reaffirmation of the primacy of political speech in the First Amendment jurisprudence. In that respect, the case has already been a constitutional game-changer. Future litigation is sure to follow, building on the success of *Citizens United* to free up the political system and strike down the still extensive web of regulation that envelops political speech.

Some of these challenges are already well under way. For example, under current federal law, an individual such as George Soros is free to spend $20 million to promote his favored candidates, but if two or more individuals get together to do the same thing, neither can contribute more than $5,000 to the effort. It is hard to see what anti-corruption purpose such a dichotomy serves, and in *SpeechNow.org v. FEC*, argued before the U.S. Court of Appeals for the District of Columbia Circuit in January, plaintiffs argue that if it is not corrupting for one person to spend unlimited sums on independent expenditures, it is not corrupting if two or more people combine their resources to promote the candidates of their choice. A decision is expected soon. Expect, too, legal challenges to the federal prohibition on contributions by corporations directly to candidates—if a $2,300 contribution from a corporate CEO or PAC is not corrupting, it is hard to see how a $2,300 contribution directly from a corporate treasury is corrupting.

Much less clear is whether *Citizens United* will be a game-changer in electoral politics. The general consensus is that *Citizens United* favors Republicans, based on the widely held perception that corporations are more likely to support Republicans than Democrats. But this perception may not be true. Even before *Citizens United*, the federal government and most states also allowed corporations to operate political action committees (PACs), which could then solicit the corporation's managers and shareholders for voluntary contributions to the PAC, which in turn could contribute limited amounts to candidates or make independent expenditures to support candidates. But whereas corporate PACs typically gave about two-thirds of their contributions to Republicans during the 1990s and the first part of the last decade, peaking in the 2004 cycle at nearly 10 to 1 for the GOP, over the past three years corporate PACs have devoted a slim majority of the contributions to Democrats.

More importantly, there is good reason to doubt that *Fortune* 500 companies are going to start making large expenditures in political campaigns. As noted, even before *Citizens United*, 28 states allowed corporate and union spending on state and local political races, yet large-scale corporate spending was very rare in those states. Another sign that corporations are not eager to jump headfirst into political spending comes from the relatively low level of activity by corporate PACs. Among the *Fortune* 500—huge corporations that are all heavily regulated by the government—only about 60 percent actually maintained PACs.

These PACs are subject to extensive regulation, which runs up operating costs to the point that the operating costs of PACs often total more than half of their total revenue. Corporations can, however, pay these operating costs directly from their corporate treasuries. Yet roughly half of these PACs' operating expenses were paid not by the corporations that established them, but out of funds donated to the PACs. In other words, even before *Citizens United*, corporate America could have roughly doubled the amount of money available in their PACs to use for political expenditures simply by paying the administrative and legal costs of operating the PAC from their general treasuries. Yet they did not. And only about 10 percent of PACs contributed the maximum legal amount in any election. All this suggests a lack of interest in political participation.

The truth is, the *Fortune* 500 prefer lobbying to campaigning. Even prior to McCain-Feingold, when corporations could support parties with "soft money," the *Fortune* 500 spent roughly 10 times as much money on lobbying as on political expenditures. As Edward Kangas, former chairman of Deloitte Touche Tohmatsu and of the Committee for Economic Development said in the *New York Times*, explaining his support for McCain-Feingold, "We have lobbyists."

But if large corporations may be reluctant to spend on political races, Big Labor is not. Labor unions also benefit from the *Citizens United* decision, and have historically been much more partisan in their political activity than has big business. The relatively small number of unions makes it easier for them to coordinate their activity. Add in the lack of any need to avoid offending a portion of their customer base, and unions are well positioned to take advantage of *Citizens United*. Indeed, within weeks of the *Citizens United* decision, three unions pledged to spend $1 million each to try to defeat U.S. senator Blanche Lincoln in the Democratic primary in Arkansas, finding her insufficiently dedicated to Big Labor's agenda.

Thus, if *Citizens United* ultimately works to favor conservatives, it may be less due to the *Fortune 500* than to the small business community. These small and midsized companies usually cannot afford the high administrative costs of maintaining a PAC, and often don't have enough employees eligible for solicitation to make forming a PAC worthwhile in any case. Moreover, unlike *Fortune 500* companies, small businesses typically do not maintain permanent large lobbying operations in Washington, and because they are less likely to be heavily regulated or engaged in government contracting, their contact with Washington is likely to be more sporadic. For these companies, the ability to speak directly to the public is potentially a great benefit.

This small business community is generally much more conservative in its politics than is the *Fortune 500*, and in particular much more hostile to government regulation. But these small companies are unlikely to undertake major campaigns on their own. Thus it may be up to trade associations and business groups, such as chambers of commerce, to organize business efforts.

Meanwhile, managers and executives, particularly of large, publicly traded companies, will need to do some serious rethinking about their obligations to shareholders. Do they have an obligation to their shareholders to try to maximize long-term value by opposing tax and spend, pro-regulatory politicians, and working to elect officials who appreciate pro-growth policies? Or do they play it safe, avoid political activity, and hope that the regulators will eat them last? The decisions they make may ultimately determine the real importance of *Citizens United*.

Matt Bai

How Much Has *Citizens United* Changed the Political Game?

"A hundred million dollars is nothing," the venture capitalist Andy Rappaport told me back in the summer of 2004. This was at a moment when wealthy liberals like George Soros and Peter Lewis were looking to influence national politics by financing their own voter-turnout machine and TV ads and by creating an investment fund for start-ups. Rappaport's statement struck me as an expression of supreme hubris. In American politics at that time, $100 million really meant something.

Eight years later, of course, his pronouncement seems quaint. Conservative groups alone, including a super PAC led by Karl Rove and another group backed by the brothers Charles and David Koch, will likely spend more than a billion dollars trying to take down Barack Obama by the time November rolls around.

The reason for this exponential leap in political spending, if you talk to most Democrats or read most news reports, comes down to two words: Citizens United. The term is shorthand for a Supreme Court decision that gave corporations much of the same right to political speech as individuals have, thus removing virtually any restriction on corporate money in politics. The oft-repeated narrative of 2012 goes like this: Citizens United unleashed a torrent of money from businesses and the multimillionaires who run them, and as a result we are now seeing the corporate takeover of American politics.

As a matter of political strategy, this is a useful story to tell, appealing to liberals and independent voters who aren't necessarily enthusiastic about the administration but who are concerned about societal inequality, which is why President Obama has made it a rallying cry almost from the moment the Citizens United ruling was made. But if you're trying to understand what's really going on with politics and money, the accepted narrative around Citizens United is, at best, overly simplistic. And in some respects, it's just plain wrong.

It helps first to understand what Citizens United did and didn't do to change the opaque rules governing outside money. Go back to, say, 2007, and pretend you're a conservative donor. At this moment, you would still have been free to write a check for any amount to a 527—so named because of the shadowy provision in the tax code that made such groups legal. (America Coming Together and the infamous Swift Boat Veterans for Truth were both 527s.) Even corporations, though they couldn't contribute to a candidate or a party, were free to write unlimited checks to something called a social-welfare group, whose principal purpose, ostensibly, is issue advocacy rather than political activity. The anti-tax Club for Growth, for instance, is a social-welfare group. So, remarkably, are the Koch brothers' Americans for Prosperity and Karl Rove's Crossroads GPS.

There were, however, a few caveats when it came to the way these groups could spend their money. Neither a 527 nor a social-welfare group could engage in "express advocacy"—that is, overtly making the case for one candidate over another. Nor could they use corporate money for "electioneering communications"—a category defined as radio or television advertising that even mentions a candidate's name within 30 days of a primary or 60 days of a general election. So under the old rules, the Club for Growth couldn't broadcast an ad that said "Vote Against Barack Obama," but it could spend that money on as many ads as it wanted that said "Barack Obama has ruined America—call and tell him to stop!" as long as it did so more than 60 days before an election. (The distinction between those two ads may sound silly and arcane to you, but that's why you don't sit on the Federal Election Commission.)

Citizens United and a couple of related court decisions changed all of this in two essential ways, and each of them was more incremental than transformational. First, the Supreme Court wiped away much of the rigmarole about "express advocacy" and "electioneering." Now any outside group can use corporate money to make a direct case for who deserves your vote and why, and they can do so right up to Election Day. The second change is that the old 527s have now been made effectively obsolete, replaced by the super PAC. The main difference between a super PAC and a social-welfare group, practically speaking, is that a super PAC has to disclose the identity of its donors, while social-welfare groups generally do not.

Those who criticize the effect of Citizens United look at these very technical changes and see an obvious causal relationship. The high court says outside groups are allowed to use corporate dollars to expressly support candidates, and suddenly we have this tidal wave of money threatening to overwhelm the airways. One must have led to the other, right?

Well, not necessarily. Legally speaking, zillionaires were no less able to write fat checks four years ago than they are today. And while it is true that corporations can now give money for specific purposes that were prohibited before, it seems they aren't, or at least not at a level that accounts for anything like the sudden influx of money into the system. According to a brief filed by Mitch McConnell, the Senate minority leader, and Floyd Abrams, the First Amendment lawyer, in a Montana case on which the Supreme Court ruled last month, not a single Fortune 100 company contributed to a candidate's super PAC during this year's Republican primaries. Of the $96 million or more raised by these super PACs, only about 13 percent came from privately held corporations, and less than 1 percent came from publicly traded corporations.

This only tells part of the story. The general election has just begun, and big energy and health care companies may still be pouring money into social-welfare groups that don't have to disclose their donors. The watchdog group Citizens for Responsibility and Ethics in Washington reported last month, for instance, that Aetna anonymously contributed more than $7 million to two such groups. We may never know precisely how much money is coming from similar companies, which should alarm anyone who cares about the integrity and transparency of government.

But the best anecdotal evidence suggests that this kind of thing isn't happening in nearly the proportions you might expect. Kenneth Gross, an election lawyer who represents an array of large corporations, told me that few of his clients have contributed to the social-welfare groups engaged in political activity this year. They know those contributions might become public at some point, and no company that sells a product wants to risk the kind of consumer reaction that engulfed Target in 2010, after it contributed $150,000 to a Minnesota group backing a conservative candidate opposing gay marriage. "If you've got a bank on every corner, if you've got stores in every strip mall, you don't want to be associated with a social cause," Gross told me.

None of this is to say that Citizens United hasn't had an impact. Gross and others point out that in the era before Citizens United, while individuals and companies could still contribute huge sums to outside groups, they were to some extent deterred by the confusing web of rules and the liability they might incur for violations. What the new rulings did, as the experts like to put it, was to "lift the cloud of uncertainty" that hung over such expenditures, and the effect of this psychological shift should not be underestimated. It almost certainly accounts for some rise in political money this year, both from individuals and companies.

Even so, the Supreme Court's ruling really wasn't the sort of tectonic event that Obama and his allies would have you believe it was. "I'd go so far as to call it a liberal delusion," Ira Glasser, the former executive director of the ACLU and a liberal dissenter on Citizens United, told me. Which leads to an obvious question: If Citizens United doesn't explain this billion-dollar blast of outside money, then what does?

You may remember that back in the '90s, the most nefarious influence in politics emanated from what was then called "soft money"—basically, unlimited contributions from rich people, corporations, and labor unions to both major parties. According to data from the Center for Responsive Politics, in 2000, the last presidential year in which soft money was legal, the two parties raised more than $450 million of it, divided almost equally between them. Only 38 percent of that came from individuals.

That all changed with the passage of the Bipartisan Campaign Reform Act of 2002, popularly known as the McCain-Feingold law. The new law stamped out soft money for good, but it also created a vacuum in political fund-raising. The parties could no longer tap an endless stream of soft money, but thanks to the advent of the 527, rich ideologues with their own agendas could write massive checks for the purpose of building what were, essentially, shadow parties—independent groups with their own turnout and advertising campaigns, limited in what they could say but accountable to no candidate or party boss. Wealthy liberals like Soros and Lewis, along with groups like MoveOn.org, were the first to spot the opportunity. All told, wealthy liberals spent something close to $200 million in an effort to oust George W. Bush in 2004, setting an entirely new standard for outside spending.

Richard L. Hasen, an expert on campaign finance at the University of California at Irvine, recently wrote an article for Slate titled, "The Numbers Don't Lie," in which he showed that total outside spending, as measured through March 8 of every election season, seemed to explode after the Citizens United decision, reaching about $15.9 million in 2010 (compared with $1.8 million in the previous midterm cycle) and $88 million this year (compared with $37.5 million at the same point in 2008). "If this was not caused by Citizens United," he wrote, "we have a mighty big coincidence on our hands."

But there are alternate ways to interpret this data. The level of outside money increased 164 percent from 2004 to 2008. Then it rose 135 percent from 2008 to 2012. In other words, while the sheer amount of dollars seems considerably more ominous after Citizens United, the percentage of change from one presidential election to the next has remained pretty consistent since the passage of McCain-Feingold. And this suggests that the rising amount of outside money was probably bound to reach ever more staggering levels with or without Citizens United. The unintended consequence of McCain-Feingold was to begin a gradual migration of political might from inside the party structure to outside it.

And in his examination of raw numbers, Hasen managed to ignore what is probably the most relevant bit of data during this period: 2010 and 2012 were the first election cycles since the enactment of McCain-Feingold in which a Democrat occupied the White House. Rich conservatives weren't inspired to invest their fortunes in 2004, when Bush ran for the second time while waging an unpopular war, or in 2008, when they were forced to endure the nomination of McCain. But now there's a president and a legislative agenda they bitterly despise (much as Soros and his friends saw the Bush presidency as an existential threat to the country), so it's not surprising that outside spending by Republicans in 2010 and 2012 would dwarf everything that came before. What we are seeing—what we almost certainly would have seen even without the court's ruling in Citizens United—is the full force of conservative wealth in America, mobilized by a common enemy for the first time since the fall of party monopolies.

A consequence of McCain-Feingold has been to flip on its head an old truism of politics, which is that incumbency comes with a fixed financial advantage. In the era of soft money, controlling the White House meant that a party could almost always leverage its considerable resources to dominate fund-raising. But today it's much easier to tap into the fury and anxiety of out-of-power millionaires than it is to amass contributions in defense of the status quo. This dynamic probably explains why wealthy Democrats who pioneered the idea of outside money during the Bush years have largely stood down this year, even while conservative fund-raising has soared. It isn't that liberals don't like Obama or grow queasy at the mention of super PACs. It's a function of human nature: nobody really gets pumped up to write a $10 million check just to keep things more or less as they are.

If you're a Democrat, there's some good news here. One persistent fear you hear from liberals is that Citizens United altered the balance between the parties in a permanent way—that corporate money will give Republicans a structural advantage that can never be overcome. What's more likely is that the boom in outside money will prove to be cyclical, with the momentum swinging toward whoever feels shut out and persecuted at the moment. Liberals dominated outside spending in 2004 and 2006. And should Romney become president, they'll most likely do so again.

It's worth asking just how much an advantage all of this outside money actually confers. The greatest impact of this year's imbalance in outside money will be felt on the state level, where a lot of House seats and control of the Senate hang in the balance, and where a sharp gust of advertising can often blow the results in one direction or another. But a presidential campaign is different, focusing as it does on a dozen or so pivotal states and a limited number of advertising markets. There's probably a limit to how many 30-second spots all of these groups can cram onto cable stations during late-night showings of *Turner & Hooch*.

I recently called Carter Eskew, a longtime Democratic adman and strategist whose clients included Al Gore in 2000, and asked him a simple question: How much did he think he would really need for a candidate today, if he could have an unlimited budget to run a national ad campaign, including all the outside money? Eskew paused before giving a declarative answer: $500 million. Anything beyond that, he said, was probably overkill.

In other words, there's a threshold below which a presidential candidate can't really compete effectively, and that number—whether it's $500 million or something less—is outlandish enough that it should give us pause. But beyond that number, it's not clear that spending an extra $200 million or $500 million will really make all that much of a difference on Election Day. More likely, the two ideological factions are now like rivals of the nuclear age, stockpiling enough bombs to destroy the same cities over and over again, when one would do the job.

You could even argue that whatever benefit a campaign derives from all this money is balanced, somewhat, by the threat it poses. Back in the days of soft money, a candidate had ownership of his party's national apparatus and the accusations it hurled on prime-time TV. He was responsible for the integrity of his argument, and his advisers ultimately controlled it. What the reform-minded architects of McCain-Feingold inadvertently unleashed, what Citizens United intensified but by no means created, is a world in which a big part of the money in a presidential campaign is spent by political entrepreneurs and strategists who are unanswerable to any institution. Candidates and parties who become the vehicles of angry outsiders, as Mitt Romney is now, don't really have control of their own campaigns anymore; to a large extent, they are the instruments of volatile forces beyond their own reckoning.

Maybe that makes for a cleaner and more democratic system than the one we had before, in the way the campaign-finance reformers intended. Standing here in 2012, it's just hard to see how.

DISCUSSION QUESTIONS

1. The actions of public officials affect corporate entities, including labor unions. Should these entities thus be free to express their views on candidates by spending independently on campaign ads in elections (i.e., not donating directly to candidates)? If so, what concerns if any would you have about the impact of this spending on democracy? If not, why is it acceptable for government officials to take actions that affect these organizations but not acceptable for these organizations to spend money to try to influence who the government officials should be?

2. Do you agree with Dworkin's argument that none of the five theories of the First Amendment apply to corporate speech? Which of the five would have the strongest basis for justifying a First Amendment protection for corporate speech?

3. Should corporations be treated as people for purposes of political speech? If yes, why isn't it sufficient that the individuals who work for the corporations can spend their own money independently in elections? If not, why should individuals give up their free speech rights just because they incorporate as a group that shares common concerns?

4. Whose arguments about the implications of *Citizens United* do you find more compelling? Do you agree with Dworkin, who sees it as a threat to democracy? Smith, who thinks the decision promotes freedom of speech? Or Bai, who believes the decision was mildly consequential but who appears to have some concerns about the amount of spending in politics?

5. The *Citizens United* ruling applies to many forms of corporate entities, including for-profit corporations, many non-profits, and labor unions. Whether you support or oppose the decision, does this wide reach increase or decrease your support or opposition?

13

Government and the Economy: Is Income Inequality a Problem?

By any measure, income and wealth are distributed unequally in the United States. That may not come as a surprise, but the degree to which wealth and income are concentrated might be. According to recent Census figures, household income at the ninetieth percentile (meaning that 10 percent of households earned more income, and 89 percent less) was nearly twelve times household income at the tenth percentile. According to the Congressional Research Service, the top 1 percent of households held 34.5 percent of the nation's wealth. The bottom 50 percent held 1.1 percent in 2010. This means that the top 1 percent held over thirty-one times the wealth of the entire bottom half of the country. In 1989, the ratio was only 10:1.

The fact of income inequality is indisputable. Whether that inequality has negative effects (and what to do about it) is a more complicated question. To many, high levels of income inequality signify gross failure of basic norms of fairness, and has harmful consequences for cohesion, civic life, and ultimately, even political stability. In this view, income inequality is both a cause and a consequence of political inequality, as the rich are better equipped to rig the system in their favor through favorable tax laws and regulations that further protect and concentrate wealth. Those who aren't wealthy wind up with the scraps:

underfunded public schools, dangerous neighborhoods, crumbling infrastructure, inadequate services, and on and on. Others maintain that inequality is not a serious problem, and that even if it were, the alternative—draconian policies that forcefully redistribute wealth—is even worse. Moreover, since nobody can say what distribution of income would be fair, any attempt to achieve balance is arbitrary.

The two readings in this debate clash directly on this point. Timothy Noah, author of *The Great Divergence*, which claims that inequality is at crisis proportions, summarized his argument in a series of columns in the online journal *Slate*. Here, he focuses on the consequences of excessive inequality. Apart from the fundamental unfairness—working class people unable to amass resources, take a day off, or achieve any sense of economic security, while the wealthy enjoy gated communities and lives of privilege—inequality has a number of corrosive effects that go well beyond this: lower economic growth, bad health outcomes for those at the bottom, and driving the middle class into the ranks of the poor. Noah specifically attacks the main arguments made by those who dismiss the idea that income inequality is either not worth worrying about, or is actually a good thing.

Did Noah provide a caricature of the argument that inequality may be a positive? Richard Epstein, a professor at New York University Law School, makes the argument that Noah dismisses: that inequality is actually a good thing, not because it gives people an incentive to work their way up the income ladder, but because the policies needed to remedy it make everybody worse off (through lower economic growth and coercive rules). The only way to reduce inequality is through tax policies that transfer wealth from those who have wealth to those who do not. Those policies not only do not work, Epstein argues, but they have the effect of eliminating aggregate wealth. Part of the problem is that when governments redistribute wealth, groups compete for the right to transfer those resources to themselves (Epstein notes the success of labor unions, big business, and agricultural interests in doing this, and suggests that income redistribution is no different). And part of the problem is that forced exchange via government coercion is, by definition, less efficient than voluntary exchange. The result may be less inequality, but also less wealth.

Timothy Noah

Why We Can't Ignore Growing
Income Inequality

> Clarence the Angel: We don't use money in heaven.
> George Bailey: Comes in pretty handy down here, bub.
> —Frank Capra's *It's A Wonderful Life* (1946)

The Declaration of Independence says that all men are created equal, but we know that isn't true. George Clooney was created better-looking than me. Stephen Hawking was born smarter, Evander Holyfield stronger, Jon Stewart funnier, and Warren Buffett better able to understand financial markets. All these people have parlayed their exceptional gifts into very high incomes—much higher than mine. Is that so odd? Odder would be if Buffett or Clooney were forced to live on my income, adequate though it might be to a petit-bourgeois journalist. Lest you conclude my equanimity is in any way unique (we Slate writers are known for our contrarianism), Barbara Ehrenreich, in her 2001 book *Nickel and Dimed*, quotes a woman named Colleen, a single mother of two, saying much the same thing about the wealthy families whose floors she scrubs on hands and knees. "I don't mind, really," she says, "because I guess I'm a simple person, and I don't want what they have. I mean, it's nothing to me."

It is easy to make too much of this, and a few conservatives have done so in seeking to dismiss the importance (or even existence) of the Great Divergence. Let's look at their arguments.

Inequality is good. Every year the American Economic Association invites a distinguished economist to deliver at its annual conference the Richard T. Ely Lecture. Ely, a founder of the AEA and a leader in the Progressive movement, would have been horrified by the 1999 lecture that Finis Welch, a professor of economics (now emeritus) at Texas A&M, delivered in his name. Its title was "In Defense of Inequality."

Welch began by stating that "all of economics results from inequality. Without inequality of priorities and capabilities, there would be no trade, no specialization, and no surpluses produced by cooperation." He invited his audience to consider a world in which skill, effort, and sheer chance played no role whatsoever in what you got paid. The only decision that would affect your wage level would be when to leave school. "After that, the clock ticks, and wages follow the experience path. Nothing else matters. Can you imagine a more horrible, a more deadening existence?"

But something close to the dystopia Welch envisioned already exists for those toiling in the economy's lower tiers. Welch should have a chat with his office receptionist. Or he could read *Nickel and Dimed*, or the 2010 book *Catching Out* by Dick J. Reavis, a contributing editor at *Texas Monthly* who went undercover as a day laborer.

Waitresses, construction workers, dental assistants, call-center operators—people in these jobs are essentially replaceable, and usually have bosses who don't distinguish between individual initiative and insubordination. Even experience is of limited value, because it's often accompanied by diminishing physical vigor.

Welch said that he believed inequality was destructive only when "the low-wage citizenry views society as unfair, when it views effort as not worthwhile, when upward mobility is impossible or so unlikely that its pursuit is not worthwhile." Colleen's comment would appear to suggest that the first of these conditions has not been met. But that's only because I omitted what she went on to say: "But what I would like is to be able to take a day off now and then . . . if I had to . . . and still be able to buy groceries the next day." Colleen may not begrudge the rich the material goods they've acquired through skill, effort, and sheer chance, but that doesn't mean she thinks her own labors secure her an adequate level of economic security. Clearly, they don't.

Welch judged the growing financial rewards accruing to those with higher levels of education a good thing insofar as they provided an incentive to go to college or graduate school. But for most of the 20th century, smaller financial incentives attracted enough workers to meet the economy's growing demand for higher-skilled labor. That demand isn't being met today, as Harvard economists Claudia Goldin and Lawrence Katz have shown. Welch also said that both women and blacks made income gains during the Great Divergence (duly noted in our installment on race and gender, though the gains by blacks were so tiny that it's more accurate to say blacks didn't lose ground). But that's hardly evidence that growing income inequality unrelated to gender or race doesn't matter. Finally, Welch argued that the welfare state has made it too easy not to work at all. But the Great Divergence had a more significant impact on the working middle class than on the destitute.

Income doesn't matter. In most contexts, libertarians can fairly be said to place income in very high regard. Tax it to even the slightest degree and they cry foul. If government assistance must be extended, they prefer a cash transaction to the provision of government services. The market is king, and what is the market if not a mighty river of money?

Bring up the topic of growing income inequality, though, and you're likely to hear a different tune. Case in point: "Thinking Clearly About Economic Inequality," a 2009 Cato Institute paper by Will Wilkinson. Income isn't what matters, Wilkinson argues; consumption is, and "the weight of the evidence shows that the run-up in consumption inequality has been considerably less dramatic than the rise in income inequality." Wilkinson concedes that the available data on consumption are shakier than the available data on income; he might also have mentioned that consumption in excess of income usually means debt—as in, say, subprime mortgages. The thought that the have-nots are compensating for their lower incomes by putting themselves (and the country) in economically ruinous hock is not reassuring.

Wilkinson further argues that consumption isn't what matters; what matters is utility gained from consumption. Joe and Sam both own refrigerators. Joe's is a $350 model from Ikea. Sam's is an $11,000 state-of-the-art Sub-Zero. Sam gets to consume a lot more than Joe, but whatever added utility he achieves is marginal; Joe's Ikea fridge "will keep your beer just as cold." But if getting rich is only a matter of spending more money on the same stuff you'd buy if you were poor, why bother to climb the greasy pole at all?

Next Wilkinson decides that utility isn't what matters; what matters is buying power. Food is cheaper than ever before. Since lower-income people spend their money disproportionately on food, declining food prices, Wilkinson argues, constitute a sort of raise. Never mind that Ehrenreich routinely found, in her travels among the lower middle class, workers who routinely skipped lunch to save money or brought an individual-size pack of junk food and called that lunch. Reavis reports that a day laborer's typical lunch budget is $3. That won't buy much. The problem isn't the cost of food per se but the cost of shelter, which has shot up so high that low-income families don't have much left over to spend on other essentials.

Declining food prices constitute a sort of raise for higher-income people too. But Wilkinson writes that the affluent spend a smaller share of their budget on food and a much larger share on psychotherapy and yoga and cleaning services. And since services like these are unaffected by foreign competition or new efficiencies in manufacturing, Wilkinson argues, providers can charge whatever they like.

Tell it to Colleen! I recently worked out with my new cleaning lady what I would pay her. Here's how the negotiation went. I told her what I would pay her. She said, "OK." According to the Bureau of Labor Statistics, the median income for a housekeeper is $19,250, which is $2,800 below the poverty line for a family of four.

A more thoughtful version of the income-doesn't-matter argument surfaces in my former *Slate* colleague Mickey Kaus' 1992 book *The End of Equality*. Kaus chided "Money Liberals" for trying to redistribute income when instead they might be working to diminish social inequality by creating or shoring up spheres in which rich and poor are treated the same. Everybody can picnic in the park. Everybody should be able to receive decent health care. Under a compulsory national service program, everybody would be required to perform some civilian or military duty.

As a theoretical proposition, Kaus' vision is appealing. Bill Gates will always have lots more money than me, no matter how progressive the tax system becomes. But if he gets called to jury duty he has to show up, just like me. When his driver's license expires, he'll be just as likely to have to take a driving test. Why not expand this egalitarian zone to, say, education, by making public schools so good that Gates' grandchildren will be as likely to attend them as mine or yours?

But at a practical level, Kaus' exclusive reliance on social equality is simply inadequate. For one thing, the existing zones of social equality are pretty circumscribed. Neither Gates nor I spend a lot of time hanging around the Department of Motor Vehicles. Rebuilding or creating the more meaningful spheres—say, public education or a truly national health care system—won't occur overnight. Nurturing the social-equality sphere isn't likely to pay off for a very long time.

Kaus would like to separate social equality from income equality, but the two go hand in hand. In theory they don't have to, but in practice they just do. Among industrialized nations, those that have achieved the greatest social equality are the same ones that have achieved the greatest income equality. France, for example, has a level of income inequality much lower than that of most other countries in the Organization for Economic Cooperation and Development. It's one of the very few places where income inequality has been going down. (Most everywhere else it's gone up, though nowhere to the degree it has in the United States.) France also enjoys what the World Health Organization calls the world's finest health care system (by which the WHO means, in large part, the most egalitarian one; this is the famous survey from 2000 in which the U.S. ranked 37th).

Do France's high marks on both social equality and income equality really strike you as a coincidence? As incomes become more unequal, a likelier impulse among the rich isn't to urge or even allow the government to create or expand public institutions where they can mix it up with the proles. It's to create or expand private institutions that will help them maintain separation from the proles, with whom they have less and less in common. According to Jonathan Rowe, who has written extensively about social equality, that's exactly what's happening in the United States. In an essay titled "The Vanishing Commons" that appeared in *Inequality Matters*, a 2005 anthology, Rowe notes that Congress has been busy extending copyright terms and patent monopolies and turning over public lands to mining and timber companies for below-market fees. "In an 'ownership' society especially," Rowe writes, "we should think about what we own in common, not just what we keep apart."

Inequality doesn't create unhappiness. Arthur C. Brooks, president of the American Enterprise Institute, argued this point in *National Review* online in June. What drives entrepreneurs, he wrote, is not the desire for money but the desire for earned success. When people feel they deserve their success, they are happy; when they do not, they aren't. "The money is just the metric of the value that the person is creating."

Brooks marshaled very little evidence to support his argument, and what evidence he did muster was less impressive than he thought. He made much of a 1996 survey that asked people how successful they felt, and how happy. Among the 45 percent who counted themselves "completely successful" or "very successful," 39 percent said they were very happy. Among the 55 percent who counted themselves at most "somewhat successful," only 20 percent said they were happy. Brooks claimed victory with the finding that successful people were more likely to be happy (or at least to say they were), by 19 percentage points, than less-successful people. More striking, though, was that 61 percent of the successful people—a significant majority—did not say they were "very happy." Nowhere in the survey were the successful people asked whether they deserved their happiness.

Let's grant Brooks his generalization that people who believe they deserve their success are likelier to be happy than people who believe they don't. It makes intuitive sense. But Brooks's claim that money is only a "metric" does not. Looking at the same survey data, Berkeley sociologist Michael Hout found that from 1973 to 2000 the difference between the affluent and the poor who counted themselves either "very happy" or "not too happy" ranged from 19 percentage points to 27. Among the poor, the percentage who felt "very happy" fell by nearly one-third from 1973 to 1994, then crept up a couple of points during the tight labor market of the late 1990s. Hout also observed that overall happiness dropped a modest 5 percent from 1973 to 2000.

Quality of life is improving. This argument has been made by too many conservatives to count. Yes, it's true that an unemployed steel worker living in the 21st century is in many important ways better off than the royals and aristocrats of yesteryear. Living conditions improve over time. But people do not experience life as an interesting moment in the evolution of human societies. They experience it in the present and weigh their own experience against that of the living. Brooks cites (even though it contradicts his argument) a famous 1998 study by economists Sara Solnick (then at the University of Miami, now at the University of Vermont) and David Hemenway of the Harvard School of Public Health. Subjects were asked which they'd prefer: to earn $50,000 while knowing everyone else earned $25,000, or to earn $100,000 while knowing everyone else earned $200,000. Objectively speaking, $100,000 is twice as much as $50,000. Even so, 56 percent chose $50,000 if it meant that would put them on top rather than at the bottom. We are social creatures and establish our expectations relative to others.

Inequality isn't increasing. This is the boldest line of conservative attack, challenging a consensus about income trends in the United States that most conservatives accept. (Brooks: "It is factually incorrect to argue that income inequality has not risen in America—it has.") Alan Reynolds, a senior fellow at Cato, made the case in a January 2007 paper. It was a technical argument hinging largely on a critique of the tax data used by Emmanuel Saez and Thomas Piketty in the groundbreaking paper we looked at in our installment about the superrich. But as Gary Burtless of Brookings noted in a January 2007 reply, Social Security records "tell a simple and similar story." A Congressional Budget Office analysis, Burtless wrote, addressed "almost all" of Reynolds's objections to Saez and Piketty's findings, and confirmed "a sizable rise in both pre-tax and after-tax inequality." Reynolds's paper didn't deny notable increases in top incomes, but he argued that these were because of technical changes in tax law and/or to isolated and unusual financial events. That, Burtless answered, was akin to arguing that, "adjusting for the weather and the season, no homeowner in New Orleans ended up with a wet basement" after Hurricane Katrina.

That income inequality very much matters is the thesis of the 2009 book *The Spirit Level*, by Richard Wilkinson and Kate Pickett, two medical researchers based in Yorkshire. The book has been criticized for overreaching. Wilkinson and Pickett relate income inequality trends not only to mental and physical health, violence, and teenage pregnancy, but also to global warming. But their larger point—that income inequality is bad not only for people on the losing end but also for society at large—seems hard to dispute. "Modern societies," they write,

> will depend increasingly on being creative, adaptable, inventive, well-informed and flexible communities, able to respond generously to each other and to needs wherever they arise. These are characteristics not of societies in hock to the rich, in which people are driven by status insecurities, but of populations used to working together and respecting each other as equals.

The United States' economy is currently struggling to emerge from a severe recession brought on by the financial crisis of 2008. Was that crisis brought about by income inequality? Some economists are starting to think it may have been. David Moss of Harvard Business School has produced an intriguing chart that shows bank failures tend to coincide with periods of growing income inequality. "I could hardly believe how tight the fit was," he told the *New York Times*. Princeton's Paul Krugman has similarly been considering whether the Great Divergence helped cause the recession by pushing middle-income Americans into debt. The growth of household debt has followed a pattern strikingly similar to the growth in income inequality (see the final graph). Raghuram G. Rajan, a business school professor at the University of Chicago, recently argued on the New Republic's Web site that "let them eat credit" was "the mantra of the political establishment in the go-go years before the crisis." Christopher Brown, an economist at Arkansas State University, wrote a paper in 2004 affirming that "inequality can exert a significant drag on effective demand." Reducing inequality, he argued, would also reduce consumer debt. Today, Brown's paper looks prescient.

Heightened partisanship in Washington and declining trust in government have many causes (and the latter slide predates the Great Divergence). But surely the growing income chasm between the poor and middle class and the rich, between the Sort of Rich and the Rich, and even between the Rich and the Stinking Rich, make it especially difficult to reestablish any spirit of *e pluribus unum*. Republicans and Democrats compete to show which party more fervently opposes the elite, with each side battling to define what "elite" means. In a more equal society, the elite would still be resented. But I doubt that opposing it would be an organizing principle of politics to the same extent that it is today.

I find myself returning to the gut-level feeling expressed at the start of this series: I do not wish to live in a banana republic. There is a reason why, in years past, Americans scorned societies starkly divided into the privileged and the destitute. They were repellent. Is it my imagination, or do we hear less criticism of such societies today in the United States? Might it be harder for Americans to sustain in such discussions the necessary sense of moral superiority?

What is the ideal distribution of income in society? I couldn't tell you, and historically much mischief has been accomplished by addressing this question too precisely. But I can tell you this: We've been headed in the wrong direction for far too long.

Richard A. Epstein

Three Cheers for Income Inequality

Taxing the top one percent even more means less wealth and fewer jobs for the rest of us.

The 2008 election was supposed to bring to the United States a higher level of civil discourse. Fast-forward three years and exactly the opposite has happened. A stalled economy brings forth harsh recriminations. As recent polling data reveals, the American public is driven by two irreconcilable emotions. The first is a deep distrust of government, which has driven the approval rate for Congress below ten percent. The second is a strong egalitarian impulse that directs its fury to the top one percent of income earners. Thus the same people who want government to get out of their lives also want government to increase taxes on the rich and corporations. They cannot have it both ways.

I voiced some of my objections to these two points in an interview on PBS, which sparked much controversy. The topic merits much more attention.

What are the origins of inequality? Start with a simple world in which all individuals own their labor. Acting in their self-interest (which includes that of family and friends), they seek to improve their lot in life. They cannot use force to advance their own position. Thus, they are left with two alternatives: individual labor and cooperative voluntary ventures.

Voluntary ventures will normally emerge only when all parties to them entertain expectations of gain from entering into these transactions. In some cases, to be sure, these expectations will be dashed. All risky ventures do not pan out. But on average and over time, the few failures cannot derail the many successes. People will make themselves better off.

The rub is that they need not do so at even rates. The legitimate origin of the inequality of wealth lies in the simple observation that successful actors outperform unsuccessful ones, without violating their rights. As was said long ago by Justice Pitney in *Coppage v. Kansas*, "it is from the nature of things impossible to uphold freedom of contract and the right of private property without at the same time recognizing as legitimate those inequalities of fortune that are the necessary result of the exercise of those rights."

So why uphold this combination of property and contract rights? Not because of atavistic fascination for venerable legal institutions. Rather, it is because voluntary exchanges improve overall social welfare. This works in three stages.

First, these transactions, on average, will make all parties to them better off. The only way the rich succeed is by helping their trading partners along the way.

Second, the successes of the rich afford increased opportunities for gain to other people in the form of new technologies and businesses for others to exploit.

Third, the initial success of the rich businessman paves the way for competitors to enter the marketplace. This, in turn, spurs the original businessman to make further improvements to his own goods and services.

In this system, the inequalities in wealth pay for themselves by the vast increases in wealth.

Any defense of wealth inequalities through voluntary means is, however, subject to a powerful caveat: The wealth must be acquired by legitimate means, which do not include aid in the form of state subsidies, state protection, or any other special gimmick. The rich who prosper from these policies do not deserve their wealth. Neither does anyone else who resorts to the same tactics.

As an empirical matter, large businesses, labor unions, and agricultural interests that have profited from government protections have drained huge amounts of wealth from the system. Undoing these protections may or may not change the various indices of inequality. But it will increase the overall size of the pie by improving the overall level of system efficiency.

The hard question that remains is this: To what extent will the United States, or any other nation, profit by a concerted effort to redress inequalities of wealth?

Again the answer depends on the choice of means. Voluntary forms of redistribution through major charitable foundations pose no threat to the accumulation of wealth. Indeed, they spur its creation by affording additional reasons to acquire levels of wealth that no rational agent could possibly consume.

Forced transfers of wealth through taxation will have the opposite effect. They will destroy the pools of wealth that are needed to generate new ventures, and they will dull the system-wide incentives to create wealth in the first place. There are many reasons for this system-wide failure.

First, the use of state coercion to remedy inequalities of wealth is not easily done. The most obvious method for doing so is by creating subsidies for people at the bottom, which are offset by high rates of taxation for people at the top. The hope is that high taxes will do little to blunt economic activity at the high end, while the payments will do little to dull initiative at the low end.

But this program is much more difficult to implement than is commonly supposed. The process of income redistribution opens up opportunities for powerful groups to secure transfers of wealth to themselves. This does nothing to redress inequalities of wealth. Even if these political players are constrained, there is still no costless way to transfer wealth up and down the income scale.

The administrative costs of running a progressive income tax system are legion. Unfortunately, that point was missed in a recent op-ed. Writing in the *New York Times*, Cornell economist Robert H. Frank plumped hard for steeper progressive income tax rates as a way to amend income inequality.

Yet matters are not nearly as simple as he supposes. In his view, the source of complexity in the current income tax code lies in the plethora of special interest provisions that make it difficult to calculate income by recognized standard economic measures. Thus, he thinks that it is "flatly wrong" to think that the flat tax will result in tax simplification. After all, it is just as easy to read a tax schedule that has progressive rates as one that has a uniform flat rate.

But more than reading tax schedules is at stake. First, one reason why the internal revenue code contains such complexity is its desire to combat the private strategies that people, especially those in the top one percent, use to avoid high levels of taxation. Anyone who has spent time in dealing with family trusts and partnerships, with income averaging, with the use of real estate shelters, and with foreign investments, knows just how hard it is to protect the progressive rate schedule against manipulation.

Second, the creation of these large tax loopholes is not some act of nature. Frank, like so many defenders of progressive taxation, fails to realize that progressive rates generate huge pressures to create new tax shelters. Lower the overall tax rates and the pressure to create tax gimmicks with real economic costs diminishes. Overall social output is higher with a flat tax than it is with a progressive one.

Third, the dangers posed by the use of progressive taxation are not confined to these serious administrative issues. There are also larger questions of political economy at stake. The initial question is just how steep the progressive tax ought to be. Keep it too shallow, and it does little to generate additional public revenues to justify the added cost of administration. Make it too steep, and it will reduce the incentives to create wealth that are always unambiguously stronger under a flat tax system. But since no one knows the optimal level of progressivity, vast quantities of wealth are dissipated in fighting over these levels. The flat tax removes that dimension of political intrigue.

Fourth, sooner or later—and probably sooner—high tax rates will kill growth. Progressives like Frank operate on the assumption that high taxation rates have little effect on investment by asking whether anyone would quit a cushy job just to save a few tax dollars. But the situation is in reality far more complex. One key to success in the United States lies in its ability to attract foreign labor and foreign capital to our shores. In this we are in competition with other nations whose tax policies are far more favorable to new investment than ours. The loss of foreign people and foreign capital is not easy to observe because we cannot identify with certainty most of the individuals who decide to go elsewhere. But we should at the very least note that there is the risk of a brain drain as the best and brightest foreign workers who came to the United States in search of economic opportunity ultimately may return home. They will likely not want to brave the hostile business climate that they see in the United States.

Fifth, sophisticated forms of tax avoidance are not limited to foreign laborers. Rich people have a choice of tax-free and taxable investments. They can increase transfers to family members in order to reduce the incidence of high progressive taxation. They can retire a year sooner, or go part-time to reduce their tax burdens. And of course, they can fight the incidence of higher taxation by using their not inconsiderable influence in the tax arenas.

Sixth, the inefficiencies created by a wide range of tax and business initiatives reduces the wealth earned by people in that top one percent, and thus the tax base on which the entire redistributive state depends. Defenders of progressive taxation, like Frank, cite the recent report of the Congressional Budget Office, which shows huge increases of wealth in the top one percent from 1979 to 2007. The top one percent increased its wealth by 275 percent in those years. The rest of the income distribution lagged far behind.

Unfortunately, the CBO report was out of date the day it was published. We now have tax data available that runs through 2009, which shows the folly of seeking to rely on heavier rates of taxation on the top one percent. The Tax Foundation's October 24, 2011 report contains this solemn reminder of the risks of soaking the rich in bad times:

> In 2009, the top 1 percent of tax returns paid 36.7 percent of all federal individual income taxes and earned 16.9 percent of adjusted gross income (AGI), compared to 2008 when those figures were 38.0 percent and 20.0 percent, respectively. Both of those figures—share of income and share of taxes paid— were their lowest since 2003 when the top 1 percent earned 16.7 percent of adjusted gross income and paid 34.3 percent of federal individual income taxes.

It is worth adding that the income of the top one percent also dropped 20 percent between 2007 and 2008, with a concomitant loss in tax revenues.

There are several disturbing implications that flow from this report. The first is that these figures explain the vulnerability in bad times of our strong dependence on high-income people to fund the transfer system. The current contraction in wealth at the top took place with only few new taxes. The decline in taxable income at the top will only shrink further if tax rates are raised. A mistake, therefore, in setting tax rate increases could easily wreck the entire system. Indeed, the worst possible outcome would be for high taxation to lower top incomes drastically. Right now, for better or worse, the entire transfer system of the United States is dependent on the continued success of high-income earners whom the egalitarians would like to punish.

Put otherwise, if a person at the middle of the income distribution loses a dollar in income, the federal government loses nothing in income tax revenues. Let a rich person suffer that decline and the revenue loss at the federal level is close to 40 percent, with more losses at the state level. The slow growth policies of the last three years have cost far more in revenue from the top one percent than any increase in progressive taxation could possibly hope to achieve. The more we move toward an equal income policy, the more we shall need tax increases on the middle class to offset the huge revenue losses at the top. Our current political economy makes the bottom 99 percent hostage to the continued success of the rich.

The dangers of the current obsession with income inequality should be clear. The rhetorical excesses of people like Robert Frank make it ever easier to champion a combination of high taxation schemes coupled with ever more stringent regulations of labor and capital markets. Together, these schemes spell the end of the huge paydays of the top one percent. Those earners depend heavily on a growth in asset value, which is just not happening today.

But what about the flat tax? Frank and others are right to note that a return to the flat tax will result in an enormous redistribution of income to the top one percent from everyone else. But why assume that the current level of progressivity sets the legitimate baseline, especially in light of the current anemic levels of economic growth? What theory justifies progressive taxation in the first place? The current system presupposes that this nation can continue to fund the aspirations of 99 percent out of the wealth of the one percent. That will prove to be unsustainable. A return to a flatter tax (ideally a flat tax) will have just the short-term consequences that Frank fears. It will undo today's massively redistributivist policies. But it will also go a long way toward unleashing growth in our heavily regulated and taxed economy.

The United States is now in the midst of killing the goose that lays the golden eggs. That current strategy is failing in the face of economic stagnation, even with no increase in tax rates. It will quickly crumble if tax increases are used to feed the current coalition of unions and farmers who will receive much of the revenue, while the employment prospects of ordinary people languish for want of the major capital investments that often depend on the wealth of the privileged one percent of the population.

The clarion call for more income equality puts short-term transfers ahead of long-term growth. Notwithstanding the temper of the times, that siren call should be stoutly resisted. Enterprise and growth, not envy and stagnation, are the keys to economic revival.

DISCUSSION QUESTIONS

1. How much inequality is too much? Can you define a standard for judging whether a given distribution of income is sufficiently unfair to justify government redress? In practical terms, if the top 1 percent of households control 34 percent of wealth, is that too much? What would a reasonable concentration be?

2. Ultimately, arguments against using government power to create a more equal (or, if you prefer, a less unequal) income distribution reduce to the position that even if inequality is bad, it is the price we must pay for a free society. Is that right? Does this mean that *all* redistributive policies are improper?

3. Are there ways of reducing income inequality that do not require the types of coercion that Epstein criticizes? What might they be?

14

Government and Society: Health Care Reform

Figuring out how to provide health care services is one of the hardest issues that confront democracies. Most industrialized countries have created "single payer" systems, in which health care is provided (either entirely or largely) by government agencies, with universal coverage and paid for through taxes. The systems in Canada and Great Britain are examples. These systems provide universal access, though critics argue that they inevitably ration care, have long wait times, and limit access to advanced treatments. Relying largely on private coverage is an attractive option for people who can afford insurance, but can result in millions of people without access to services.

One thing is certain, though: health care is expensive, and increasing costs pose significant problems for individuals and governments. In the United States, we spend about one-sixth of GDP on health care services, close to $3 trillion in 2011. Per capita, we spend about twice what other industrialized countries spend. Yet about 50 million Americans lacked health insurance, and we do worse on key measures of public health, such as life expectancy and infant mortality, than many other countries.

The passage of the Affordable Care Act (ACA, or "Obamacare" to its critics) did not end the controversy over what to do about health care in the United States, and the reaction since its 2010 passage has been a continuation of longstanding disputes over affordability, access, and the reach of government. The key feature of the new law is a mandate that everyone purchase health insurance; those who do not will have to pay a fine. Other elements include an expansion of Medicaid and new rules that prohibit insurance companies from denying coverage or charging higher premiums based on pre-existing conditions.

Supporters of the law say it achieves the goal of providing universal access to health care, will help slow the growth of health care costs, and will ease the problem of paying for the costs of providing services to the uninsured. Some are unhappy that the law did not create a "single payer" system; in this view, leaving insurance companies intact—even giving them millions of new customers through the mandate—perpetuates the problem of profit-driven business providing services.

Critics see it very differently: they insist that "insurance" is not the same as "access," and believe that the law will result in higher costs, longer wait times, and less innovation. Many object strongly to the mandate, arguing that it expands government power by forcing people to purchase a product (health insurance) that they may not want or need. In 2012, the Supreme Court ruled in *National Federation of Independent Business v. Sebelius* that the mandate was a constitutional exercise of Congress's taxation power, ending the main effort to overturn the law. In Congress, Republicans introduced bills to repeal the law altogether (none passed).

The readings here provide different perspectives on the ACA. Serafini offers the views of health care experts, most of whom think that the law will provide nearly universal coverage, though they are less confident about the law's effect on costs and quality. Levin sees the law as a complete disaster that will increase costs, reduce access, and distort the entire health care system. He argues that we need to restore a degree of market discipline—where individuals have a direct incentive to make efficient decisions about their own care—and insists that there is no way to improve the ACA. The only option is outright repeal.

Condon addresses the concern that a major piece of social legislation was adopted on a pure party line vote. Unlike earlier laws—Social Security, Medicare, Civil Rights, Voting Rights—the ACA was passed without a single Republican voting for the bill on final passage (one House Republican voted for an earlier version of the bill). There are risks, he concludes, to this kind of process, although he believes that the burden is on Republicans to offer an option instead of repeal.

Marilyn Werber Serafini

Grading Health Reform: Experts Assess Whether the Bill Delivers on Its Promises

The primary objectives of health care reform were clear long before Congress took up the issue last year: slow the growth of health care spending, insure more people, improve the quality of care—and do it all without busting the federal budget. *National Journal* this week asked twenty health care experts across the political spectrum how the bill that President Obama signed into law on Tuesday measures up against those yardsticks.

The experts generally agreed that the new law comes close to achieving the objective of providing insurance to all Americans and does a fairly good job of making coverage affordable and available to consumers. But the experts also said that the law falls short of promises to lower skyrocketing health care spending, and they concluded that it doesn't do enough to improve the quality of health care.

* * *

Our judges gave each candidate's plan a series of numerical grades, from 1 to 10, depending on how close they thought it would come to achieving a given goal, such as covering the uninsured. A score of 10 indicated that the plan would come extremely close to reaching the goal, while a score of 1 meant that it would not come at all close.

National Journal tried to craft the survey questions to elicit objective assessments rather than partisan or ideological views. Regarding the uninsured, for example, we asked the judges how close each proposal would come to providing health insurance for all Americans. *NJ* did not want answers that reflected the judges' political leanings or personal views about whether a given plan was the best—or even a good—approach.

* * *

A Big Step Toward Universal Coverage

The Congressional Budget Office estimates that the health care reform law will provide coverage to 31 million of the 47 million Americans currently uninsured.

Many of the people who won't be covered are illegal immigrants who are ineligible for federal assistance in obtaining insurance.

None of the twenty experts gave the law a perfect score of 10 for providing coverage, although all but two gave it high marks. Indeed, in this category, President Obama received the same grade that he did as a candidate.

During the campaign Obama recommended a narrower mandate requiring only that parents purchase insurance for their children; in contrast, the new law requires many adults to also get coverage. Most people without health insurance will have to pay one of two penalties, whichever is greater: either a fixed fine, starting at $95 in 2014, rising to $325 in 2015, and to $695 in 2016; or a percentage of taxable income, starting at 1.0 percent in 2014 and rising to 2.5 percent in 2016.

People with annual incomes below 100 percent of the federal poverty line ($10,830 for an individual and $22,050 for a family of four) are exempt from the penalties.

The law will significantly expand Medicaid, the federal-state health care program for the poor, to as many as 13 million additional beneficiaries. Beginning in 2014, Medicaid eligibility will extend to people with annual earnings lower than 133 percent of the federal poverty line ($14,440 for an individual).

Some judges took 1 or 2 points off their scores in this category because they advocated tougher penalties for failure to purchase insurance. Paul Ginsburg, president of the Center for Studying Health System Change, said, "I expect that the mandate will be refined in response to experience."

Ed Howard, executive vice president of the Alliance for Health Reform, called the law "a good start," and Jeffrey Levi, executive director of the Trust for America's Health, agreed. "Clearly, a significant group of people will be left out of this reform," he said. "But the addition of over 30 million Americans to the insurance roll is a monumental step of major proportions. But those who are left out will continue to need a safety net—hence the importance of the provisions expanding funding for community health centers and public health."

Gail Wilensky, a senior fellow at Project Hope who was Medicare administrator during the presidency of George H. W. Bush, noted that according to CBO estimates, "the percentage of people without insurance would drop from the current 15 percent to 5 percent, which is two-thirds of the way to universal coverage."

Elizabeth McGlynn, associate director of the health program at Rand, said that based on her think tank's microsimulation modeling, the percentage of uninsured would be reduced by 53 to 57 percent. She called that "a substantial improvement," although she added that it "would not achieve universal coverage." McGlynn concluded, "A large portion of the uninsured would be eligible for, but not enrolled in, Medicaid."

The Lewin Group actuary, John Sheils, said that his firm's model indicates that the law covers 60 percent of the uninsured population but only 43 percent of care that is currently uncompensated. "Very-low-income people exempt from the mandate account for much of this," he said.

According to Joe Antos, an American Enterprise Institute scholar, the goal shouldn't be reducing the number of uninsured but increasing the number of people who have access to appropriate care. "There is nothing in the bill that assures this," he said. Over time, Heritage Foundation Vice President Stuart Butler cautioned, although almost all citizens and legal residents will get coverage, "it may not be of the type, cost, and quality that they would like."

Some conservative opponents argue that an insurance mandate is unconstitutional and sets a worrisome precedent for government power. More than a dozen states have already filed lawsuits challenging the constitutionality of the requirement.

Many health reform advocates are also concerned, but for different reasons. They worry that some people will ignore the mandate—especially those who are young and healthy and see little need for health insurance. America's Health Insurance Plans, which represents insurers, shares this apprehension. Insurers agreed early on to stop denying policies to people with pre-existing conditions and in poor health in exchange for universal coverage.

Minor Impact on Quality of Care

Many of National Journal's health care experts are disappointed that the new law won't do more to improve the quality of health care. "The main focus of the legislation is on coverage expansion, not on improving quality or consumer decision-making," said Elizabeth McGlynn, associate director of the health program at Rand. "The bill contains provisions that would increase the information available to consumers; however, there are no direct incentives for consumers to use that information or to change the decisions they would have otherwise made."

The key, said Paul Ginsburg, president of the Center for Studying Health System Change, is implementing research into medical effectiveness. The new law funds research on so-called comparative effectiveness to evaluate the success of various medical treatments.

But American Enterprise Institute scholar Joe Antos worries that even the most-sophisticated [sic] consumers will have trouble interpreting and applying comparative-effectiveness results. "Sensible consumers will continue to rely on the advice of their doctors, which depends on the community standard of practice, the patient's specific circumstances, how services are paid for, and other factors. Patients are increasingly also seeking information on the Internet, which can lead some to demand inappropriate treatments."

Jeffrey Levi, executive director of Trust for America's Health, shares Antos's concern. "It's one thing to do the comparative-effectiveness research and quality assessment; it's another for consumers to take that information to heart and apply it to their own situations."

Quality may also differ for those getting insurance through an exchange and those in employer-sponsored plans, said Heritage Foundation Vice President Stuart Butler. Those in exchanges will have "a lot more choice and information," he said, predicting that employers will react to extra fees by restricting coverage and shifting costs.

Few experts were optimistic that doctors, hospitals, and other medical providers will gain the tools to improve care using best practices. "The bill promotes comparative-effectiveness research but does nothing to increase adherence to guidelines," said Lewin Group actuary John Sheils. "Adherence is the problem. There is overwhelming evidence in the literature showing that doctors do not follow guidelines."

Former Senate Majority Leader Tom Daschle noted that changes resulting from the research will not come "for some time." And even when the results of comparative-effectiveness research are more readily available, "probably past the 10-year mark," according to Antos, "their appropriate application depends critically on the specific patient's circumstances. Judgment will remain the driving factor, unless future Congresses attempt to impose uniform standards on medical practice."

Grace-Marie Turner, president of the Galen Institute, worries that comparative-effectiveness studies "are historically out of date long before the studies are finalized." What may have a greater effect on quality of care is the funding that President Obama included in last year's economic stimulus law to encourage doctors to adopt electronic medical records. "Considerable work must be done to help physicians who are in solo and small group practice use emerging tools," she said.

Although former Medicare Administrator Gail Wilensky called the law's direction positive, she stressed that much depends on what happens with pilot and demonstration projects that the law establishes for Medicare. The law authorizes pilot projects to test so-called accountable care organizations and the bundling of payments to medical providers. The idea is to get medical providers to better coordinate patient care. The government and private insurers, in turn, could then more effectively base payments on performance.

The experts were somewhat skeptical that the reforms will encourage medical providers to compete for patients based on quality and price. Conservatives were especially critical, but liberals didn't give high scores either.

Competition will change, Butler said, but not to meet that goal. "In Medicaid, Medicare, and in the more regulated private system, the incentive will increase to compete by cutting costs and avoiding certain patients to achieve a reasonable return amid tighter fee schedules," he said.

Bill Gets Low Score For Cost Control

Bringing health care spending in line with the economy's growth rate has been a priority since Washington began talking about health reform decades ago. During the 2008 presidential campaign, judges gave Barack Obama's proposal a score of only 3 for controlling costs.

In rating the newly passed reforms, the scores were nearly as low. Former Medicare Administrator Gail Wilensky noted that the law will institute some "promising" pilot projects for coordinating medical care in Medicare and for testing ways to pay doctors and hospitals. Still, Heritage Foundation Vice President Stuart Butler said that the law will increase, not decrease, the growth rate of total health spending.

"While the bill contains provisions that may ultimately lead to reductions," Elizabeth McGlynn, Rand health program associate director said, her think tank's projections indicate that, "with the exception of payment reform options, most would have a relatively small effect on the growth rate in health spending."

The actuary for the Centers for Medicare and Medicaid Services "reports that health spending will continue to grow faster than the economy, even assuming that future Congresses cut Medicare spending as prescribed in the bill," American Enterprise Institute scholar Joe Antos contended, adding, "This objective is probably impossible to meet even over the long term given the aging populace."

Brookings Institution senior fellow Henry Aaron is more optimistic about the long-term forecast; and Ed Howard, executive vice president of the Alliance for Health Reform, said that "most of what is possible is at least put in place, but will take time to have impact."

Many health care economists had high hopes for a so-called Cadillac tax to discourage employers from offering overly generous benefits. With less coverage, the theory goes, people will have to pay more out of their own pockets and thus become thriftier about purchasing medical services. But the final law watered down the tax and delayed its implementation. The tax on high-end insurance plans will apply to health plan premiums greater than $10,200 for individual coverage and $27,500 for families; it won't kick in until 2018.

Scores were somewhat higher, although mixed, when *National Journal* asked whether the federal government will get its money's worth from the law. "In terms of government spending per net newly insured individual, the expected value of the services obtained should exceed the cost to the federal government," McGlynn responded.

Butler, however, argued that the law is based on a "very high taxpayer cost for coverage expansions that could have been achieved at much lower cost." In scoring the law on its cost, Butler wanted to know whether zero was an option. "It has been 'funded' with new taxes and 'savings' that will not materialize. It is thus actually being funded with debt obligations on future generations."

Grace-Marie Turner, president of the Galen Institute, particularly worries about Medicare savings, which mostly come from decreasing payments to the Medicare Advantage program.

One-quarter of Medicare recipients get their insurance coverage from health maintenance organizations, preferred provider groups, and even some private fee-for-service plans as part of Medicare Advantage. But the program has been controversial because the government pays participating insurers about 14 percent more per beneficiary than it pays for the care of seniors in Medicare's traditional fee-for-service program.

"Richard Foster, Medicare's chief actuary, warned Congress that making the deep cuts to Medicare contained in the Senate bill 'represent an exceedingly difficult challenge' and, if sustained, would cause one out of five hospitals and nursing homes to become unprofitable," Turner said. "Congress is highly unlikely to allow this to happen, requiring even more tax dollars and deficit spending. This legislation is not paid for, even with half a trillion dollars in cuts to Medicare and half a trillion in new taxes. Political pressures will intensify to provide ever larger subsidies to more and more people and to impose strict price controls on providers. Coverage restrictions inevitably will follow. So, no, reform is not funded with existing health care dollars."

Paul Ginsburg, president of the Center for Studying Health System Change, countered that the government would have cut Medicare Advantage costs even if reform legislation had not passed, "although perhaps less sharply."

Yuval Levin

Repeal: Why and How Obamacare Must Be Undone

In the days since the enactment of their health care plan, Democrats in Washington have been desperately seeking to lodge the new program in the pantheon of American public-policy achievements. House Democratic whip James Clyburn compared the bill to the Civil Rights Act of 1964. Vice President Biden argued it vindicates a century of health reform efforts by Democrats and Republicans alike. House speaker Nancy Pelosi said "health insurance reform will stand alongside Social Security and Medicare in the annals of American history."

Even putting aside the fact that Social Security and Medicare are going broke and taking the rest of the government with them, these frantic forced analogies are preposterous. The new law is a ghastly mess, which began as a badly misguided technocratic pipe dream and was then degraded into ruinous incoherence by the madcap process of its enactment.

The appeals to history are understandable, however, because the Democrats know that the law is also exceedingly vulnerable to a wholesale repeal effort: Its major provisions do not take effect for four years, yet in the interim it is likely to begin wreaking havoc with the health care sector—raising insurance premiums, health care costs, and public anxieties. If those major provisions do take effect, moreover, the true costs of the program will soon become clear, and its unsustainable structure will grow painfully obvious. So, to protect it from an angry public and from Republicans armed with alternatives, the new law must be made to seem thoroughly established and utterly irrevocable—a fact on the ground that must be lived with; tweaked, if necessary, at the edges, but at its core politically untouchable.

But it is no such thing. Obamacare starts life strikingly unpopular and looks likely to grow more so as we get to know it in the coming months and years. The entire House of Representatives, two-thirds of the Senate, and the president will be up for election before the law's most significant provisions become fully active. The American public is concerned about spending, deficits, debt, taxes, and over-active government to an extent seldom seen in American history. The excesses of the plan seem likely to make the case for alternative gradual and incremental reforms only stronger.

And the repeal of Obamacare is essential to any meaningful effort to bring down health care costs, provide greater stability and security of coverage to more Americans, and address our entitlement crisis. Both the program's original design and its contorted final form make repairs at the edges unworkable. The only solution is to repeal it and pursue genuine health care reform in its stead.

From Bad to Worse

To see why nothing short of repeal could suffice, we should begin at the core of our health care dilemma.

Conservative and liberal experts generally agree on the nature of the problem with American health care financing: There is a shortage of incentives for efficiency in our methods of paying for coverage and care, and therefore costs are rising much too quickly, leaving too many people unable to afford insurance. We have neither a fully public nor quite a private system of insurance, and three key federal policies—the fee-for-service structure of Medicare, the disjointed financing of Medicaid, and the open-ended tax exclusion for employer-provided insurance—drive spending and costs ever upward.

The disagreement about just how to fix that problem has tended to break down along a familiar dispute between left and right: whether economic efficiency is best achieved by the rational control of expert management or by the lawful chaos of open competition.

Liberals argue that the efficiency we lack would be achieved by putting as much as possible of the health care sector into one big "system" in which the various irregularities could be evened and managed out of existence by the orderly arrangement of rules and incentives. The problem now, they say, is that health care is too chaotic and answers only to the needs of the insurance companies. If it were made more orderly, and answered to the needs of the public as a whole, costs could be controlled more effectively.

Conservatives argue that the efficiency we lack would be achieved by allowing price signals to shape the behavior of both providers and consumers, creating more savings than we could hope to produce on purpose, and allowing competition and informed consumer choices to exercise a downward pressure on prices. The problem now, they say, is that third-party insurance (in which employers buy coverage or the government provides it, and consumers almost never pay doctors directly) makes health care too opaque, hiding the cost of everything from everyone and so making real pricing and therefore real economic efficiency impossible. If it were made more transparent and answered to the wishes of consumers, prices could be controlled more effectively.

That means that liberals and conservatives want to pursue health care reform in roughly opposite directions. Conservatives propose ways of introducing genuine market forces into the insurance system—to remove obstacles to choice and competition, pool risk more effectively, and reduce the inefficiency in government health care entitlements while helping those for whom entry to the market is too expensive (like Americans with pre-existing conditions) gain access to the same high quality care. Such targeted efforts would build on what is best about the system we have in order to address what needs fixing.

Liberals, meanwhile, propose ways of moving Americans to a more fully public system, by arranging conditions in the health care sector (through a mix of mandates, regulations, taxes, and subsidies) to nudge people toward public coverage, which could be more effectively managed. This is the approach the Democrats originally proposed last year. The idea was to end risk-based insurance by making it essentially illegal for insurers to charge people different prices based on their health, age, or other factors; to force everyone to participate in the system so that the healthy do not wait until they're sick to buy insurance; to align various insurance reforms in a way that would raise premium costs in the private market; and then to introduce a government-run insurer that, whether through Medicare's negotiating leverage or through various exemptions from market pressures, could undersell private insurers and so offer an attractive "public option" to people being pushed out of employer plans into an increasingly expensive individual market.

Conservatives opposed this scheme because they believed a public insurer could not introduce efficiencies that would lower prices without brutal rationing of services. Liberals supported it because they thought a public insurer would be fairer and more effective.

But in order to gain sixty votes in the Senate last winter, the Democrats were forced to give up on that public insurer, while leaving the other components of their scheme in place. The result is not even a liberal approach to escalating costs but a ticking time bomb: a scheme that will build up pressure in our private insurance system while offering no escape. Rather than reform a system that everyone agrees is unsustainable, it will subsidize that system and compel participation in it—requiring all Americans to pay ever-growing premiums to insurance companies while doing essentially nothing about the underlying causes of those rising costs.

Liberal health care mavens understand this. When the public option was removed from the health care bill in the Senate, Howard Dean argued in the *Washington Post* that the bill had become merely a subsidy for insurance companies, and failed completely to control costs. Liberal health care blogger Jon Walker said, "The Senate bill will fail to stop the rapidly approaching meltdown of our health care system, and anyone is a fool for thinking otherwise." Markos Moulitsas of the Daily Kos called the bill "unconscionable" and said it lacked "any mechanisms to control costs."

Indeed, many conservatives, for all their justified opposition to a government takeover of health care, have not yet quite seen the full extent to which this bill will exacerbate the cost problem. It is designed to push people into a system that will not exist—a health care bridge to nowhere—and so will cause premiums to rise and encourage significant dislocation and then will initiate a program of subsidies whose only real answer to the mounting costs of coverage will be to pay them with public dollars and so increase them further. It aims to spend a trillion dollars on subsidies to large insurance companies and the expansion of Medicaid, to micromanage the insurance industry in ways likely only to raise premiums further, to cut Medicare benefits without using the money to shore up the program or reduce the deficit, and to raise taxes on employment, investment, and medical research.

The case for averting all of that could hardly be stronger. And the nature of the new law means that it must be undone—not trimmed at the edges. Once implemented fully, it would fairly quickly force a crisis that would require another significant reform. Liberals would seek to use that crisis, or the prospect of it, to move the system toward the approach they wanted in the first place:

arguing that the only solution to the rising costs they have created is a public insurer they imagine could outlaw the economics of health care. A look at the fiscal collapse of the Medicare system should rid us of the notion that any such approach would work, but it remains the left's preferred solution, and it is their only plausible next move—indeed, some Democrats led by Iowa senator Tom Harkin have already begun talking about adding a public insurance option to the plan next year.

Because Obamacare embodies a rejection of incrementalism, it cannot be improved in small steps. Fixing our health care system in the wake of the program's enactment will require a big step—repeal of the law before most of it takes hold—followed by incremental reforms addressing the public's real concerns.

The Case for Repeal

That big step will not be easy to take. The Democratic party has invested its identity and its future in the fate of this new program, and Democrats control the White House and both houses of Congress. That is why the conservative health care agenda must now also be an electoral agenda—an effort to refine, inform, and build on public opposition to the new program and to the broader trend toward larger and more intrusive, expensive, and fiscally reckless government in the age of Obama. Obamacare is the most prominent emblem of that larger trend, and its repeal must be at the center of the conservative case to voters in the coming two election cycles.

The design of the new law offers some assistance. In an effort to manipulate the program's Congressional Budget Office score so as to meet President Obama's goal of spending less than $1 trillion in its first decade, the Democrats' plan will roll out along a very peculiar trajectory. No significant entitlement benefits will be made available for four years, but some significant taxes and Medicare cuts—as well as regulatory reforms that may begin to push premium prices up, especially in the individual market—will begin before then. And the jockeying and jostling in the insurance sector in preparation for the more dramatic changes that begin in 2014 will begin to be felt very soon.

To blunt the effects of all this, the Democrats have worked mightily to give the impression that some attractive benefits, especially regarding the rules governing insurance companies, will begin immediately. This year, they say, insurance companies will be prevented from using the pre-existing medical condition of a child to exclude that child's parents from insurance coverage, and a risk-pool program will be established to help a small number of adults who are excluded too. Additionally, insurance policies cannot be cancelled retroactively when someone becomes sick, some annual and lifetime limits on coverage are prohibited, and "children" may stay on their parents' insurance until they turn 26. Obamacare's champions hope these reforms might build a constituency for the program.

But these benefits are far too small to have that effect. The pre-existing condition exclusion prohibits only the refusal to cover treatment for a specific disease, not the exclusion of a family from coverage altogether, and applies only in the individual market, and so affects almost no one. More than half the states already have laws allowing parents to keep adult children on their policies—through ages varying from 24 to 31. And the other new benefits, too, may touch a small number of people (again, mostly in the individual market, where premiums will be rising all the while), but will do nothing to affect the overall picture of American health care financing. CBO scored these immediate reforms as having no effect on the number of uninsured or on national health expenditures.

The bill will also have the government send a $250 check to seniors who reach the "donut hole" gap in Medicare prescription drug coverage this year—and the checks will go out in September, just in time for the fall elections. But the checks will hardly make up for the significant cuts in Medicare Advantage plans that allow seniors to choose among private insurers for their coverage. Those cuts begin in 2011, but the millions of seniors who use the program will start learning about them this year—again, before the election—as insurance companies start notifying their beneficiaries of higher premiums or cancelled coverage.

We are also likely to see some major players in health insurance, including both large employers and large insurers, begin to take steps to prepare for the new system in ways that employees and beneficiaries will find disconcerting. Verizon, for instance, has already informed its employees that insurance premiums will need to rise in the coming years and retiree benefits may be cut. Caterpillar has said new taxes and rules will cost the company $100 million in just the next year, and tractor maker John Deere has said much the same. Such announcements are likely to be common this year, and many insurers active in the individual market are expected to begin curtailing their offerings as that market looks to grow increasingly unprofitable under new rules.

These early indications will help opponents of the new law make their case. But the case will certainly need to focus most heavily on what is to come in the years after this congressional election: spending, taxes, rising health care costs, cuts in Medicare that don't help save the program or reduce the deficit, and a growing government role in the management of the insurance sector.

The numbers are gargantuan and grim—even as laid out by the Congressional Budget Office, which has to accept as fact all of the legislation's dubious premises and promises. If the law remains in place, a new entitlement will begin in 2014 that will cost more than $2.4 trillion in its first ten years, and will grow faster than either Medicare or private-sector health care spending has in the past decade.

Rather than reducing costs, Obamacare will increase national health expenditures by more than $200 billion, according to the Obama administration's own HHS actuary. Premiums in the individual market will increase by more than 10 percent very quickly, and middle-class families in the new exchanges (where large numbers of Americans who now receive coverage through their employers will find themselves dumped) will be forced to choose from a very limited menu of government-approved plans, the cheapest of which, CBO estimates, will cost more than $12,000. Some Americans—those earning up to four times the federal poverty level—will get subsidies to help with some of that cost, but these subsidies will grow more slowly than the premiums, and those above the threshold will not receive them at all. Many middle-class families will quickly find themselves spending a quarter of their net income on health insurance, according to a calculation by Scott Gottlieb of the American Enterprise Institute.

Through the rules governing the exchanges and other mechanisms (including individual and employer insurance mandates, strict regulation of plan benefit packages, rating rules, and the like), the federal government will begin micromanaging the insurance sector in an effort to extend coverage and control costs. But even CBO's assessment does not foresee a reduction in costs and therefore an easing of the fundamental source of our health care woes.

To help pay for the subsidies, and for a massive expansion of Medicaid, taxes will rise by about half a trillion dollars in the program's first ten years— hitting employers and investors especially hard, but quickly being passed down to consumers and workers. And the law also cuts Medicare, especially by reducing physician and hospital payment rates, by another half a trillion dollars—cuts that will drastically undermine the program's operation as, according to the

Medicare actuary, about 20 percent of doctors and other providers who participate in the program "could find it difficult to remain profitable and, absent legislative intervention, might end their participation." And all of this, CBO says, to increase the portion of Americans who have health insurance from just under 85 percent today to about 95 percent in ten years.

Of course, this scenario—for all the dark prospects it lays out—assumes things will go more or less as planned. CBO is required to assume as much. But in a program so complex and enormous, which seeks to take control of a sixth of our economy but is profoundly incoherent even in its own terms, things will surely not always go as planned. The Medicare cuts so essential to funding the new entitlement, for instance, are unlikely to occur. Congress has shown itself thoroughly unwilling to impose such cuts in the past, and if it fails to follow through on them in this case, Obamacare will add hundreds of billions of additional dollars to the deficit. By the 2012 election, we will have certainly begun to see whether the program's proposed funding mechanism is a total sham, or is so unpopular as to make Obamacare toxic with seniors. Neither option bodes well for the program's future.

Some of the taxes envisioned in the plan, especially the so-called Cadillac tax on high-cost insurance, are also unlikely to materialize quite as proposed, adding further to the long-term costs of the program. And meanwhile, the bizarre incentive structures created by the law (resulting in part from the elimination of the public insurance plan which was to have been its focus) are likely to cause massive distortions in the insurance market that will further increase costs. The individual market will quickly collapse, since new regulations will put it at an immense disadvantage against the new exchanges. We are likely to see significant consolidation in the insurance sector, as smaller insurers go out of business and the larger ones become the equivalent of subsidized and highly regulated public utilities. And the fact that the exchanges will offer subsidies not available to workers with employer-based coverage will mean either that employers will be strongly inclined to stop offering insurance, or that Congress will be pressured to make subsidies available to employer-based coverage. In either case, the program's costs will quickly balloon.

Perhaps worst of all, the law not only shirks the obligation to be fiscally responsible, it will also make it much more difficult for future policy-makers to do something about our entitlement and deficit crisis. Obamacare constructs a new entitlement that will grow more and more expensive even more quickly than Medicare itself. Even if the program were actually deficit neutral, which it surely won't be, that would just mean that it would keep us on the same budget trajectory we are on now—with something approaching trillion-dollar deficits in each of the next ten years and a national debt of more than $20 trillion by 2020—but leave us with much less money and far fewer options for doing anything about it.

In other words, Obamacare is an unmitigated disaster—for our health care system, for our fiscal future, and for any notion of limited government. But it is a disaster that will not truly get under way for four years, and therefore a disaster we can avert.

This is the core of the case the program's opponents must make to voters this year and beyond. If opponents succeed in gaining a firmer foothold in Congress in the fall, they should work to begin dismantling and delaying the program where they can: denying funding to key provisions and pushing back implementation at every opportunity. But a true repeal will almost certainly require yet another election cycle, and another president.

The American public is clearly open to the kind of case Obamacare's opponents will need to make. But keeping voters focused on the problems with the program, and with the reckless growth of government beyond it, will require a concerted, informed, impassioned, and empirical case. This is the kind of case opponents of Obamacare have made over the past year, of course, and it persuaded much of the public—but the Democrats acted before the public could have its say at the polls. The case must therefore be sustained until that happens. The health care debate is far from over.

Toward Real Reform

Making and sustaining that case will also require a clear sense of what the alternatives to Obamacare might be—and how repeal could be followed by sensible incremental steps toward controlling health care costs and thereby increasing access and improving care.

Without a doubt, the Democrats' program is worse than doing nothing. But the choice should not be that program or nothing. The problems with our health care system are real, and conservatives must show the public how repealing Obamacare will open the way to a variety of options for more sensible reforms— reforms that will lower costs and help those with pre-existing conditions or without affordable coverage options, but in ways that do not bankrupt the country, or undermine the quality of care or the freedom of patients and doctors to make choices for themselves.

Republicans this past year offered a variety of such approaches, which varied in their ambitions, costs, and forms. A group led by representatives Paul Ryan and Devin Nunes and senators Tom Coburn and Richard Burr proposed a broad measures that included reforms of Medicare, Medicaid, the employer-based coverage tax exclusion, and malpractice liability and would cover nearly all of the uninsured. The House Republican caucus backed a more modest first step to make high-risk pools available to those with pre-existing conditions, enable insurance purchases across state lines, pursue tort reform, and encourage states to experiment with innovative insurance regulation. Former Bush administration official Jeffrey Anderson has offered an approach somewhere between the two, which pursues incremental reforms through a "small bill." Other conservatives have offered numerous other proposals, including ways of allowing small businesses to pool together for coverage, the expansion of Health Savings Accounts and consumer-driven health care (which Obamacare would thoroughly gut), and various reforms of our entitlement system.

All share a basic commitment to the proposition that our health care dilemmas should be addressed through a series of discrete, modest, incremental solutions to specific problems that concern the American public, and all agree that the underlying cause of these problems is the cost of health coverage and care, which would be best dealt with by using market forces to improve efficiency and bring down prices.

The approach to health care just adopted by President Obama and the Democratic Congress thoroughly fails to deal with efficiency and cost, and stands in the way of any meaningful effort to do so. It is built on a fundamental conceptual error, suffers from a profound incoherence of design, and would make a bad situation far worse. It cannot be improved by tinkering. It must be removed before our health care crisis can be addressed.

If we are going to meet the nation's foremost challenges—ballooning debt, exploding entitlements, out-of-control health care costs, and the task of keeping America strong and competitive—we must begin by making Obamacare history. We must repeal it, and then pursue real reform.

George E. Condon, Jr.

Even After Big Victory, Health Care Future Uncertain

President Obama's stunning victory on Thursday in the Supreme Court is a surprising validation of his dogged refusal to give ground on his 2008 campaign promise to provide health insurance for the millions of Americans who live in daily dread of disease or sickness. Just about everybody not on the White House staff expected a conservative high court to invalidate key parts of the law Obama pushed through Congress in 2010. But the president prevailed, dealing a severe blow to Republican hopes to ride "Obamacare" to big victories in November.

But before the White House gets too carried away in celebration, the reality is that the Court's decision, as historic as it is, does not guarantee the survival of the law that is the signature accomplishment of Obama's first term in office. This big legal victory gives the president a second chance to do what he flubbed the first time—persuade the country that this is not a partisan exercise. For even after this decision, the health care law still is far from the permanent reform he envisioned when he hailed its passage as answering "the call of history." More than two years later, it remains deeply unpopular despite surviving this legal challenge. Its implementation faces threats of sabotage and its repeal is only as far away as the next election that empowers Republicans to keep their promises. And it is far from a sure political winner in the upcoming election.

This was not how the White House expected it to be. They believed that the country would come to like the new law once they saw that it provided them benefits and understood that it did not threaten their own health insurance plans. But what was an article of faith in 2010 and 2011 has run aground in 2012. Polling shows that individual components are popular. But, as indicated in an ABC News/ *Washington Post* poll released on Wednesday, that doesn't mean people like the overall bill any better. In fact, the survey, conducted June 20–24, shows that 52 percent dislike what has been dubbed "Obamacare" while only 36 percent view it favorably.

That the president now understands these numbers was evident from his statement in the East Room. In victory, he was restrained and serious—no dancing in the end zone when the game is only in the third quarter. And there were certainly no claims that the law has been a political winner, only open acknowledgment that the long debate has been "divisive" and the wry observation that "it should be pretty clear by now that I didn't do this because it was good politics." He well knows the political challenges ahead.

Even on a day when the president's lawyers celebrate doing their job well, it is clear that most of these political and practical problems could have been averted or at least moderated if Obama had taken a different approach when he was crafting the legislation. He might have heard that "call from history." But he didn't heed the lessons of history. He was willing to be the first president since the Civil War to attempt to ram through a major social change—a program that would touch just about every American—on a party-line vote with no support in Congress from the opposing party. Full of hubris and with complete control of both Congress and the White House, the president's advisers did not feel the need for bipartisanship in 2009. They viewed it as a luxury, not a necessity.

Other presidents pushing big programs grasped the futility of trying to shut out the minority party. Even those who had large enough majorities to force their wishes on Congress understood that they needed their accomplishments to appear legitimate to the people and so survive the inevitable change in political cycles that would shift power in Washington. Certainly, Presidents Franklin Roosevelt and Lyndon Johnson understood that. Roosevelt settled for far less than he wanted in Social Security in 1935, complaining privately that it "had been chiseled down to a conservative pattern." But he won over sixteen of the twenty-one Republicans in the Senate and eighty-one of the ninety-six Republicans in the House. In the next election, in 1936, those who campaigned to repeal Social Security seemed out of the mainstream. GOP presidential nominee Alf Landon was in a minority when he argued that the law was "unjust, unworkable, stupidly drafted, and wastefully financed." He lost all but two states.

Three decades later, Johnson, who won his first congressional race in that 1936 election and had studied FDR, showed he had learned the lesson. Again, he had big majorities. But Johnson made sure that he did not pass the Civil Rights Bill of 1964, Medicare in 1965, or the Voting Rights Act of 1965 without significant Republican votes. On both civil rights bills, the GOP margins were even bigger than the Democratic margins. Medicare was closer, but drew thirteen Republican votes in the Senate and seventy in the House. "We had overwhelming Democratic majorities in the House and the Senate," recalled former Democratic Rep. Lee Hamilton, who was a freshman from Indiana in 1965. "He could have passed any bill he wanted to. He had the votes. But he chose to negotiate with the Republicans because he did not want to pass such an important bill on a party-line vote ... As a result, Medicare was able to be implemented effectively. It had legitimacy."

That, added Hamilton, who now heads the Center on Congress at Indiana University, "has to be the model." When you pass a major piece of legislation on a party-line vote, he said, "It makes it extremely difficult to implement the legislation effectively, because there are so many ways the opposition can interfere, disrupt, delay, or block the implementation of the legislation." Certainly, that has been the case with health care. And it remains a threat even after Thursday's Supreme Court ruling. Finding a way to win over some Republicans will be a major imperative after November's election.

The White House, of course, howls in protest at any suggestion the president did not make a good-faith effort to enlist Republicans. Aides point to the much-ballyhooed seven-hour bipartisan health care "summit" at Blair House in February 2010 and to repeated invitations to Republicans to come on board. But the process was flawed from the beginning when the White House left the writing of the bill to Democrats, gave little support to the "Gang of Fourteen" or the "Gang of Six", and made it clear that there would be no give on medical–malpractice reform even though that could have wooed Republicans. And there was very little personal reaching out by the president to individual GOP members or senators.

But this Court decision, said former Democratic Rep. Tony Coelho, gives the president something he needed going into the election. "It makes him look strong and look like a leader," he said. "It helps diminish the notion that it is a partisan political deal." Coelho, who was in the House for eleven years representing a California district, was a House staffer when Medicare passed. He places the blame for the lack of Republican votes on the 2010 health care law on the early decision by GOP leaders to oppose anything the president offered.

"Today's leadership has a hard time cutting deals with Democrats," he said.

Now, because of the Supreme Court, the pressure shifts back to Republicans to explain why they want to repeal a measure that the Court has judged to be constitutional and that offers some attractive things to voters. And the opportunity is there for Democrats to show skeptical voters—especially those crucial independents who now may be willing to take a second look—that there is something in this law for them.

DISCUSSION QUESTIONS

1. One way of thinking about the tradeoffs inherent in health care is to imagine that there are three main goals of any system: access to services, affordability, and advanced treatments. But you can only choose two. How should we manage these tradeoffs? Are there any ways to select an optimal balance?

2. The conservative case for reform argues that the only way to achieve it is to put individuals back in control of their own decisions, and making them accountable for the costs. The liberal case for reform argues that this is impossible, because there is no way that people can ever make these decisions. (If you were offered the choice of an advanced MRI for $1,000, or a less sensitive CT scan for $200, how would you choose?) Is there any way to resolve this?

3. If you could design a health care system from scratch, what would it look like— private, public, or a combination? What role would values and attitudes about government play?

15

Foreign Policy and World Politics:
Is the World Still a Dangerous Place?

September 11, 2001 was a defining moment in American history. People will forever remember where they were on that date, much as people in an earlier generation recall where they were when they learned President Kennedy had been shot. The attacks were an emphatic demonstration that the world was a dangerous place.

A common belief in the intelligence community before 9/11 was that terror groups might actually possess a nuclear weapon, but none would dare to use it. After 9/11, this changed to a belief that terror groups did not possess a nuclear weapon, but would not hesitate to use one if they did. In response, the United States launched wars in Afghanistan and Iraq (the first of which became the longest war ever fought in American history, and the latter of which was extremely controversial), created a new security apparatus, reorganized entire swaths of society and the economy (as anyone who has flown in the last twelve years knows), and spent trillions of dollars in the fight against terrorism. Critics of these efforts argued that we were overreacting, as the threat was far less grave than perceived. Supporters countered that the new vigilance stopped many subsequent efforts to attack targets in the United States, from efforts to bring down airliners to plots to set off bombs in Times Square and destroy the New York Federal Reserve building.

After twelve years, can we say anything about how safe we are? The readings here consist of a debate that took place in the pages of the journal *Foreign Affairs*. Zenko and Cohen maintain that the United States is far safer than most realize, and that political leaders are exaggerating the threat for their own purposes, mostly electoral gain. It is not just the United States that is safer: they argue that the world is in fact a safer place to be than at any time in the past sixty years. There are fewer armed conflicts, fewer terrorist attacks, zero prospects for a superpower confrontation, unquestioned U.S. military supremacy, and more free nations. Even the nightmare scenario of a nuclear attack—whether from Iran, North Korea, or a terrorist group—is more a function of previous anxiety over a nuclear war with the Soviet Union than a realistic assessment of current threats. What the United States needs now, they conclude, is a balanced security policy that deals with actual problems that exist instead of the remote chance (the "1 percent doctrine") of a serious threat.

Miller disagrees. Even though the United States does not face any meaningful challenge to its military superiority, that does not mean that dangers are entirely absent. Given the instability of existing and potential nuclear powers, there is a threat that a crisis could lead to a nuclear confrontation (as well as the possibility that a rogue state may soon have both a nuclear weapon and the missile technology to threaten the United States directly). China and Russia as well could easily pose a threat to Asia or Europe. Add to this the unstable mix of failed states and non-state actors, and the world remains a dangerous place.

Micah Zenko and Michael A. Cohen

"Clear and Present Safety: The United States Is More Secure Than Washington Thinks"

Last August, the Republican presidential contender Mitt Romney performed what has become a quadrennial rite of passage in American presidential politics: he delivered a speech to the annual convention of the Veterans of Foreign Wars. His message was rooted in another grand American tradition: hyping foreign threats to the United States. It is "wishful thinking," Romney declared, "that the world is becoming a safer place. The opposite is true. Consider simply the jihadists, a near-nuclear Iran, a turbulent Middle East, an unstable Pakistan, a delusional North Korea, an assertive Russia, and an emerging global power called China. No, the world is not becoming safer."

Not long after, U.S. Secretary of Defense Leon Panetta echoed Romney's statement. In a lecture last October, Panetta warned of threats arising "from terrorism to nuclear proliferation; from rogue states to cyber attacks; from revolutions in the Middle East to economic crisis in Europe, to the rise of new powers such as China and India. All of these changes represent security, geopolitical, economic, and demographic shifts in the international order that make the world more unpredictable, more volatile and, yes, more dangerous." General Martin Dempsey, chairman of the Joint Chiefs of Staff, concurred in a recent speech, arguing that "the number and kinds of threats we face have increased significantly." And U.S. Secretary of State Hillary Clinton reinforced the point by claiming that America resides today in a "very complex, dangerous world."

Within the foreign policy elite, there exists a pervasive belief that the post–Cold War world is a treacherous place, full of great uncertainty and grave risks. A 2009 survey conducted by the Pew Research Center for the People and the Press found that 69 percent of members of the Council on Foreign Relations believed that for the United States at that moment, the world was either as dangerous as or more dangerous than it was during the Cold War. Similarly, in 2008, the Center for American Progress surveyed more than 100 foreign policy experts and found that 70 percent of them believed that the world was becoming more dangerous. Perhaps more than any other idea, this belief shapes debates on U.S. foreign policy and frames the public's understanding of international affairs.

There is just one problem: It is simply wrong. The world that the United States inhabits today is a remarkably safe and secure place. It is a world with fewer violent conflicts and greater political freedom than at virtually any other point in human history. All over the world, people enjoy longer life expectancy and greater economic opportunity than ever before. The United States faces no plausible existential threats, no great-power rival, and no near-term competition for the role of global hegemon. The U.S. military is the world's most powerful, and even in the middle of a sustained downturn, the U.S. economy remains among one of the world's most vibrant and adaptive. Although the United States faces a host of international challenges, they pose little risk to the overwhelming majority of American citizens and can be managed with existing diplomatic, economic, and, to a much lesser extent, military tools.

This reality is barely reflected in U.S. national security strategy or in American foreign policy debates. President Barack Obama's most recent National Security Strategy aspires to "a world in which America is stronger, more secure, and is able to overcome our challenges while appealing to the aspirations of people around the world." Yet that is basically the world that exists today. The United States is the world's most powerful nation, unchallenged and secure. But the country's political and policy elite seem unwilling to recognize this fact, much less integrate it into foreign policy and national security decision-making.

The disparity between foreign threats and domestic threatmongering results from a confluence of factors. The most obvious and important is electoral politics. Hyping dangers serves the interests of both political parties. For Republicans, who have long benefited from attacking Democrats for their alleged weakness in the face of foreign threats, there is little incentive to tone down the rhetoric; the notion of a dangerous world plays to perhaps their greatest political advantage. For Democrats, who are fearful of being cast as feckless, acting and sounding tough is a shield against GOP attacks and an insurance policy in case a challenge to the United States materializes into a genuine threat. Warnings about a dangerous world also benefit powerful bureaucratic interests. The specter of looming dangers sustains and justifies the massive budgets of the military and the intelligence agencies, along with the national security infrastructure that exists outside government— defense contractors, lobbying groups, think tanks, and academic departments.

There is also a pernicious feedback loop at work. Because of the chronic exaggeration of the threats facing the United States, Washington overemphasizes military approaches to problems (including many that could best be solved by nonmilitary means). The militarization of foreign policy leads, in turn, to further dark warnings about the potentially harmful effects of any effort to rebalance U.S. national security spending or trim the massive military budget—warnings that are inevitably bolstered by more threat exaggeration. Last fall, General Norton Schwartz, the U.S. Air Force chief of staff, said that defense cuts that would return military spending to its 2007 level would undermine the military's "ability to protect the nation" and could create "dire consequences." Along the same lines, Panetta warned that the same reductions would "invite aggression" from enemies. These are puzzling statements given that the U.S. defense budget is larger than the next 14 countries' defense budgets combined, and that the United States still maintains weapons systems designed to fight an enemy that disappeared 20 years ago.

Of course, threat inflation is not new. During the Cold War, although the United States faced genuine existential threats, American political leaders nevertheless hyped smaller threats or conflated them with larger ones. Today, there are no dangers to the United States remotely resembling those of the Cold War era, yet policy-makers routinely talk in the alarmist terms once used to describe superpower conflict. Indeed, the mindset of the United States in the post–9/11 world was best (albeit crudely) captured by former Vice President Dick Cheney. While in office, Cheney promoted the idea that the United States must prepare for even the most remote threat as though it were certain to occur. The journalist Ron Suskind termed this belief "the one percent doctrine," a reference to what Cheney called the "one percent chance that Pakistani scientists are helping al Qaeda build or develop a nuclear weapon." According to Suskind, Cheney insisted that the United States must treat such a remote potential threat "as a certainty in terms of our response."

Such hair-trigger responsiveness is rarely replicated outside the realm of national security, even when the government confronts problems that cause Americans far more harm than any foreign threat. According to an analysis by the budget expert Linda Bilmes and the economist Joseph Stiglitz, in the ten years since 9/11, the combined direct and indirect costs of the U.S. response to the murder of almost 3,000 of its citizens have totaled more than $3 trillion. A study by the Urban Institute, a nonpartisan think tank, estimated that during an overlapping period, from 2000 to 2006, 137,000 Americans died prematurely because they lacked health insurance. Although the federal government maintains robust health insurance programs for older and poor Americans, its response to a national crisis in health care during that time paled in comparison to its response to the far less deadly terrorist attacks.

Rather than Cheney's one percent doctrine, what the United States actually needs is a 99-percent doctrine: a national security strategy based on the fact that the United States is a safe and well-protected country and grounded in the reality that the opportunities for furthering U.S. interests far exceed the threats to them. Fully comprehending the world as it is today is the best way to keep the United States secure and resistant to the overreactions that have defined its foreign policy for far too long.

Better Than Ever

The United States, along with the rest of the world, currently faces a period of economic and political uncertainty. But consider four long-term global trends that underscore just how misguided the constant fear-mongering in U.S. politics is: the falling prevalence of violent conflict, the declining incidence of terrorism, the spread of political freedom and prosperity, and the global improvement in public health. In 1992, there were 53 armed conflicts raging in 39 countries around the world; in 2010, there were 30 armed conflicts in 25 countries. Of the latter, only four have resulted in at least 1,000 battle-related deaths and can therefore be classified as wars, according to the Uppsala Conflict Data Program: the conflicts in Afghanistan, Iraq, Pakistan, and Somalia, two of which were started by the United States.

Today, wars tend to be low-intensity conflicts that, on average, kill about 90 percent fewer people than did violent struggles in the 1950s. Indeed, the first decade of this century witnessed fewer deaths from war than any decade in the last century. Meanwhile, the world's great powers have not fought a direct conflict in more than 60 years—"the longest period of major power peace in centuries," as the Human Security Report Project puts it. Nor is there much reason for the United States to fear such a war in the near future: no state currently has the capabilities or the inclination to confront the United States militarily.

Much of the fear that suffuses U.S. foreign policy stems from the trauma of 9/11. Yet although the tactic of terrorism remains a scourge in localized conflicts, between 2006 and 2010, the total number of terrorist attacks declined by almost 20 percent, and the number of deaths caused by terrorism fell by 35 percent, according to the U.S. State Department. In 2010, more than three-quarters of all victims of terrorism—meaning deliberate, politically motivated violence by nonstate groups against noncombatant targets—were injured or killed in the war zones of Afghanistan, Iraq, Pakistan, and Somalia. Of the 13,186 people killed by terrorist attacks in 2010, only 15, or 0.1 percent, were U.S. citizens. In most places today—and especially in the United States—the chances of dying from a terrorist attack or in a military conflict have fallen almost to zero.

As violence and war have abated, freedom and democratic governance have made great gains. According to Freedom House, there were sixty-nine electoral democracies at the end of the Cold War; today, there are 117. And during that time, the number of autocracies declined from 62 to 48. To be sure, in the process of democratizing, states with weak political institutions can be more prone to near-term instability, civil wars, and interstate conflict. Nevertheless, over time, democracies tend to have healthier and better-educated citizens, almost never go to war with other democracies, and are less likely to fight nondemocracies.

Economic bonds among states are also accelerating, even in the face of a sustained global economic downturn. Today, 153 countries belong to the World

Trade Organization and are bound by its dispute-resolution mechanisms. Thanks to lowered trade barriers, exports now make up more than 30 percent of gross world product, a proportion that has tripled in the past 40 years. The United States has seen its exports to the world's fastest-growing economies increase by approximately 500 percent over the past decade. Currency flows have exploded as well, with $4 trillion moving around the world in foreign exchange markets every day. Remittances, an essential instrument for reducing poverty in developing countries, have more than tripled in the past decade, to more than $440 billion each year. Partly as a result of these trends, poverty is on the decline: in 1981, half the people living in the developing world survived on less than $1.25 a day; today, that figure is about one-sixth. Like democratization, economic development occasionally brings with it significant costs. In particular, economic liberalization can strain the social safety net that supports a society's most vulnerable populations and can exacerbate inequalities. Still, from the perspective of the United States, increasing economic interdependence is a net positive because trade and foreign direct investment between countries generally correlate with long-term economic growth and a reduced likelihood of war.

A final trend contributing to the relative security of the United States is the improvement in global health and well-being. People in virtually all countries, and certainly in the United States, are living longer and healthier lives. In 2010, the number of people who died from AIDS-related causes declined for the third year in a row. Tuberculosis rates continue to fall, as do the rates of polio and malaria. Child mortality has plummeted worldwide, thanks in part to expanded access to health care, sanitation, and vaccines. In 1970, the global child mortality rate (deaths of children under five per 1,000) was 141; in 2010, it was 57. In 1970, global average life expectancy was 59, and U.S. life expectancy was 70. Today, the global figure is just under 70, and the U.S. figure is 79. These vast improvements in health and well-being contribute to the global trend toward security and safety because countries with poor human development are more war-prone.

Phantom Menace

None of this is meant to suggest that the United States faces no major challenges today. Rather, the point is that the problems confronting the country are manageable and pose minimal risks to the lives of the overwhelming majority of Americans. None of them—separately or in combination—justifies the alarmist rhetoric of policy-makers and politicians or should lead to the conclusion that Americans live in a dangerous world.

Take terrorism. Since 9/11, no security threat has been hyped more. Considering the horrors of that day, that is not surprising. But the result has been a level of fear that is completely out of proportion to both the capabilities of terrorist organizations and the United States' vulnerability. On 9/11, al Qaeda got tragically lucky. Since then, the United States has been preparing for the one percent chance (and likely even less) that it might get lucky again. But al Qaeda lost its safe haven after the U.S.-led invasion of Afghanistan in 2001, and further military, diplomatic, intelligence, and law enforcement efforts have decimated the organization, which has essentially lost whatever ability it once had to seriously threaten the United States.

According to U.S. officials, al Qaeda's leadership has been reduced to two top lieutenants: Ayman al-Zawahiri and his second-in-command, Abu Yahya al-Libi. Panetta has even said that the defeat of al Qaeda is "within reach." The near collapse of the original al Qaeda organization is one reason why, in the decade since 9/11, the U.S. homeland has not suffered any large-scale terrorist assaults. All subsequent attempts have failed or been thwarted, owing in part to the incompetence of their perpetrators. Although there are undoubtedly still some terrorists who wish to kill Americans, their dreams will likely continue to be frustrated by their own limitations and by the intelligence and law enforcement agencies of the United States and its allies."

As the threat from transnational terrorist groups dwindles, the United States also faces few risks from other states. China is the most obvious potential rival to the United States, and there is little doubt that China's rise will pose a challenge to U.S. economic interests. Moreover, there is an unresolved debate among Chinese political and military leaders about China's proper global role, and the lack of transparency from China's senior leadership about its long-term foreign policy objectives is a cause for concern. However, the present security threat to the U.S. mainland is practically nonexistent and will remain so. Even as China tries to modernize its military, its defense spending is still approximately one-ninth that of the United States. In 2012, the Pentagon will spend roughly as much on military research and development alone as China will spend on its entire military.

While China clumsily flexes its muscles in the Far East by threatening to deny access to disputed maritime resources, a recent Pentagon report noted that China's military ambitions remain dominated by "regional contingencies" and that the People's Liberation Army has made little progress in developing capabilities that "extend global reach or power projection." In the coming years, China will enlarge its regional role, but this growth will only threaten U.S. interests if Washington attempts to dominate East Asia and fails to consider China's legitimate regional interests. It is true that China's neighbors sometimes fear that China will not resolve its disputes peacefully, but this has compelled Asian countries to cooperate with the United States, maintaining bilateral alliances that together form a strong security architecture and limit China's room to maneuver.

The strongest arguments made by those warning of Chinese influence revolve around economic policy. The list of complaints includes a host of Chinese policies, from intellectual property theft and currency manipulation to economic espionage and domestic subsidies. Yet none of those is likely to lead to direct conflict with the United States beyond the competition inherent in international trade, which does not produce zero-sum outcomes and is constrained by dispute-resolution mechanisms, such as those of the World Trade Organization. If anything, China's export-driven economic strategy, along with its large reserves of U.S. Treasury bonds, suggests that Beijing will continue to prefer a strong United States to a weak one.

Nuclear Fear

It is a matter of faith among many American politicians that Iran is the greatest danger now facing the country. But if that is true, then the United States can breathe easy: Iran is a weak military power. According to the International Institute for Strategic Studies, Iran's "military forces have almost no modern armor, artillery, aircraft or major combat ships, and UN sanctions will likely obstruct the purchase of high-technology weapons for the foreseeable future."

Tehran's stated intention to project its interests regionally through military or paramilitary forces has made Iran its own worst enemy. Iran's neighbors are choosing to balance against the Islamic Republic rather than fall in line behind its leadership. In 2006, Iran's favorability rating in Arab countries stood at nearly 80 percent; today, it is under 30 percent. Like China's neighbors in East Asia, the Gulf states have responded to Iran's belligerence by participating in an emerging regional security arrangement with the United States, which includes advanced conventional weapons sales, missile defenses, intelligence sharing, and joint military exercises, all of which have further isolated Iran.

Of course, the gravest concerns about Iran focus on its nuclear activities. Those fears have led to some of the most egregiously alarmist rhetoric: at a

Republican national security debate in November, Romney claimed that an Iranian nuclear weapon is "the greatest threat the world faces." But it remains unclear whether Tehran has even decided to pursue a bomb or has merely decided to develop a turnkey capability. Either way, Iran's leaders have been sufficiently warned that the United States would respond with overwhelming force to the use or transfer of nuclear weapons. Although a nuclear Iran would be troubling to the region, the United States and its allies would be able to contain Tehran and deter its aggression—and the threat to the U.S. homeland would continue to be minimal.

Overblown fears of a nuclear Iran are part of a more generalized American anxiety about the continued potential of nuclear attacks. Obama's National Security Strategy claims that "the American people face no greater or more urgent danger than a terrorist attack with a nuclear weapon." According to the document, "international peace and security is threatened by proliferation that could lead to a nuclear exchange. Indeed, since the end of the Cold War, the risk of a nuclear attack has increased."

If the context is a state-against-state nuclear conflict, the latter assertion is patently false. The demise of the Soviet Union ended the greatest potential for international nuclear conflict. China, with only 72 intercontinental nuclear missiles, is eminently deterrable and not a credible nuclear threat; it has no answer for the United States' second-strike capability and the more than 2,000 nuclear weapons with which the United States could strike China.

In the past decade, Cheney and other one-percenters have frequently warned of the danger posed by loose nukes or uncontrolled fissile material. In fact, the threat of a nuclear device ending up in the hands of a terrorist group has diminished markedly since the early 1990s, when the Soviet Union's nuclear arsenal was dispersed across all of Russia's 11 time zones, all 15 former Soviet republics, and much of eastern Europe. Since then, cooperative U.S.–Russian efforts have resulted in the substantial consolidation of those weapons at far fewer sites and in comprehensive security upgrades at almost all the facilities that still possess nuclear material or warheads, making the possibility of theft or diversion unlikely. Moreover, the lessons learned from securing Russia's nuclear arsenal are now being applied in other countries, under the framework of Obama's April 2010 Nuclear Security Summit, which produced a global plan to secure all nuclear materials within four years. Since then, participants in the plan, including Chile, Mexico, Ukraine, and Vietnam, have fulfilled more than 70 percent of the commitments they made at the summit.

Pakistan represents another potential source of loose nukes. The United States' military strategy in Afghanistan, with its reliance on drone strikes and cross-border raids, has actually contributed to instability in Pakistan, worsened U.S. relations with Islamabad, and potentially increased the possibility of a weapon falling into the wrong hands. Indeed, Pakistani fears of a U.S. raid on its nuclear arsenal have reportedly led Islamabad to disperse its weapons to multiple sites, transporting them in unsecured civilian vehicles. But even in Pakistan, the chances of a terrorist organization procuring a nuclear weapon are infinitesimally small. The U.S. Department of Energy has provided assistance to improve the security of Pakistan's nuclear arsenal, and successive senior U.S. government officials have repeated what former Secretary of Defense Robert Gates said in January 2010: that the United States is "very comfortable with the security of Pakistan's nuclear weapons."

A more recent bogeyman in national security debates is the threat of so-called cyberwar. Policy-makers and pundits have been warning for more than a decade about an imminent "cyber-Pearl Harbor" or "cyber-9/11." In June 2011, then Deputy Defense Secretary William Lynn said that "bits and bytes can be as threatening as bullets and bombs." And in September 2011, Admiral Mike Mullen, then chairman of the Joint Chiefs of Staff, described cyber attacks as an "existential" threat that "actually can bring us to our knees."

Although the potential vulnerability of private businesses and government agencies to cyber attacks has increased, the alleged threat of cyberwarfare crumbles under scrutiny. No cyber attack has resulted in the loss of a single U.S. citizen's life. Reports of "kinetic-like" cyber attacks, such as one on an Illinois water plant and a North Korean attack on U.S. government servers, have proved baseless. Pentagon networks are attacked thousands of times a day by individuals and foreign intelligence agencies; so, too, are servers in the private sector. But the vast majority of these attacks fail wherever adequate safeguards have been put in place. Certainly, none is even vaguely comparable to Pearl Harbor or 9/11, and most can be offset by common sense prevention and mitigation efforts.

A New Approach

Defenders of the status quo might contend that chronic threat inflation and an overmilitarized foreign policy have not prevented the United States from preserving a high degree of safety and security and therefore are not pressing problems. Others might argue that although the world might not be dangerous now, it could quickly become so if the United States grows too sanguine about global risks and reduces its military strength. Both positions underestimate the costs and risks of the status quo and overestimate the need for the United States to rely on an aggressive military posture driven by outsized fears.

Since the end of the Cold War, most improvements in U.S. security have not depended primarily on the country's massive military, nor have they resulted from the constantly expanding definition of U.S. national security interests. The United States deserves praise for promoting greater international economic interdependence and open markets and, along with a host of international and regional organizations and private actors, more limited credit for improving global public health and assisting in the development of democratic governance. But although U.S. military strength has occasionally contributed to creating a conducive environment for positive change, those improvements were achieved mostly through the work of civilian agencies and nongovernmental actors in the private and nonprofit sectors. The record of an overgrown post–Cold War U.S. military is far more mixed. Although some U.S.-led military efforts, such as the NATO intervention in the Balkans, have contributed to safer regional environments, the U.S.-led wars in Afghanistan and Iraq have weakened regional and global security, leading to hundreds of thousands of casualties and refugee crises (according to the Office of the UN High Commissioner for Refugees, 45 percent of all refugees today are fleeing the violence provoked by those two wars). Indeed, overreactions to perceived security threats, mainly from terrorism, have done significant damage to U.S. interests and threaten to weaken the global norms and institutions that helped create and sustain the current era of peace and security. None of this is to suggest that the United States should stop playing a global role; rather, it should play a different role, one that emphasizes soft power over hard power and inexpensive diplomacy and development assistance over expensive military buildups.

Indeed, the most lamentable cost of unceasing threat exaggeration and a focus on military force is that the main global challenges facing the United States today are poorly resourced and given far less attention than "sexier" problems, such as war and terrorism. These include climate change, pandemic diseases, global economic instability, and transnational criminal networks—all of which could serve as catalysts to severe and direct challenges to U.S. security interests. But these concerns are less visceral than alleged threats from terrorism and rogue nuclear states. They require long-term planning and occasionally painful solutions, and they are not constantly hyped by well-financed interest groups. As a result, they are given short shrift in national security discourse and policy making.

To avoid further distorting U.S. foreign policy and to take advantage of today's relative security and stability, policy-makers need to not only respond to a 99 percent world but also solidify it. They should start by strengthening the global architecture of international institutions and norms that can promote U.S. interests and ensure that other countries share the burden of maintaining global peace and security. International institutions such as the UN (and its affiliated agencies, such as the International Atomic Energy Agency), regional organizations (the African Union, the Organization of American States, the European Union, and the Association of Southeast Asian Nations), and international financial institutions can formalize and reinforce norms and rules that regulate state behavior and strengthen global cooperation, provide legitimacy for U.S. diplomatic efforts, and offer access to areas of the world that the United States cannot obtain unilaterally.

American leadership must be commensurate with U.S. interests and the nature of the challenges facing the country. The United States should not take the lead on every issue or assume that every problem in the world demands a U.S. response. In the majority of cases, the United States should "lead from behind"—or from the side, or slightly in the front—but rarely, if ever, by itself. That approach would win broad public support. According to the Chicago Council on Global Affairs' most recent survey of U.S. public opinion on international affairs, less than 10 percent of Americans want the country to "continue to be the preeminent world leader in solving international problems." The American people have long embraced the idea that their country should not be the world's policeman; for just as long, politicians from both parties have expressed that sentiment as a platitude. The time has come to act on that idea.

If the main challenges in a 99 percent world are transnational in nature and require more development, improved public health, and enhanced law enforcement, then it is crucial that the United States maintain a sharp set of nonmilitary national security tools. American foreign policy needs fewer people who can jump out of airplanes and more who can convene roundtable discussions and lead negotiations. But owing to cuts that began in the 1970s and accelerated significantly during its reorganization in the 1990s, the U.S. Agency for International Development (USAID) has been reduced to a hollow shell of its former self. In 1990, the agency had 3,500 permanent employees. Today, it has just over 2,000 staffers, and the vast majority of its budget is distributed via contractors and nongovernmental organizations. Meanwhile, with 30,000 employees and a $50 billion budget, the State Department's resources pale in comparison to those of the Pentagon, which has more than 1.6 million employees and a budget of more than $600 billion. More resources and attention must be devoted to all elements of nonmilitary state power—not only USAID and the State Department but also the Millennium Challenge Corporation, the National Endowment for Democracy, and a host of multilateral institutions that deal with the underlying causes of localized instability and ameliorate their effects at a relatively low cost. As U.S. General John Allen recently noted, "In many respects, USAID's efforts can do as much—over the long term—to prevent conflict as the deterrent effect of a carrier strike group or a marine expeditionary force." Allen ought to know: He commands the 100,000 U.S. troops fighting in Afghanistan.

Upgrading the United States' national security toolbox will require reducing the size of its armed forces. In an era of relative peace and security, the U.S. military should not be the primary prism through which the country sees the world. As a fungible tool that can back up coercive threats, the U.S. military is certainly an important element of national power. However, it contributes very little to lasting solutions for 99 percent problems. And the Pentagon's enormous budget not only wastes precious resources; it also warps national security thinking and policy making. Since the military controls the overwhelming share of the resources within the national security system, policy-makers tend to perceive all challenges through the distorting lens of the armed forces and respond accordingly. This tendency is one reason the U.S. military is so big. But it is also a case of the tail wagging the dog: the vast size of the military is a major reason every challenge is seen as a threat.

More than 60 years of U.S. diplomatic and military efforts have helped create a world that is freer and more secure. In the process, the United States has fostered a global environment that bolsters U.S. interests and generally accepts U.S. power and influence. The result is a world far less dangerous than ever before. The United States, in other words, has won. Now, it needs a national security strategy and an approach to foreign policy that reflect that reality.

Paul D. Miller

National Insecurity: Just How Safe Is the United States?

Micah Zenko and Michael Cohen ("Clear and Present Safety," March/April 2012) argue that "the world that the United States inhabits today is a remarkably safe and secure place." The country faces no "existential" threats, great-power war is unlikely, democracy and prosperity have spread, public health has improved, and few international challenges place American lives at risk." In light of these developments, they argue, the United States is safer today than it was during the Cold War.

The biggest problem with this argument is the authors' narrow definition of what constitutes a threat to the United States: a situation that poses existential danger or causes immediate bodily harm or death to U.S. citizens. This threshold is shortsighted and unrealistically high. If the same framework were applied to the twentieth century, then the outbreak of World War I and the German invasion of Poland in 1939 would not have been considered threats to the United States. But U.S. strategists then understood that because their country was a primary beneficiary and architect of the world order, any threat to that order was a threat to the United States itself.

So, too, today, there are major challenges to the global order that endanger U.S. national security, whether or not they pose existential or immediate threats. They include nuclear-armed autocracies, the spread of failed states and the rogue actors who operate from within them, and a global Islamist insurgency. Because the United States has lacked a single superpower rival and has focused chiefly on defeating terrorism and al Qaeda, it has underestimated the danger from all three.

Atomic Autocracies

The single greatest danger to global peace and to the United States is the presence of powerful autocratic states armed with nuclear weapons. Democracies, including those with atomic weapons, generally share a similar view of the world as the United States and thus rarely pose threats. Unlike during the Cold War, when the United States faced only two nuclear-armed autocratic adversaries, China and the Soviet Union, now it may soon face five: Russia, China, North Korea, Pakistan (if civilian rule there proves illusory and relations with the

United States continue to deteriorate), and Iran (should its nuclear program succeed). All these countries are at least uncooperative with, if not outright hostile to, the United States. Zenko and Cohen are sanguine about the prospects of great-power war, but a militarized crisis involving nuclear weapons states is more likely today than at any time in decades.

Russia no longer purports to lead a global revolution aimed at overthrowing all capitalist states, but its contemporary ideology—authoritarian, nationalist, and quasi-imperialist—threatens Europe's future freedom and territorial integrity. The Kremlin was likely involved in the 2007 cyberattack on Estonia, a NATO ally, which targeted the country's parliament, government offices, banks, and media organizations. And in 2008, Russia invaded Georgia, which had been promised future NATO membership. As his popularity at home erodes, Russian president Vladimir Putin may once again allow a foreign crisis to escalate to win nationalist plaudits. For more than seventy years, U.S. policy-makers have equated Europe's security with that of the United States; it is that notion that gives credence to the U.S. presidential candidate Mitt Romney's contention that Russia is the United States' "number one geopolitical foe."

Meanwhile, China clearly poses a greater danger today than it did during the Cold War. The United States and China fought to a bloody stalemate in the Korean War and remained enemies for the next two decades. But crippled by economic weakness, in 1972, Beijing embraced diplomatic relations with Washington. China's power quickly grew as the country liberalized its economy and modernized its military. It is now a formidable power, armed with nuclear weapons and a ballistic missile capability, and it has invested heavily in building up its navy. Its increasing strength has emboldened it to aim more overtly at reducing U.S. influence in East Asia. The same Pentagon report that Zenko and Cohen cite to calm fears about China also notes that "Beijing is developing capabilities intended to deter, delay, or deny possible U.S. support for [Taiwan] in the event of conflict. The balance of cross-Strait military forces and capabilities continues to shift in the mainland's favor." And because U.S. relations with China are prone to regular crises, as during the Tiananmen Square massacre in 1989 and after the accidental U.S. bombing of the Chinese embassy in Belgrade in 1999, a militarized confrontation with China is more likely today than at any point since the Korean War.

In addition to Russia and China, there may soon be up to three more nuclear autocracies hostile to the United States. North Korea and Iran are avowed enemies of the United States, and distrust between the United States and Pakistan has never been higher. Pakistan and North Korea tested nuclear weapons in 1998 and 2006, respectively, and Iran will almost certainly develop a nuclear weapons capability. (To be sure, a U.S. or Israeli strike could temporarily delay Iran's nuclear program. But such an attack might well provoke a wider war, illustrating once again the dangers rife in the international system.) All three states have invested in medium and long-range ballistic missiles that could hit U.S. allies, and despite the failure of North Korea's recent missile test, the United States must take seriously the possibility that any of these three states could soon be able to produce missiles that could hit the U.S. homeland. North Korea's nuclear arsenal is very small, and it would take years for Iran to accumulate a nuclear stockpile. But these states need only a few dozen warheads to pose a major challenge to the United States. What is more, because of their technological and conventional military weakness, North Korea, Pakistan, and Iran have sought to level the playing field by investing in unconventional capabilities or terrorist organizations, the latter of which could be used to carry out a nuclear attack.

Pirates and Terrorists and Hackers, Oh My!

In addition to traditional threats from nuclear-armed states, the United States faces dangers that it rarely or never encountered during the Cold War: failed states and the rogue actors that operate from within them, including pirates, organized criminals, drug cartels, terrorists, and hackers.

Zenko and Cohen correctly observe that these kinds of dangers have often been overblown. There is nothing new about pirates and terrorists, for example, and they have rarely been more than a nuisance. What is new are their increased capabilities to threaten the United States, capabilities magnified by technology, globalization, and state failure. Travel and communication have become easier, weapons technology is more lethal, and the growing number of lawless countries offers fertile ground for rogue actors to operate with impunity. At the same time, U.S. border, port, and infrastructure security has not kept up. Osama bin Laden harmed the United States in a way that would have been inconceivable for a nonstate actor during the Cold War. And even if the United States can prevent another 9/11 or a crippling cyberattack, the aggregate effects of an increasing number of malicious nonstate actors include rising costs of sustaining the global liberal order, a slowing of the gears of normal diplomatic and economic exchange, and heightened public suspicion and uncertainty.

The most dangerous threat of this type is what the counterterrorism scholar David Kilcullen has called the global Islamist insurgency, consisting of campaigns by Islamist militants to erase Western influence in Muslim countries, replace secular governments in the Muslim world with hard-line regimes, and eventually establish the supremacy of their brand of Islam across the world. Some Islamist organizations have directly targeted the United States and its allies in dozens of attacks and attempted attacks over the last decade. Of these groups, Zenko and Cohen mention only al Qaeda, and they repeat the Obama administration's claim that the organization is near defeat. The claim is wrong, but even if it were true, it would be irrelevant: al Qaeda is only the most famous member of a global network of Islamist movements that oppose the United States. If such a movement were to take over any country, that country would offer a safe haven to al Qaeda and its affiliates, allies, and copycats. But if one were to seize control of Pakistan, with its nuclear weapons, or Saudi Arabia, with its oil wealth, the resulting regime would pose a major threat to global order.

During the Cold War, the only phenomenon comparable to today's proliferation of militant Islamist groups was the Soviet Union's sponsorship of communist insurgencies around the world. But the Islamist movements will likely prove more resilient and more dangerous, because they are decentralized, their ideology does not rest on the fate of one particular regime, and globalization has made it easier for them to operate across borders. There is also a greater risk that Islamists will acquire and use weapons of mass destruction, since they are not accountable to one particular sponsoring power that can be deterred.

Zenko and Cohen are right that the United States needs to reinvest in its tools of soft power, including diplomacy and development. But those tools are not enough to cope with hostile states armed with nuclear weapons, rogue actors empowered by technology and globalization, and a worldwide network of insurgent and terrorist groups that claim they have a religious duty to oppose the United States. In attempting to manage or defeat these threats, the United States cannot afford to reduce its military capabilities, as Zenko and Cohen advise. Waiting to respond to dangers only once they threaten the very existence of the United States, instead of trying to prevent them from materializing, is an irresponsible basis for foreign policy.

Zenko and Cohen Reply

In "Clear and Present Safety," we argued that the world the United States inhabits is a remarkably safe place and that politicians, government officials, military leaders, and national security experts regularly overstate threats to the country. In this regard, Paul Miller's response is not an indictment of our thesis but a strong corroboration.

Indeed, it is hard to imagine a better example than Miller's response of how potential challenges are regularly inflated in order to justify an ever-expanding national security infrastructure. Miller relies on alarmist, worst-case scenarios and dubious historical analogies. Even worse, he displays a surprising lack of confidence in the United States' ability to respond to emerging challenges.

In Miller's dystopian worldview, every potential provocation, no matter how far-fetched, both is likely to occur and requires a militarized response.

Take his approving citation of Mitt Romney's claim that Russia is the United States' "number one geopolitical foe." Despite his halfhearted caveat that Moscow "no longer purports to lead a global revolution aimed at overthrowing all capitalist states," he still seems to believe that a demographically, economically, and diplomatically weakened Russia is bent on imperiling European security. Reading Miller, one would never know that a massive, 28-state military alliance, comprising 3.5 million active-duty troops and close to 2,500 nuclear weapons, exists in large measure to block Russian revanchist aspirations.

Miller claims that "Iran will almost certainly develop a nuclear weapons capability." That Tehran has decided to pursue nuclear weapons, however, would be news to the Office of the Director of National Intelligence and the International Atomic Energy Agency, neither of which shares Miller's view. Even if Iran did go nuclear, there is little reason to believe that the United States could not contain it, just as it has contained numerous other nuclear powers since World War II.

Miller speaks of a global Islamist insurgency and warns grimly that Pakistan or Saudi Arabia could be taken over by radical Islamists. These are doomsday scenarios that have been batted around for the last decade but are unlikely to materialize. This is largely because jihadist groups have shown little actual ability to seize power in these countries, where they enjoy paltry public support.

Miller also argues that any authoritarian state with a few dozen nuclear weapons would "pose a major challenge to the United States." But he omits the motive for these countries to seek nuclear weapons—defense—and discounts the United States' own formidable nuclear deterrent. In the past ten years, North

Korea has developed a small nuclear capability, but that acquisition has had little effect on the strategic balance on the Korean Peninsula because of U.S. conventional and nuclear weapons deployed in the theater. What is striking, although Miller mentions the failure of Pyongyang's most recent missile test, it seems to have had no impact on his dire prediction of a North Korean missile threat to the U.S. homeland.

Finally, Miller argues that "a militarized confrontation with China is more likely today than at any point since the Korean War." His basis for this assertion is that U.S.–Chinese relations "are prone to regular crises," such as those during the Tiananmen Square massacre in 1989 and following the accidental U.S. bombing of the Chinese embassy in Belgrade in 1999. But neither of these disputes, nor the many others that have occasionally roiled relations in the last two decades, came even close to provoking a militarized conflict.

The reason is both obvious and important: neither Washington nor Beijing has any interest in going to war, and both have employed formal and informal mechanisms to prevent conflict, including the exchange of special envoys, the Military Maritime Consultative Agreement, and mutual membership in the World Trade Organization. Indeed, the U.S.–Chinese relationship has been defined by intermittent cooperation and mutual interest on such issues as curbing nuclear proliferation, enhancing global economic stability, and even putting in place sanctions against Iran. And as the recent incident involving the Chinese dissident Chen Guangcheng demonstrated, neither side wants to openly confront the other. So it remains a mystery why Miller contends that "China clearly poses a greater danger today than it did during the Cold War."

Just as Miller overestimates the threats the United States faces, he also underestimates Washington's ability to respond to those challenges. The United States has unmatched intelligence and analytic capabilities and some of the world's best diplomats. Its defense budget is larger than those of the next fourteen countries combined and supports over 2,000 operationally deployed nuclear weapons; an air force of some 4,000 aircraft; a navy with 285 ships, including 11 carrier strike groups; and 770,000 active-duty soldiers and marines. Even if this budget is reduced by eight percent over the coming decade, as Congress agreed it would be as part of the 2011 debt-limit agreement, the men and women who protect the country and its interests will still be able to meet the challenges that may come their way.

Miller is right to conclude that "waiting to respond to dangers only once they threaten the very existence of the United States, instead of trying to prevent them from materializing, is an irresponsible basis for foreign policy." He is wrong, however, about the appropriate strategy and tools to stop these dangers from emerging.

Our essay argued that the United States must rebalance its national security strategy to de-emphasize the currently dominant role of the military. Miller apparently disagrees, but he never explains why a highly militarized foreign policy can best manage the challenges facing the United States in the twenty-first century. Even if one accepts Miller's darkly pessimistic worldview, it does not necessarily follow that the armed forces should take the lead in carrying out U.S. foreign policy. If the past decade demonstrated anything, it is that military action is not always the best way to keep the country safe and healthy, especially if one wants to avoid the accompanying cost in blood and treasure and a host of unintended consequences.

Since September 11, 2001, U.S. defense spending has grown by 70 percent, intelligence spending by 100 percent, and homeland security spending by 300 percent. Miller implicitly argues that these efforts have not made the United States any safer. But he refuses to provide any alternatives, sticking to the same pattern of overreaction that our essay addressed. It makes little sense to continue to base U.S. national security strategy on such a flawed premise and yet expect a different outcome.

DISCUSSION QUESTIONS

1. Is it useful to think in terms of probabilities—a 1 percent chance of an attack, or even a 0.01 percent chance—when the consequences of a nuclear detonation in New York, or Tokyo, or London would be unthinkable? Shouldn't governments do everything possible to prevent this? Or is it necessary to think in terms of costs and benefits?

2. What do you see as the major security threats to the United States over the next ten years? Twenty-five years? Fifty years? Is there any realistic way of assessing such threats, and planning how to deal with them?

Permissions Acknowledgments

Kevin Johnson: "The debate over immigration reform is not over until it's over. SCOTUSblog (June 25, 2012), http://www.scotusblog.com/2012/06/online-symposium-the-debate-over-immigration-reform-is-not-over-until-its-over.

John B. Judis: "Tea Minus Zero," *The New Republic,* May 27, 2010. Reprinted by permission of *The New Republic,* © 2010 TNR II, LLC.

Eric Lane and Michael Oreskes: From *The Genius of America: How the Constitution Saved Our Country and Why It Can Again.* Copyright © 2007 by Eric Lane and Michael Oreskes. Reprinted by permission of Bloomsbury USA.

Yuval Levin: "Repeal: Why and how Obamacare must be undone." This article is reprinted with permission of *The Weekly Standard,* where it first appeared on 4/5-12/2010. For more information visit www.weeklystandard.com.

Sanford Levinson: Chapter 1, "The Ratification Referendum," *Our Undemocratic Constitution: Where the Constitution Goes Wrong (And How We the People Can Correct It)* by Sanford Levinson, pp. 11–24. Copyright © 2006 by Oxford University Press, Inc. Reprinted with permission of Oxford University Press.

Eric Liu: "Sworn Again Americans." This essay originally appeared in *Democracy: A Journal of Ideas,* issue #24.

Paul Miller: "National Insecurity: Just How Safe is the United States?" Reprinted by permission of *Foreign Affairs,* (no. 3, July/August 2012). Copyright 2012 by the Council on Foreign Relations, Inc. www.ForeignAffairs.com.

Timothy Noah: "The United States of Inequality, Part 10: Why We Can't Ignore Growing Income Inequality." From *Slate,* © 2010 The Slate Group All rights reserved. Used by permission and protected by the Copyright Laws of the United States. The printing, copying, redistribution, or retransmission of the Material without express written permission is prohibited.

Richard Peltz-Steele: "Dismantling Federalism Is A Shortcut With A Very Steep Price," Forbes, 7/08/2012. Reprinted by permission of Richard J. Peltz-Steele, U Mass Law School.

Justin Raimondo: "The Libertarian Case Against Gay Marriage," *The American Conservative,* April 1, 2011. Reprinted with permission, Copyright *The American Conservative.*